PROBLEMS
AND
PARABLES OF LAW

SUNY Series in Judaica: Hermeneutics, Mysticism, and Religion
Michael Fishbane, Robert Goldenberg, and Elliot Wolfson, Editors

PROBLEMS
AND
PARABLES OF LAW

Maimonides and Nahmanides
on Reasons for the
Commandments
(*Ta'amei Ha-Mitzvot*)

JOSEF STERN

State University
of New York
Press

Published by
State University of New York Press, Albany

Production by Susan Geraghty
Marketing by Fran Keneston

Printed in the United States of America

For information, address State University of New York
Press, State University Plaza, Albany, N.Y., 12246

Library of Congress Cataloging-in-Publication Data

Stern, Josef, 1949–
    Problems and parables of law : Maimonides and Nahmanides on
reasons for the commandments (ta'amei ha-mitzvot) / Josef Stern.
        p.   cm. — (SUNY series in Judaica)
    Includes bibliographical references.
    ISBN 0-7914-3823-6 (hardcover : alk. paper). — ISBN 0-7914-3824-4
(pbk. : alk. paper)
    1. Commandments (Judaism) 2. Philosophy, Jewish. 3. Maimonides,
Moses, 1138–1204—Contributions in understanding the commandments of
Judaism. 4. Nahmanides, ca. 1195–ca. 1270—Contributions in
understanding the commandments of Judaism. I. Title. II. Series.
BM520.7.S75 1998
296.1'8—dc21   97-40713
                                                                                         CIP

10 9 8 7 6 5 4 3 2 1

In memory of my mother, Florence Sherman Stern,
zikhronah livrakhah,
and for my father, Kurt Stern,
yibadeil lehayim arukim

CONTENTS

ACKNOWLEDGMENTS

The chapters in this volume, with the exception of chapter 1, all originated as independent papers presented and written over the last thirteen
years. On some points they overlap, on others they collide, on yet others they complement one another. Together they trace the coming of age
of my own thinking about Maimonides and Nahmanides on *ta'amei ha-
mitzvot*. I have not attempted to eliminate all repetition among the chapters, but I have made significant revisions in chapters 3, 4, and 5 where
I thought that my original argument could now be clarified or strength-
ened. I have noted these changes in the endnotes, which themselves have
been revised for all the chapters. Chapter 3, which originally appeared
only in Hebrew, appears here in English for the first time.

Ancestors of a number of these chapters were first presented to col-
leagues at the annual Philosophy Conference of the Shalom Hartman
Institute, Jerusalem; the Academy for Jewish Philosophy; the Sixth
Jerusalem Philosophical Encounter (sponsored by the Bergmann Center,
the Hebrew University of Jerusalem); and the Conference on Myth and
Ritual, New York University. I am grateful to their critical but supportive
audiences for their reactions on those occasions. Zev Harvey, Jonathan
Malino, and David Shatz are three of the best guides to the *Guide* that a
lost soul could hope to meet in his moments of perplexity. I want to thank
them for their many discussions, criticisms, and patience as I have labored
over these papers. I am also indebted for valuable comments and advice
to Gad Freudenthal, Martin Golding, Arthur Hyman, Moshe Idel, Alfred
Ivry, Menahem Kellner, Joel Kraemer, Tzvi Langermann, Ralph Lerner,
Jeffrey Macy, Charles Manekin, the late Shlomo Pines, Peretz Segal, David
Stern, Sarah Stroumsa, and Shabsai Wolfe. It was Sidney Morgenbesser
who, when I was still an undergraduate and graduate student at Columbia
back in the seventies, first convinced a group of us that it was possible to
do Jewish *philosophy*. It would be impossible to acknowledge in detail the
extent to which discussions with him, then and since, have influenced my
thinking about the topics in this volume (especially about "problematic"
commandments and the rational explanation of the Law) and indeed all
my subsequent work in Jewish philosophy.

I wish to thank Michael Fishbane and Elliot Wolfson, two of the
editors of the distinguished series in which this volume appears, for their

invitation to put together this volume, their advice in the course of its execution, and their friendship and encouragement. Susan Geraghty and Kay Bolton of SUNY Press were consistently helpful throughout the final stages of publication; I am most grateful for their efforts. It is also a pleasure to acknowledge the material support of the Lady Davis Fellowship Trust, Jerusalem during 1984–1985 (when the earliest of these chapters was written) and both the United States National Endowment for the Humanities and the Memorial Foundation for Jewish Culture during 1996–1997 (when the last of these chapters was composed). The final work on this volume was completed in the remarkable atmosphere of the Library of the Van Leer Institute, Jerusalem, my home away from home.

Back at home, my own Stern gang—Amitai, Rephael, and Yonatan—has constantly provided problems and parables to rival those of this book. The original stimulus for chapter 5 was the *brit milah* of the youngest of them, Yoni, but, as I write these words in Jerusalem, I pray that all three will grow up to be full partners in a peaceful Israel in Abrahamic covenant with its neighbors. Of a completely different order of magnitude is my gratitude to and love for Cheryl Newman, my own partner. Without her questioning and curiosity, alone I never could have conceived many of these thoughts and, without her support of every kind, none of them would have made it into writing.

Aharon aharon haviv. It is with deep thanks and love that I wish to dedicate this volume to my late mother, Florence Sherman Stern, *zikhronah livrakhah*, and my father, Kurt Stern, *yibadeil lehayim arukim*. May this book be a small token of gratitude for the values they taught me by example: to strive for integrity, intellectual and moral, and to pursue truth, as Maimonides would add, whatever its source.

Chapters 2 through 6 originally appeared as independent essays and appear here by permission:

Chapter 2 was first published as "The Idea of a *Hoq* in Maimonides' Explanation of the Law," in S. Pines and Y. Yovel, eds., *Maimonides and Philosophy* (Dordrecht: Martinus Nijhoff/Kluwer 1986), pp. 92–130; reprinted here with the kind permission of Kluwer Academic Publishers.

Chapter 3 was first published as "On an Alleged Contradiction between Maimonides' *Guide of the Perplexed* and *Mishneh Torah*" (Heb.), *Shenaton Ha-Mishpat Ha-Ivri* (*Annual of the Institute for Research in Jewish Law*), Hebrew University, Israel, 1989, pp. 283–98; reprinted here by permission of the editor of *Shenaton Ha-Mishpat Ha-Ivri* ©1989.

Chapter 4 was first published as "Nahmanides' Conception of *Ta'amei Mitzvot* and its Maimonidean Background," in Daniel Frank, ed., *Community and Covenant: New Essays in Jewish Political and Legal Philosophy* (Albany: State University of New York Press, 1994): 141–71; reprinted here with the permission of the State University of New York Press ©1994.

Chapter 5 was first published as "Maimonides on the Covenant of Circumcision and the Unity of God," in Michael Fishbane, ed., *The Midrashic Imagination: Jewish Exegesis, Thought and History* (Albany: State University of New York Press, 1993): 131–54; reprinted here with the permission of the State University of New York Press ©1994.

Chapter 6 was first published as "The Fall and Rise of Myth in Ritual: Maimonides versus Nahmanides on the Huqqim, Astrology, and the War Against Idolatry," *Jewish Thought and Philosophy*, vol. 6 (1997), pp. 185–263; reprinted here by permission of Harwood Academic Publishers ©1997.

I wish to thank the above publishers for permission to reprint these essays in revised form.

ABBREVIATIONS OF FREQUENTLY CITED PRIMARY SOURCES

I. RABBINIC TEXTS

BT: *Talmud Bavli* (1886), Vilna, repr. frequently.

JT: *Talmud Yerushalmi* (n.d.), Krotozhin, repr. Jerusalem; cited by chapter and halakhah.

Sifra: *Sifra on Leviticus* (1983), ed., L. Finkelstein, New York.

Tanhuma: *Midrash Tanhuma* (1879), Warsaw.

Torat Kohanim: *Sifra De-Bei Rab* (1862), ed., I. H. Weiss (Vienna; repr. Jerusalem, n.d.).

II. WORKS OF MOSES MAIMONIDES

Blau: *Responsa of R. Moses b. Maimon* (Heb.) (1958–60), 3 vols., ed., Jehoshua Blau, Jerusalem: Mekize Nirdamim.

EC: *Shemonah Peraqim* (1963), in PM; English trans. as *Eight Chapters*, in *Ethical Writings of Maimonides* (1975), trans. and eds., Raymond L. Weiss and Charles Butterworth, New York: New York University Press, 59–104.

Guide: *The Guide of the Perplexed* (*Dalālat al-Ha'irīn*) (1963), trans., Shlomo Pines, Chicago: University of Chicago Press. All unmarked parenthetic references are to this translation, by part, chapter, and page; e.g., (I:2:23) refers to Part I, chap. 2, p. 23.

LA: "Letter on Astrology" (Heb.) (1926), ed., Alexander Marx, *Hebrew Union College Annual* III: 349–58; English trans. by R. Lerner in *Medieval Political Philosophy* (1963), eds., Ralph Lerner and Muhsin Mahdi, Ithaca, N.Y.: Cornell University Press, 227–36.

MN: *Moreh Nevukhim* (Heb.) (1904/1960), trans., Samuel Ibn Tibbon, with four commentaries: Efodi, Shem Tob, Crescas, and Don Isaac Abrabanel, Vilna/Jerusalem.

MT: *Mishneh Torah* (Heb.) (repr. frequently); Eng. trans. by Moses Hyamson of *Book of Knowledge and Book of Adoration* (1962),

Jerusalem: Boys Town; *The Code of Maimonides*, Yale Judaica
Series (1949–72), New Haven, Conn.: Yale University Press.

Munk: *Le Guide des Égarés* (1856–66), trans., Solomon Munk, 3 vols.,
Paris: G.-P. Maisonneuve & Larose.

PM: *Mishnah im Peirush Rabeinu Moshe ben Maimon* (Heb.) (1963), 7
vols., trans., J. Kafih, Jerusalem: Mossad HaRav Kook.

SMN: *Sefer Moreh Nevukhim* (Heb.) (1928), trans., R. Judah b.
Solomon Al-Harizi. Vilna, reprint London, 1851, ed., L. Schlossberg, notes by Scheyer.

Shailat: *Letters and Essays of Maimonides* (Heb.) (1987), 2 vols., trans.
and ed., Isaac Shailat, Ma'ale Adumim, Israel: Ma'aliyot.

SHM: *Sefer Ha-Mitzvot (Book of Commandments), with Nachmanides'
Notes* (Heb.) (1981), ed., C. Chavel, Jerusalem: Mossad HaRav
Kook.

III. WORKS OF MOSES NAHMANIDES

K: *Kitvei ha-RaMBaN (Writings of Nahmanides)* (Heb.) (1960), 2 vols.,
ed., C. Chavel, Jerusalem: Mossad HaRav Kook.

C: *Perush ha-RaMBaN 'al ha-Torah, (Commentary on the Torah)*
(Heb.) (1959–63), 3 vols, ed., C. Chavel, Jerusalem: Mossad HaRav
Kook.

CHAPTER 1

Ta'amei Ha-Mitzvot *and the Philosophical Foundations of Judaism*

A recurring topic since the beginning of Jewish philosophical thought has been the subject of *ta'amei ha-mitzvot,* literally: "reasons for the commandments." Unlike many other issues studied by Jewish philosophers—for example, the existence and attributes of God, theodocy, creation and miracles, or providence—*ta'amei ha-mitzvot* is not part of the received canon of natural, or philosophical, theology. To be sure, it raises epistemological and metaphysical questions that also apply to theism or religion in general. However, the philosopher investigating *ta'amei ha-mitzvot* does not begin with a general question, like the problem of evil, about which he turns to the intellectual tradition of Judaism to learn what it has to say. He begins instead with the "data" of Judaism—its scriptural commandments and their rabbinic interpretation—in an attempt to articulate their philosophical or theoretical presuppositions. Analogues to the place of *ta'amei ha-mitzvot* within Jewish philosophy would be akin to the place of the logic of quantum mechanics in the philosophy of physics or of the theory of evolution in the philosophy of biology. To introduce a terminological distinction to mark the difference, *ta'amei ha-mitzvot* falls under the philosophical foundations of Judaism rather than in Jewish philosophy simpliciter.

Like many topics addressed by medieval Jewish philosophers, *ta'amei ha-mitzvot* entered their repertoire through the writings of Saadiah Gaon under the influence of Islamic Kalam.[1] As Jewish thinkers attempted to "rationalize"—in various of the many senses of this difficult expression—the objects of divine revelation and prophecy, their attention naturally shifted to reasons for the Mosaic commandments. These reasons could be of two kinds: either those of the legislator (or Legislator), explanations why the commandments were legislated, or those of the performer, reasons that would justify or move an agent to perform the commandments. Some thinkers focus on one kind of reason rather than the other; others do not distinguish the two; still others make the second a condition to be met by candidates of the first kind. Sometimes but not always, the two kinds of reasons coincide. When they do not, problems like antinomianism raise their head.

The study of *ta'amei ha-mitzvot*, like most other received subjects he touched, was radically and thoroughly transformed in the hands of Moses Maimonides who devotes to it the largest self-contained bloc of the *Guide of the Perplexed* dedicated to a single theme: chapters 25 to 49 (and possibly also including chap. 51) of the third part. These twenty-five chapters consist of eleven introductory chapters in the last of which Maimonides divides the commandments into fourteen classes. Maimonides first defends his view that all commandments have reasons why they were legislated and that it is proper, even obligatory, to study them. Next he lays out the general aims of the Law—to create conditions for the practical and intellectual well-being of the community-at-large—and the assumptions that guide his assignments of particular reasons to individual commandments. Among these guiding premises is his controversial hypothesis that many of the cultic and ritual Mosaic commandments should be explained in light of the historical context—in particular the star-worshipping Sabian culture—in which they were legislated. These introductory chapters are then followed by fourteen chapters, one for each class, which propose reasons for individual commandments. What is remarkable about this account is not only the highly contextualized and contingent conception of the Law that emerges, but also the thoroughness, detail, and consistency with which Maimonides applies his general principles to particular commandments. By the time Maimonides is done, very few of his promisory notes remain unpaid, or so it seems.

This is not Maimonides' only excursion into *ta'amei ha-mitzvot* in his many writings. Even within the *Guide*, the long, detailed account in III:25–49 is immediately followed, in Part III, chapters 51–52, by a second sketch according to which the commandments, or "practices of worship," furnish "training" for certain perfected individuals to "occupy [themselves] with His commandments" rather than with "matters pertaining to this world" (III:51:622), an explanation that differs sharply from the preceding account that aims at the this-worldly welfare of the general community. And while Maimonides does not give a systematic theory of *ta'amei ha-mitzvot* in either the *Commentary on the Mishnah* or *Mishneh Torah*, both of these legal works are full of *ta'amei ha-mitzvot* and their reasons frequently do not cohere with, even if they do not contradict, those given in the *Guide*. A recurring problem for students of the Maimonidean corpus is the relation among the different accounts of *ta'amei ha-mitzvot* in these different works.

Maimonides' reconception of *ta'amei ha-mitzvot* not only revolutionized the subject he received; it also precipitated strong reactions among subsequent Jewish thinkers, both philosophers—Gersonides, Crescas, Albo, and Arama, to name a few—and mystics in the various Spanish kabbalistic traditions.[2] Possibly the most significant among these nach-Maimonideans, and the one who put forth the most important competing account of *ta'amei ha-mitzvot* in medieval Jewish thought, was Moses Nahmanides, one of the leading talmudists of the thirteenth century and a seminal figure in the emerging kabbalah, whose writings, largely in the form of biblical commentary, span, combine, and fall somewhere in between philosophy and kabbalah. Scholars have tended traditionally to set the two Moseses in stark opposition to each other; but in recent years a more subtle, nuanced picture of their relation has begun to emerge, one that acknowledges the degree to which Nahmanides adapted as well as criticized Maimonidean theses and his considerable ambivalence toward the "Rav."

This book focuses on two elements in the Maimonidean revolution in the study of *ta'amei ha-mitzvot* and their impact on Nahmanides. The first is Maimonides' idea of the problematic commandment. The second is his idea that explanations of commandments—both individual laws and the Law, or totality of commandments, as a whole—should be modelled after the multilevelled interpretation of parables. Both of these ideas are concerned with the *form* of *ta'amei ha-mitzvot*, the explanatory structures for the reasons Maimonides offers for certain classes of commandments. Both structures are then adopted by Nahmanides and adapted by him to fit the substantively very different reasons he proposes to explain the same commandments. Despite the differences between the contents of Maimonides' and Nahmanides' respective *ta'amei ha-mitzvot*, I argue that their shared models of explanation are as significant.

The idea of a problematic commandment grows out of Maimonides' treatment of the *huqqim*, the subject of the second and last chapters. The *huqqim* are commandments—like the burning of the red heifer, the prohibition against wearing garments woven from linen and wool (*sha'atnez*), and sending forth the scapegoat—that in classic rabbinic Judaism are said to have no reason. Even though the rabbis seem to have regarded the *huqqim* as exceptions to the rule, Maimonides views the existence of *any* arbitrary commandments of this kind as a violation of his most basic metaphysical assumptions about the necessary order and high purposefulness of divine creation, including the Mosaic Law, which he describes as a divine (i.e., natural) law that aims at the highest well-being of the community. The same metaphysical issue underlies chapter 3, which takes off from Maimonides' ruling in the *Mishneh Torah* that the commandment to send forth the mother bird before taking her young (Deut. 22, 6–7) is a "decree of Scripture" [*gezerat ha-katuv*], a phrase traditionally used to mean that the commandment is arbitrary, or without reason.

Against the idea that a commandment may be arbitrary, or reasonless, Maimonides holds that the *huqqim* (and "decrees of scripture") all have reasons why they were legislated. But their reasons are not the objects of the intellect or faculty of reason; instead they make reference to the contingent historical context out of which the Mosaic Law emerged, the idolatrous Sabian culture from which the Law aimed to free the Israelites and whose beliefs it aimed to eradicate. Moreover, Maimonides uses this model of explanation not only for the handful of apparently exceptional commandments enumerated by the rabbis; he expands, or generalizes, the *huqqim* to include all laws of sacrifice and the Temple, purity and impurity, agriculture, and various other individual laws he links to Sabian rites. For Maimonides, in short, the *huqqim* are all those commandments that refute the *huqqot ha-goyim*, the idolatrous way of life of the nations of the world.

Maimonides does not hesitate to propose these historically sensitive, context-dependent reasons, or explanations, for the legislation of the *huqqim* but he also recognizes that they are problematic, especially for certain constituencies in the community. They raise several problems. First, it may be evident *why* the *huqqim* are legislated—namely, to worship the deity—but it is highly problematic, given the idolatrous character and associations of the particular rites they prescribe, *how* a divine law *could* legislate them. Given its general opposition to everything associated with idolatry, the Law ought to exclude all acts like these; instead it requires them. Maimonides' solution to this problem is to show how the Law aimed to reeducate the ancient Israelites by adopting the external means of idolatrous modes of worship, to which the people were habituated, in order to wean them from the objects of idolatry. Thus the Mosaic Law hoped to draw the Israelites to monotheism while respecting their psychological needs as creatures of habit who resist radical change.

A second problem is a consequence of the first solution. If the *huqqim* are commandments whose particular forms were shaped by their historical context of legislation, why should agents—in the twelfth century or nowadays, living in contexts vastly different from that of the ancient Israelites—be obligated to continue to perform them? More generally, what justifies the performance of context-oriented commandments like the *huqqim* once the historical conditions that motivated their legislation have lapsed? This problem, of course, exemplifies the situation where the legislator's and performer's reasons for a commandment sharply diverge. It is also a difficulty that is inevitable once one attempts, as does Maimonides, to naturalistically explain the Law, that is, explain the legislation of the Law using the same kinds of conditions and factors one would employ to explain other natural phenomena, say, as means toward achieving human practical and theoretical welfare. Any such explanation runs the risk of rendering some commandments "obsolete."[3] Maimonides, I argue, sees this difficulty as the potential grounds for a form of philosophical antinomianism, opposition to the commandments and rejection of the Law. And because of this danger, he thinks it is better for the multitude, or community at large, not to know the reasons for these commandments. The *huqqim* emerge, then, as commandments, not without reasons or with reasons we just don't know, but with reasons it is best not to *make known*, or reveal, to the multitude.

Maimonides does not, to the best of my knowledge, anywhere in his writings give a general account of the grounds of obligatoriness of the commandments, an account that would also apply to the "obsolete" commandments that he explains historically such as the *huqqim*. Part of the reason, I suspect, is that the very idea that one performs commandments because one is *obligated* would strike Maimonides as a mistaken view of one's responsibility to perform the Law. A community aims to educate or cultivate a character type or personality type among its members for whom performance of the Law is a natural means, the best of all legal means, toward achieving the kinds of ends that constitute communal welfare and that enable the creation of an environment in which individuals can achieve their respective states of happiness and perfection. It is, of course, another matter to show that the Mosaic Law actually is such a mechanism that is the best of all means.

There is also a further question, not to be confused with this first one, which concerns the "eternity," or necessity, of the Mosaic Law. Why, if the Law assumed its present form because of historical circumstances that obtained at its time of legislation, must it remain eternally the same when those historical circumstances themselves change? Why cannot the Law be superceded by other laws more suitable to later circumstances? Or why can't the community change the Law to fit changing circumstances of performance?[4]

In this volume, I explore neither this last issue nor general reasons (for Maimonides) why any agent at any time and in any context ought to perform the Mosaic commandments. Instead I focus on specific arguments the *Guide* contains to counter the antinomianism implicit in its explanation of the *huqqim*.

In chapter 2, I argue that Maimonides hints at one reply in his second account of *ta'amei ha-mitzvot* in III:51–52. There he is explicitly concerned with yet a third problem that is formally analogous to the obsolescence of the *huqqim*. This is the problem why, or how, the philosopher who is engaged in constant (or as constant as possible) intellectual contemplation of the divine, the highest form of divine worship, should perform bodily acts of worship such as the commandments.[5] His answer is that the perfected agent should exploit the commandments' very pointlessness (relative to his state of intellectual perfection) to make them a form of "training" to occupy oneself with God *rather than with matters of this world,* that is, rather than with matters that lead to one's actual well-being or happiness that do *give* a point to every other (rational) act we perform. In other words, Maimonides suggests a way in which agents can and should transform their *reasons* for *performing* commandments to fit their respective contexts and states of perfection, while the commandments themselves remain constant. Likewise for the *huqqim,* once their legislative reasons no longer motivate agents to perform them.

In chapter 6, I discuss a different response Maimonides also gives: that the Sabianism the commandments were legislated to counteract is not (only) a historical reality in the past but a live threat that the Law is still actively engaged in combatting. Based on a number of passages in which Maimonides seems intent on drawing our attention to the fact that Sabianism still survives in various myths, superstitions, and practices, I argue that what he means by the title is not just the ancient starworshipping cult-nation but also an ongoing twelfth-century mix of fatalistic astrology, magic, popular religion, and hermetic Neoplatonism. If this is so, the *huqqim* are not at all obsolete. Their legislative reasons are still at work. And just as those reasons had to be concealed from the ancient Israelites, it may still be necessary to conceal them from the twelfth-century multitude.

This last solution to the antinomian problem posed by the *huqqim* may serve as one important point of contrast between Maimonides and Nahmanides. Maimonides explains the *huqqim* as commandments designed to counter astrology, magic, and their way of life, based on his deep belief that what is primarily wrong with astrology and magic is that they are absolutely false and ineffective. Nahmanides holds the very opposite view of these "sciences": they are true and effective and, for that very reason, forbidden by the divine law. Precisely because the powers on which they rest, for example, the stars and their celestial lords, are real, there is a serious danger that they might be worshipped. Therefore the Torah prohibits all such practices. The *huqqim,* he explains, are devices to acknowledge and deal with these real powers in ways compatible with the requirements of the divine law that only God and not they be worshipped. But because of the controversial nature of this distinction between acknowledgment and worship, Nahmanides, like Maimonides, also argues that the rabbis wished to conceal the reasons for these commandments.

As sharply opposed as they are in their underlying views of astrology and magic, Nahmanides nonetheless adopts and develops Maimonides' idea that the *huqqim*—which he conservatively restores to the small number enumerated by the rabbis—are commandments, not without reasons, but whose reasons are problematic. Nahmanides, however, articulates this notion in terms of structural properties of the explanations of these commandments that are considerably more abstract than Maimonides' original idea. By enabling the same form of explanation to apply to commandments of rather different kinds, Nahmanides radically improves upon the Maimonidean idea of a problematic commandment, in each instance (ironically) expressing a decidedly anti-Maimonidean content. In the theories of *ta'amei ha-mitzvot* of both authors, however, the *huqqim* assume a unprecedented central place.

There is also a second broad ground shared by Maimonides and Nahmanides in their respective approaches to *ta'amei ha-mitzvot*. Both give multiple reasons for many commandments, using a common structure. The structure of these multiple or multilevelled reasons is modelled after that of the parable (sing.: Ar: *mathal*/Heb: *mashal*; pl.: Ar: *amthal*/Heb: *meshalim*), which Maimonides describes, using parables, in the Introduction to the *Guide*. In the first of these two parables, about a man who loses a pearl in his house, Maimonides says that the "external meaning [*zahir*] of a parable is worth nothing" (I:Intro.:11). In the second parable, based on Prov. 25, 11, "*A word fitly spoken is like apples of gold in settings of silver*," he says that the external meaning [*zahir*] is as "beautiful as silver" and "contains wisdom that is useful in many respects, among which is the welfare of human societies." This external meaning, he next contrasts with the "internal meaning" [*batin*], which is even "more beautiful" and "contains wisdom that is useful for beliefs concerned with the truth as it is" (ibid., 12).

In chapters 4 and 5, I propose that, by way of these two parables, Maimonides demarcates three levels of meaning or interpretation he believes characterize a parable. I call these (1) the vulgar external meaning, (2) the parabolic external meaning, and (3) the parabolic internal meaning. That there is this difference between (1) and (2) can be seen in the open contradiction, side by side, between the two evaluations of "external meaning" [*zahir*] in the two parables. From this I conclude that Maimonides uses the expression "external meaning" [*zahir*] equivocally or amphibolously.

Where the external meaning is said to be worthless, he intends by it the meanings of the words uttered, both as the vulgar understand them through the medium of their imagination and their lexical meaning as comparative-philological analyses reveal. For example, the vulgar external meaning of *zelem*, the well-known topic of the first chapter of the

Guide, is bodily, sensible shape; this is both what the vulgar multitude take the word to mean and what Maimonides suggests is in fact its lexical meaning through his own selective choice of prooftexts.[6] Similarly, in I:2, the external meaning of Genesis 2–3 is the "learned man's" interpretation. This meaning is worthless insofar as it contains no wisdom: at best it is concerned with material words rather than with what we ought to believe (I:50:111) and at worst (as in these examples) it expresses falsehoods no one should believe.

The silver-lined parabolic external meaning, on the other hand, is a kind of wisdom that ought to be believed. In the case of *zelem*, its parabolic external meaning is the idea of a (Aristotelian) natural, or specific, form; in the case of humanity, its intellect. In I:2, it is Maimonides' proposed interpretation of the story: Humanity was originally, and ideally, a pure intellect engaged in contemplation of theoretical truths and, only as a result of inclining to its bodily desires and imagination (expressed as eating of the fruit of the tree of knowledge), came to know the lower, and conflicting, knowledge of good and bad, knowledge concerned with communal welfare. The moral of this interpretation of the story is that the natural perfection of humanity is theoretical rather than merely practical or moral. Hence, the best community is one that aims not merely at the political and social welfare of its citizens but also at their intellectual welfare, that they acquire correct beliefs.

The golden internal meaning [*batin*], Maimonides' third kind of parabolic meaning or interpretation, is also a kind of wisdom that expresses what ought to be believed. It differs from the external parabolic meaning only in the *content* of its wisdom. Whereas parabolic external meaning expresses wisdom that is (especially, though perhaps not exclusively) conducive to the well-being of a community, parabolic internal meaning expresses wisdom related to the highest obtainable theoretical perfection of the individual: "wisdom that is useful for beliefs concerned with the truth as it is." Now, this last characterization is somewhat awkward, vague, and circumlocutious: the wisdom is not said to be knowledge *of* the truth, but wisdom "useful" for beliefs "concerned with" the truth "as it is." Let me add a few words that may throw some light on this description of parabolic internal meaning and its relation to parabolic external meaning.

Let me begin by emphasizing what the distinction between external and internal parabolic meaning is *not*. Because it is a distinction solely between two kinds of *contents*, or wisdoms, the external/internal distinction is not a function of presentation or style or audience. It does not mark the difference between the revealed and concealed. It does not mark the difference between two kinds of intended readers: the community or multitude or 'general run of men' corresponding to the external, the philosophers or elite or 'those who are able to understand by themselves' for the internal. It does not reflect a difference in the author's attitude toward the contents of the two meanings: the internal meaning is not what the author 'really' believes, the external what he merely says for public consumption or as a political strategem. And while there may sometimes be tensions between particular external and internal meanings, there is no suggestion that there is a *general* opposition between them such as a deep conflict between Law and Philosophy. In short, the distinction between the external and internal is not the distinction between the *esoteric* and *exoteric* as those terms have been applied for the last fifty years.[7]

Maimonides describes both external and internal parabolic meanings as kinds of *wisdom*. Hence, they are both kinds of philosophy, albeit one is oriented toward the welfare of the community, the other toward the highest (theoretical) perfection of the individual. Both express contents he thinks ought to be accepted, and assented to where true, or, more generally, to which an agent ought to commit himself. They are also both, equally, what is *meant* by the parable, what the author intends it to communicate and intends the reader to understand by the text.[8] Futhermore, while the identity of the intended reader or readers of the *Guide* remains a difficult open question (that I cannot discuss here), there is no reason to assume that there are (systematically) *different* readers or audiences for the external and internal. Finally, the exoteric/esoteric distinction in ancient thought was a distinction between two classes of *texts*: one popular, elementary, nontechnical, and sometimes practical; the other advanced, for a closed audience, technical, and typically theoretical.[9] The external/internal distinction, on the other hand, is a distinction between levels of meaning *within* a single text.

This is not to say that Maimonides does not conceal certain meanings or contents in the *Guide*. He explicitly tells the reader in the introduction to the *Guide* that he employs various devices for this purpose, most famously, deliberately contradictory claims but also ellipsis, disorganization, and the literary form of the parable and other figures. But the distinction between the concealed and revealed is perpendicular to the external/internal distinction. That is, there may be concealed external meanings as well as concealed internal ones, and revealed internal meanings as well as revealed external ones. (Where the external or internal meaning is revealed, it may also coincide with the vulgar external meaning; i.e., it may be expressed explicitly by the lexical meanings of the words used.) To represent Maimonides' hermeneutics, we need a matrix with at least four cells. Moreover, Maimonides' motivations for concealment and for the use of the parable, or parabolic interpretation, are entirely different. Concealment is necessary either to protect the community-at-large from premature exposure to certain contents that, without the right kind of preparation, might harm them (I:33:70–72) or to protect the philosopher from the multitude who may harm him when his claims are not properly understood or appreciated (I:17:43). The use of the parable whose multiple levels of interpretation go beyond the meaning of explicit, linear, sustained discursive speech is a function of the typically incomplete, limited character of the lighteninglike apprehension and understanding of the philosopher-prophet and of his attempts to communicate that content. According to Maimonides, it was this character of their intellectual experiences that led the prophets to express their contents in the flashlike, allusive form of the parable (I:Intro.:7–8).

Maimonides' notion of a parable, or of texts that deserve parabolic interpretation, is rather different, then, than the literary notion of a parable—that is, a narrative with a certain structure. Admittedly, some parables Maimonides himself constructs in the *Guide*—for example, the parable of the palace in III:51–52, the parable of the ruler in I:46, and the parable of the free man and slave in III:8—themselves follow the narrative model of the rabbinic king-parable (*mashal le-melekh*). But he also applies the term *parable* (*mathal, mashal*) more generally to *any* text, narrative or not, with multiple levels of external and internal meaning.[10] And not only to texts or discursive speeches. To return to *ta'amei ha-mitzvot,* he extends his idea of a parable and of parabolic interpretation from texts to commandments. Just as parabolic texts have multiple levels of meanings or interpretation, so certain commandments have multiple reasons or (legislative) explanations structured in exactly the same way as the parable—one is the vulgar external reason, the second a parabolic external reason, and the third a parabolic internal reason.

In chapters 4 and 5, I explore Maimonides' application of his model of parabolic interpretation to *ta'amei ha-mitzvot.* In chapter 4, I show how Maimonides applies the model to the explanation of the totality of the commandments, the Law as a whole. The parabolic external explanation of the Law is stated programmatically in chapter III:27 and elaborated in detail throughout III:26–49 (as Maimonides states in III:41:567): on this account, the commandments lead to the welfare, both of the body and of the soul, of the community. In III:51–52, I suggest (taking a different line from my analysis in chapter 2) that we are given the parabolic internal reason for the commandments: to serve as the kind of training that enables the perfected individual to engage in constant (or as constant as possible) intellectual apprehension of theoretical truths.

In chapter 5, I show how Maimonides applies the parabolic model of interpretation to the explanation of an individual commandment: the covenant of circumcision. He rejects the vulgar reason (which was also given by the rabbis and by Saadiah) that the act physically perfects the individual's body. As its parabolic external reason, he proposes instead that circumcision communicates or expresses belief in the unity of God, a belief that every member of the community ought to hold and that thereby contributes to the "welfare of the communal soul." And as its internal reason, he argues that circumcision restrains the person's sexual passions (among, or perhaps representative of, his other desires and needs) that prevent him from exclusively and completely engaging in intellectual apprehension as a fully actualized intellect. Ideally, indeed, Maimonides seems to hold that it would be best if the person simply had no such desires or needs. But this is impossible both because metaphysically there is no form, or intellect, without matter, or body, and because of the necessities of human nature and procreation. Hence, circumcision is an accommodation of the ideal to reality. Circumcision is not the only individual commandment for which Maimonides offers parabolic multi-levelled explanations, although he does not do it for all. Instead it seems that he applies the parabolic model specifically to commandments that focus on bodily organs, functions, or actions such as the commandment to rest one's body on the Sabbath and the commandment to bury one's excrement when at war (Deut. 23:13–14).[11]

In light of Maimonides' extension of the parabolic model to the explanation of commandments, it may also be possible now to say why he describes the internal meaning of a parable, as we saw earlier, in such vague terms: "wisdom that is useful for beliefs concerned with the truth as it is." The reason may have to do with the different kinds of things he counts as parables and therefore have an internal meaning/reason: stories (like the *Aqedah* or the episode of the tree of knowledge), speeches or non-narrative texts (like the speeches of the Book of Job and certain chapters of the *Guide* which Maimonides also wrote as parables), and commandments. (For obvious reasons, it is much easier to produce a homogeneous set of parabolic external meanings/reasons for all these objects.)

The internal meanings of parabolic *texts*—stories and speeches—either express a truth about physics, or the governance of the sublunar world, or a statement *about* the limited character of human apprehension of metaphysical truths and the consequences of those limitations. In the latter case, the interpretations are determined in significant part by considerations related to Maimonides' skepticism about human knowledge of metaphysics and divine science, something that might be described as "wisdom that is useful for beliefs concerned with the truth as it is," though it is not itself wisdom *about* the metaphysical truth, or metaphysical knowledge.[12] The internal reasons of parabolic *command-ments*, on the other hand, explain their performance as means that enable individual members of the community to achieve theoretical per-fection—apprehension of intelligible truth—to the extent possible, often as training or exercises designed to restrain, if not eliminate, bodily needs and desires. In this latter case, the internal reason is, again, not itself wisdom or knowledge of the truth or a true belief per se, but "wis-dom that is useful for beliefs concerned with the truth as it is."

Parabolic commandments and, in particular, the *huqqim*, I would add, are also good examples of laws whose parabolic *external* meaning must be *concealed*. Maimonides' explanation, for example, that sacri-fices were legislated to put an end to Sabian idolatry—by adopting the external forms of that very idolatry in order to accommodate the psy-chological needs of the ancient Israelites—is their parabolic external rea-son: it aims at the welfare of the community and, in particular, its the-oretical welfare—to inculcate the correct kind of belief that must be held by everyone. However, Moses, according to Maimonides' interpretation of the rabbis, concealed this explanation (like that of all the *huqqim*) from the multitude, or community-at-large, on pain that, if he did not, it would have rendered the sacrifices ineffective. Had the multitude believed that they were performing these outwardly idolatrous acts only in order to wean themselves away from all such worship, the actions would have been self-defeating and the people would never have been led through that means to deny idolatry and embrace monotheism. Here, then, we have a concealed parabolic external reason. A similar story can be told about the argument of chapter 6—that the *huqqim* aim to refute star worship more generally, including contemporary astrology and magic. In that case, the same kind of reason for concealment applies now as then. And if the explanation for the *huqqim* is, on the other hand, now obsolete (because there is no Sabianism to combat), there still remains an anti-antinomian reason to conceal that explanation for their legislation. For if this context-dependent historical reason for the *huqqim* was revealed to the multitude, they would reject those com-mandments on the grounds that the reason for their legislation no longer obtains. Finally, we might note that Maimonides himself explicitly reveals his explanation for the *huqqim* only insofar as he presents the Sabians as if they were only a historical reality of the past. He himself conceals his further view that Sabianism qua astrology, Neoplatonic hermeticism, magic and contemporary popular religion is still alive and remains the present live target of the *huqqim*. In all these alternatives, it is the external reason for the *huqqim* that must be concealed.

Maimonides' discussion of the metaphysical presuppositions of the *huqqim* and, more specifically, his explanation of the commandment of *shiluah ha-ken* (Deut. 22, 6–7)—the locus of chapter 3—is also the point from which Nahmanides takes off to present his general theory of *ta'amei ha-mitzvot*. As with the idea of a problematic commandment, Nahmanides adopts and develops the Maimonidean parabolic model of multiple reasons or explanations for each commandment by preserving its structure while changing the contents of its levels of reasons/meanings. In chapter 4, I discuss two ways in which Nahmanides departs from Maimonides. First, his parabolic internal reasons are theosophic and theurgic rather than philosophical: the commandments are explained as means to satisfy, complete, or perfect the deity or divine nature. Second, unlike Maimonides who considers the vulgar external meaning/reason of a parable to be worthless, Nahmanides reclaims this level of interpretation, which he identifies with *peshat*. In so doing, he enriches the notion of *peshat* to include much more than did his Spanish predecessors. But he maintains its distinctiveness from both levels of parabolic meaning/reason while restoring to it the cognitive value of which Maimonides had divested it. Despite these differences, the positive influence of Maimonides on Nahmanides' conception of the structure of *ta'amei ha-mitzvot* should not be obscured. Only against the background of their shared common approach can we clearly discern their particular disagreements and evaluate the true impact of the Maimonidean revolution.

CHAPTER 2

Problematic Commandments I: Maimonides on the Huqqim *and Antinomianism*

According to a view widely held in Rabbinic literature and medieval Jewish philosophy and scriptural exegesis, there exist a small number of Mosaic commandments, the *huqqim* (literally: "statutes"), which are said either to have no reasons or to have reasons which we do not, and perhaps cannot, know.[1] The existence of this class of laws, it was further believed, is already indicated in the language of the Torah, which appears to distinguish the *huqqim* from the *mishpatim* (literally: "ordinances" or "judgments") by juxtaposing the two in many verses.[2] Although the Torah itself gives no principle of differentiation for this division, the *mishpatim* came to be identified with those laws that are rationally necessary, according to some, or that are conventionally but universally accepted, according to others; while the *huqqim* were identified with those laws whose validity depends essentially on divine decree or which we know only by divine revelation.[3]

As with many other received notions in the tradition of Judaism, Maimonides took over these categories of *hoq* and *mishpat* and reconceived them in light of his own philosophical assumptions and purposes. Whereas previous figures in the tradition took the *huqqim* to consist of no more than eight or nine apparently unrelated individual commandments, Maimonides takes them to comprise a broad and central portion of the Law. And whereas others took the *huqqim* to be *exceptions* to the general rule of commandments for which reasons can, and should, be given, Maimonides holds that not only do the *huqqim* have reasons but that their explanation serves as a model for his conception of *ta'amei ha-mitzvot*, the project of giving reasons for, or explaining, the commandments of the Torah.

In this chapter I shall trace the development of this notion of a *hoq* in Maimonides' writings, concentrating on the *Guide of the Perplexed*. Because this subject arises in the context of his general discussion of *ta'amei ha-mitzvot*, I begin with a brief discussion of Maimonides' conception of this traditional enterprise. Against this background, I then turn to a close reading of chapter III:26 of the *Guide* where Maimonides introduces the notion of a *hoq* and restricts its traditional characterization to "particulars" rather than "generalities" of commandments. Since he claims that "the true reality of particulars of commandments is illustrated by the sacrifices" (III:26:509), I turn next to his well-known use of historical explanations for these and certain other laws. This discussion will lead us to the central issue underlying Maimonides' account of a *hoq*: the nature of the authority of the Law and the dangers of antinomianism. That his use of historical explanations tends to undermine the authority of the Law has been frequently raised as an objection to Maimonides' account; I will argue that, not only does he respond to this difficulty in the *Guide*, but that indeed it motivates his conception of a *hoq*.

I

Inquiries into *ta'amei ha-mitzvot*, the rationale or explanation of the commandments of the Torah, are concerned with either or both of two different questions: (1) Why did God legislate a particular commandment, or the Law as a whole, to Israel at the time of the Mosaic revelation?[4] and (2) Why should I, or any member of the community of Israel, perform a particular commandment or the Law as a whole? The first question—which I shall call the "commandment question"—sees the project of *ta'amei ha-mitzvot* as a matter of explaining, or demonstrating, the rationality of the Mosaic legislation; the second—the "performance question"—sees it as the task of furnishing reasons that a human agent can use to justify his own performance of the commandments. In most cases, these two types of reasons go hand in hand: Any reason why God commanded Israel to perform a commandment C will also be a reason for any member of Israel to perform C. Inversely (with some natural assumptions about God, say, that He is altruistic), any reason that an agent can use to justify his own performance of C will also be serviceable as a reason why God commanded C or why C was legislated. But there are also certain critical cases where these two types of reasons come apart: in particular, where a reason or explanation why God commanded a certain law cannot function as a reason for a member of the community of Israel at some time to justify his own performance of that very same commandment. These cases cannot be overlooked for they threaten to undermine the authority of the Law and, I shall argue, they lie at the heart of Maimonides' concern with the *huqqim*.

Although the "commandment" and "performance" questions are

clearly different, they have not always been explicitly distinguished by inquirers into *ta'amei ha-mitzvot*. In part this is because most authors have pursued both questions, though usually one is emphasized and only its implications for the other probed. Maimonides' concern in the *Guide*, as his opening statements in chapter III:26 make absolutely clear, is primarily with the "commandment" question, but the question of "performance," as we shall see, is also just off stage. He begins by drawing a parallel between the Law and God's works or acts, which had been the topic of the previous chapter.

> Just as there is disagreement among the men of speculation among the adherents of Law whether His works . . . are consequent upon wisdom or upon the will alone without being intended toward any end at all, there is also the same disagreement among them regarding our Laws, which He has given to us. Thus there are people who do not seek for them any cause at all, saying that all Laws are consequent upon the will alone. There are also people who say that every commandment and prohibition in these Laws is consequent upon wisdom and aims at some end, and that all Laws have causes and were given in view of some utility. (III:26:506)

After classifying all actions into four types, Maimonides had argued in chapter 25—against the Ash'arites who maintain that all of God's acts are consequent upon His will alone and aim at no end—that "all [of God's] actions are good and excellent," that is, all His actions aim at an end which is, furthermore, noble, either necessary or useful.[5] Alluding to his own identification of the divine attributes of action with the governance of nature (I:54), he adds that "the philosophic opinion is similar, holding . . . that in all natural things . . . some end is sought, regardless of whether we do or do not know that end" (III:25).[6] Thus, given the parallel between the two chapters, the subject of III:25 is the explanation of God's acts in general, or of nature; that of III:26, the explanation of a particular type of divine act, namely, the divine legislation of the Mosaic commandments to Israel.

There is a second, equally important, parallel between chapters III:25 and 26. Together with the metaphysical or ontological claim that all of God's acts are consequent upon His wisdom, and therefore have reasons, Maimonides makes the epistemological claim that "we, however, are ignorant of many of the ways in which wisdom is found in His works" and, as prooftext for this opinion, he cites Deut. 32:4: *The Rock, His Work Is Perfect* (III:25). Similarly, when he introduces his own position concerning the Law, Maimonides distinguishes the ontological thesis that all commandments have reasons from the epistemological thesis that the reasons for the commandments are all humanly knowable or known. "It is, however, the doctrine of all of us—both of the multitude and of the elite—that all the Laws have a cause, though we are ignorant of the causes for some of them and we do not know the manner in which they conform to wisdom." And when he concludes his discussion of *ta'amei ha-mitzvot*, he emphasizes the same parallel between the divine acts, that is, nature, and commandments, repeating the prooftext he had cited earlier in chapter 25.

> Marvel exceedingly at the wisdom of His commandments . . . just as you should marvel at the wisdom manifested in the things He had made. It says: *The rock, His works is perfect; for all His ways are judgment.* (Deut. 32:4) It says that just as the things made by Him are consummately perfect, so are His commandments consumately just. However, our intellects are incapable of apprehending the perfection of everything that He has made and the justice of everything He has commanded. We only apprehend the justice of some of His commandments just as we only apprehend some of the marvels in the things He has made, in the parts of the body of animals and in the motions of the spheres. What is hidden from us in both these classes of things is much more considerable than what is manifest. (III:49:605)

It should be stressed that the epistemic limitations concerning our knowledge of *ta'amei ha-mitzvot* to which Maimonides refers throughout these passages bear on *all* commandments, classic instances of *mishpatim* as well as *huqqim*. In III:26 it is only after he draws this general metaphysical/epistemic distinction that Maimonides first mentions the *huqqim*; the scriptural prooftexts of III:26 and III:49 refer to *mishpatim* and *huqqim*; and the commandments at whose wisdom he specifically tells us to marvel in the passage of III:49 are the punishments meted out to the husband who defames his wife, to the thief, and to the false witness, all typical examples of *mishpatim*. Analogously, in the realm of God's works or nature, the marvels Maimonides mentions range from the biological to the astronomical, from the terrestrial, for which he believed that Aristotelian natural science was as a rule fully adequate, to the celestial, concerning which he arguably believed that man can have no knowledge.[7] In nature as well as in the Law, the wisdom Maimonides believes "is hidden from us" can be found in all categories of objects of scientific inquiry. Thus, while the claim that all commandments have reasons but some may not be humanly known, or perhaps knowable, is central to Maimonides' conception of the Law, this claim applies across the board to all laws. There is no indication thusfar that there are special epistemic limitations that apply to certain classes of commandments, such as, the *huqqim*, that do not apply to the others.

As we have now seen, and will repeatedly encounter in Maimonides' discussion, underlying his conception of *ta'amei ha-mitzvot* is a deep parallel between the Law and nature. The same ontological and epistemological theses hold for both.⁸ To understand the full significance of this correspondence, we must ask ourselves, What, according to Maimonides, is the meaning of the explanandum statement that God commanded such-and-such a law? And to answer this, we must turn back to the lexicographical chapters of Part I of the *Guide* where Maimonides provides us with the key to understanding terms, not only as they are used in the Torah, but also as they are used in the *Guide* itself.⁹

Because predicates like *say*, *speak*, and *command* cannot be literally attributed to God, Maimonides tells us that they are instead "used to denote either will and volition or a notion that has been grasped by the understanding having come from God" (I:65:158). In particular, "the term 'command' is figuratively used of God with reference to the coming to be of that which He has willed" (I:65:159). Thus the statement that God commanded some law L to Israel should be rephrased, or translated into a philosophically purified language, to say that God willed the commandment L to Israel into existence, that is, that He is the efficient cause of its existence. In the same way, Maimonides explains that God is "designated as the *Rock*"—incidentally, in the same verse, Deut. 32:4, cited in both III:25 and III:49 as prooftext that all of God's acts and commandments have reasons even where we are ignorant of them (III:25:506)—inasmuch as "He is the principle and the *efficient* cause of all things other than himself" (I:16:42; my emphasis).

Now, having told us the meaning of the divinely attributed predicate 'command,' Maimonides goes on to explicate "in what respect it is said of Him . . . that He is the efficient cause" of something—and, similarly, its final cause (I:69:168). To say that God is such a cause is not to deny nature or natural causality. On the contrary, "everything that is produced in time must necessarily have a proximate cause which has produced it. In its turn that cause has a cause and so forth till finally one comes to the First Cause of all things, I mean God's will and free choice" (II:48:409). That is, God—His will and wisdom, which are identical with His essence—is said to be the cause of any action produced in time only insofar as He is the first, ultimate, or remotest of its causes, *presupposing* rather than *excluding* a series of proximate or intermediate causes that lie within the natural order. It is merely the characteristic manner of prophetic writing to omit the intermediate natural causes and ascribe the effect to the direct agency of God: "For all these things the *expressions to say, to speak, to command, to call,* and *to send* are used" (II:48:410).

We can now see exactly how Maimonides conceived of the project of *ta'amei ha-mitzvot* in the *Guide*. What is primarily to be explained is why God legislated the commandments—rather than the "performance" question—and this object of explanation is, in turn, to be understood as the statement that the commandments are the final effects of a series of proximate natural causes of which God, as in any full Aristotelian explanation, is simply the first cause. The substantive work of any particular explanation why certain commandments came to be legislated to Israel will, therefore, consist in discovering the intermediate natural causes. Furthermore, although such explanations will necessarily have recourse to the acts of individual humans, prophets, and legislators, there is good reason to suppose that Maimonides did not believe that for this reason they would be any less deterministic than explanations in the physical domain, that human volition and choice are any less subject to causation than natural phenomena and "form in this respect a domain governed by different laws or by no laws at all."[10] Thus, the parallel Maimonides constantly emphasizes between the Law and divine (i.e., natural) acts is not a parallel between two *different* domains but within *one* domain. Just as knowledge of God's attributes of action, His governance of nature, is attained through study of natural science, so one understands the *ta'amei ha-mitzvot*, why and how the Mosaic commandments came to be legislated, by studying their *natural* causes. Maimonides' presentation of *ta'amei ha-mitzvot* in Part III of the *Guide* might, in short, be described as the natural science of the Law, on a par with Aristotelian natural science of the physical world.[11] And from this perspective, his use of historical explanations to account for the characteristics of certain laws is not only not puzzling but entirely natural. However, given this conception of *ta'amei ha-mitzvot*, the *huqqim* raise a particular problem to which we now turn.

II

The *huqqim* are first introduced on the grounds that, as they are described by the Rabbis, they appear to contradict the thesis that all commandments have causes, reasons, or useful ends. To this objection, Maimonides immediately responds that "the multitude of Sages" in fact believed that "there indubitably is a cause for them . . . but that it is hidden from us either because of the incapacity of our intellects or the deficiency of our knowledge" (III:26:507). The only sense, in other words, in which the Rabbis thought that the *huqqim* have no causes is epistemological, though it is not yet clear whether this lack of knowledge associated with the *huqqim* is meant to be the same as or in addition to the general epistemic limitations already emphasized for all *ta'amei ha-mitzvot*.

Having reaffirmed the (metaphysical) thesis that all commandments have reasons, Maimonides then redescribes the *huqqim*, this time, however, in contrast to the *mishpatim* and with a significant but easily overlooked qualification: "Those commandments whose utility is clear to the multitude are called *mishpatim* and those whose utility is not clear to the multitude are called *huqqim*" (ibid.).

Here the sense in which the *huqqim* are said to lack a utility or reason is not merely epistemic but also relative to the understanding of the multitude. That is, when the Torah distinguishes certain laws as *huqqim* and others as *mishpatim*, and when the Rabbis elaborate this distinction, according to Maimonides, this is entirely as the multitude understand these commandments. Although he does not explicitly mention in this context his well-known pedagogical-political principle of exegesis, "The Torah speaks according to the language of the sons of man [*Dibrah Torah ke-lashon benei adam*]," this way of interpreting the *hoq*/*mishpat* distinction, both as it occurs in Scripture and in Rabbinic *midrashim*, is simply an application of that rule, taken as a claim not just about literally inapplicable divine predicates used in the Torah but about its concepts and distinctions generally. As Maimonides elsewhere explicates this principle, the Torah is written in language that allows the multitude and those for whom "it is not within their power to understand these matters [i.e., divine science] as they truly are" nonetheless to "to learn from" it according to their respective capacities. Furthermore, had these truths of divine science, which are only figuratively expressed or implied in the Torah, been explicitly revealed to those who are not prepared to grasp them, these people would have been genuinely harmed. What would result would be not "mere confusion" but "absolute negation" (I:33:70–71 and n.1). For the *huqqim* in particular, then, what Maimonides is saying is also twofold: (1) that their Rabbinic description, in contrast to the *mishpatim*, as having no clear reasons is meant specifically with respect to the understanding of the multitude, not with respect to the reader who apprehends "reality as it truly is," and (2) that were the actual truth concerning the *huqqim*—their true reasons or utilities— made clear to the multitude, it would not merely confuse but harm them.

What is the harm that Maimonides anticipates would befall the multitude if they knew the reasons for the *huqqim*? Immediately following this description of the *huqqim*, and after warning that if they appear to lack reasons it is only because "the deficiency resides in your apprehension," he adds:

> You already know the tradition that is widespread among us according to which the causes for all the commandments, with the exception of that concerning the red heifer, were known to Solomon; and also their dictum that God hid the causes for the commandments in order that they should not be held in little esteem, as happened to Solomon with regard to the three commandments whose causes are made clear. (III:26:507–508)

Here Maimonides proposes that *knowledge* of *ta'amei ha-mitzvot* can lead to antinomianism—"holding the commandments in little esteem."[12] Although he does not explicitly single them out, the commandments he specifically has in mind, I wish to suggest in light of the passage in which this statement occurs, are the *huqqim*. But what these reasons might be, and why knowing them should have this antinomian effect, Maimonides does not tell us, at least not yet. First we must understand the explanation or reasons for the *huqqim*; only then will we be in a position to identify the problem of antinomianism Maimonides anticipates.[13]

For a glimpse of these reasons, we must continue with the second half of chapter III:26, where Maimonides' argument appears to take a remarkable turn. After having defended the "universally agreed upon principle . . . that one should seek in all the laws an end that is useful in regard to being," Maimonides tells us that he

> found in *Bereshith Rabbah* a text of the Sages . . . from which it appears when one first reflects on it that some of the commandments have no other cause than merely to prescribe a law, without there having been in view in them any other end or any real utility. This is their dictum in that passage: *What does it matter to the Holy One, blessed be He, that animals are slaughtered by cutting their neck in front or in the back? Say therefore that the commandments were only given in order to purify the people. For it is said: the word of the Lord is purified.*

In reaction to this text, Maimonides purports to take back his earlier thesis; instead what "everyone endowed with a sound intellect ought to believe" is that only

> the generalities of the commandments [*kellal ha-mitzvah*] necessarily have a cause and have been given because of a certain utility; their details [*helkeha*] are that in regard to which it was said of the commandments that they were given merely for the sake of commanding something. (III:26:508)

On the face of it Maimonides here denies his earlier thesis that all commandments without qualification have reasons or causes. However, a closer look reveals that this revision is not in reality what it appears to be. Let me mention three considerations.

First, the problematic claim Maimonides attributes to *Bereshith Rabbah* is not the only, or even the most plausible, reading of that text. The more obvious interpretation of the *midrash* is rather that the commandments serve to benefit mankind—whom they "purify," say, by inculcating moral traits—rather than God, not that they have no rather than some cause or purpose. That Maimonides does not give the *midrash* this interpretation is all the more puzzling since his own opinion, as he later emphasizes, is also that "the whole purpose [of the Law] consists in what is useful for *us*" mankind (III:31:524, my emphasis). Hence, the question arises why he does not give the passage this more plausible interpretation, which conforms to his own position, rather than the textually unlikely reading that forces him to retract his general thesis.

Second, even if the *midrash* did unequivocally contradict Maimonides' view, he might have overruled it as a minority or individual opinion. As he puts it himself, "this dictum is very strange and has no parallel in their other dicta" (III:26:508). That he does not do this here is, again, all the more puzzling because he *does* adopt this strategy later in chapter 48. After giving the reason for the commandment "to let [the mother] go from the nest [*shiluah ha-ken*]"—which, incidentally, is the same as his reason for the laws of slaughtering, the example explicitly mentioned in the *midrash* of *Bereshith Rabbah* in chapter 26—Maimonides dismisses "as an objection" the Mishnaic dictum that he who says: "Thy mercy extendeth to young birds [should be silenced]. For this is one of the two opinions mentioned by us—I mean the opinion of those who think that there is no reason for the Law except only the will [of God]—but as for us, we follow only the second opinion" (III:48:600). Just as Maimonides sets this Rabbinic opinion aside in deference to his own position, he might have set aside the problematic *midrash* cited in chapter 26 without revising his own view.[14]

Third, after proposing the distinction between "generalities" and "particulars" of commandments in order to reconcile his earlier metaphysical thesis with the passage from *Bereshith Rabbah*, Maimonides begins to illustrate his new position with the law of slaughtering—the example mentioned in the *midrash*—only to undercut the very example in the same breath:

> I have mentioned this example to you merely because one finds [it] in their text . . . However, if one studies the truth of the matter, one finds it to be as follows: As necessity occasions the eating of animals, the commandment was intended to bring about the easiest death in an easy manner. The true reality of particulars of commandments is illustrated by the sacrifices.

In sum, after having made a strong and convincing case for his initial thesis that there exist reasons for all laws without qualification, Maimonides claims to reject it on the basis of a Rabbinic opinion which he himself describes as "strange" and "unparalleled," whose interpretation is far from unequivocal, and whose one example—the details of slaughtering—he himself challenges. Whether or not the distinction between generalities and particulars is substantively real remains to be seen, but this much is already clear from the rhetoric of this passage. It is not because Maimonides has *discovered* a conflicting Rabbinic opinion that he is led to revise the universally held thesis with which he began the chapter. Rather he interjects the *midrash* in order to lend its traditional authority both to the novel and controversial distinction between particulars and generalities which he uses it to introduce and to the example of sacrifices with which he next illustrates that distinction.[15]

According to Maimonides, the sacrifices exemplify "the true reality of particulars of commandments." While the general institution of sacrifices has a "great and manifest utility, . . . no cause will ever be found for the fact that one particular sacrifice consists in a lamb and another in a ram and that the number of the victims should be one particular number" (III:26:509). But as any reader of the coming chapters of the *Guide* knows, it is simply not true that no cause will be given for why a particular sacrifice requires a particular type of animal (Cf. III:39:552; III:46:581, 588). What distinguishes Maimonides' discussion of sacrifices is not that their details are shown to have no reason or cause, but rather the *type* of reason—referring to the historical circumstances in which they were commanded—which *is* given to them. Again, his real concern is not that inquiry into the reasons for these commandments will be vain or empty, but with the types of causes that will be uncovered and the possible consequences if a certain audience knows them.

What are these consequences, and who is this audience? Once again, to answer these questions fully, we must look more closely at Maimonides' actual explanation of sacrifices and related commandments. But one hint is already given here. In chapter 26, discussion of the *huqqim* is not explicitly related to the problem raised by the text of *Bereshith Rabbah* and its solution in terms of the distinction between generalities and particulars. In chapter 28, however, in summarizing his position, Maimonides connects the two. There he tells us that where a commandment is a direct means toward the inculcation of one of the three main ends of the Law—either a true belief ["the welfare of the soul"] or a noble moral quality or political well-being [both elements of "the welfare of the body"]—it "has a clear cause" and "no question concerning [its] end need be posed" (III:28:513).[16] On the other hand, where the commandment does not appear from its "external meaning" [*peshutam*] to be directly useful in one of these three ways people are "perplexed and opinions disagree." Now, those whose understanding is limited to the external meaning of Scripture are the multitude, the same people relative to whose understanding Maimonides states in III:26 that certain laws are labelled *huqqim*. It is specifically these commandments, the *huqqim*, about which, he now says, people dispute whether "there is no utility in them at all except the fact of mere command" or whether "there is a utility in them that is hidden from us" and about which, he adds, "you will hear . . . my exposition of the correct and demonstrated causes for them all *with the sole exception . . . of details and particular commandments*" (III:28:513, my emphasis). Furthermore, his examples are either the same examples cited earlier of *huqqim* or laws for which he later gives historical explanations (See III:37, 39, 40, 46, 48). Maimonides thus hints here at a series of (extensional) correspondences between the following classes of commandments: (i) the *huqqim*, (ii) those commandments whose reason is not grasped from the external meaning of Scripture and by the multitude, (iii) those believed by some to have no end and by others to have an end we do not know, (iv) those knowledge of whose reasons requires historical knowledge, and (v) those whose particulars "have" no reasons (however that claim is understood). The moral I wish to draw is this: Just as Maimonides was concerned that the multitude's knowledge of the *ta'amei ha-mitzvot* of the *huqqim* might lead to antinomianism, so his concern with the reasons for the particulars of certain commandments is motivated by fears of antinomianism among the multitude. Why there should be that concern, and how it is to be dealt with, will be the subject of section V.

III

Thus far I have argued on largely rhetorical grounds that Maimonides' "revised" thesis that only the generalities of commandments have causes, but not necessarily all their particulars, is nothing more than a smokescreen. In this section I will develop this interpretation in greater depth by examining more closely the substance of Maimonides' distinction between "generalities" and "particulars" and the arguments he explicitly gives in support of his alleged revision. Is his claim that particulars "have" no causes a metaphysical, or ontological, thesis—that there exist no causes for at least some particulars, that they are arbitrary, or (as some recent commentators have put it) that there exists "indeterminacy" and "contingency" in the Law (and nature)? Or is it simply an epistemological claim—that there are some particulars whose causes we will probably never know? Similarly, is the distinction between generalities [*kellalim, kellalei ha-mitzvah*] and particulars [*halakim, peratim*] ontological or merely methodological? What is Maimonides' criterion for distinguishing the two?

    Maimonides' first example—the difference between "the offering of sacrifices," a generality which he says has a "great and manifest utility," and "the fact that one particular sacrifice consists in a lamb and another in a ram and that the number of the victims should be one particular number," particulars that he claims have no reason[17]—suggests the ontological interpretation. The relation of the class of sacrifices in general to individual offerings with their respective variations seems analogous to the relation of a species or natural kind to its members with their individual accidental traits or of a whole to its parts.[18] Just as there are laws or causes that hold of species or wholes and not of their individual members or parts, so there might be causes why a generality is commanded but not some of its particulars.

Nonetheless, this interpretation also does not survive a closer look. As we have already mentioned, on at least three different occasions in the coming chapters on *ta'amei ha-mitzvot*, Maimonides gives reasons why only certain species—sheep, goats, and oxen—were sacrificed, why certain types of sacrifices required certain species, and why some sacrifices required males, others females. In each case, the explanation refers to the historical circumstances in which the law was commanded and, specifically, to idolatrous practices current at that time. So, while Maimonides does not explicitly explain why a ram and not a lamb is required for some particular sacrifice, it is not hard to imagine what his explanation would be.

Furthermore, only paragraphs after making the purportedly ontological claim that particulars have no causes, Maimonides adds that "some of the particulars of, and conditions for, some of the commandments have also become clear to me" (II:26:510). And, in concluding his exposition of the reasons for the commandments, he repeats that "there are only a few and some slight details for which I have not given reasons, even though in truth we have virtually given reasons also for these to him who is attentive and comprehending" (III:49:612; cf. also LA). Indeed we cannot give complete reasons for all commandments, Maimonides explains, only because we no longer know all the particulars of the idolatrous practices the Torah was meant to counteract, implying that if we did know all those particulars we would also know the reasons for all particulars of the Law (see III:49:612). Of course, it is not surprising that Maimonides does not dwell on cases where he has nothing to say, nor does he ever claim more than that *some* (not that all) particulars have no reasons. But, at the very least, these statements should make us wonder whether the same author really meant that particulars of commandments have no causes in a straightforward ontological sense.

Add to this the fact that such an ontological thesis does absolutely no *substantive* work in the subsequent account of *ta'amei ha-mitzvot* in chapters 36–49. Nowhere, for example, does Maimonides appeal to such a principle in order to show that some aspect of a commandment *needs* no further explanation or to show that it *cannot* be explained.

Moreover, if the claim were ontological, one would expect it to have a basis in nature, in the particulars of natural phenomena as well. On the contrary, however, Maimonides states that "the belief of the multitude of the men of knowledge in our Law," of the prophets, and of the philosophers is "that the *particulars* of natural acts are all well arranged and ordered and bound up with one another, all of them being causes and effects; and that none of them is futile or frivolous or vain, being acts of perfect wisdom" (III:25:505, my emphasis). Given the parallel he establishes between the explanation of natural phenomena and commandments of the Law, one would expect nothing less to hold for the latter.

Furthermore, the very distinction between generalities and particulars, as Maimonides actually puts it to use, is not fixed or absolute, as one would expect of an ontological distinction like the species/member relation. The identification of a commandment or aspect of a commandment as a "particular" is relative to a choice of "generality," each of which, in turn, is relative to the use of a given system of classification or categorization. Something that is a generality in one categorization might be a particular in another, and within a given system of classification something ordered as a generality relative to one thing might itself be ordered as a particular relative to another. Relativity of this type is exactly what we find in Maimonides' actual explanations of the Law. Generalities of commandments are aspects explained in terms of what Maimonides calls "first" intentions which are "not dependent on time or place" (III:34:535), while particulars are explained (also) in terms of "second" intentions which take into account the historical circumstances in which the commandment was originally promulgated. Now, the same thing that in one context in the *Guide* is a generality to be explained in terms of a first intention, in another context becomes a particular to be explained by a second intention. For example, in chapter 26 the institution of sacrifice is the generality relative to which the sacrifice of a ram is a particular, presumably to be explained by a second intention having to do with actual idolatrous practices. But in chapter 32 the *institution* of sacrifice tout cour is treated as a particular, explained in terms of a second intention having to do with the Israelites' habituation to such a form of worship, relative to which *any* mode of worship of God is the corresponding generality.[19]

In short, the entire import of the generality/particular distinction seems to be methodological and epistemological. For the purposes of the account of *ta'amei ha-mitzvot* that follows in chapters 36–49, the generalities of the commandments correspond to the fourteen classes into which Maimonides divides them in chapter 35, while the particulars correspond to the individual commandments that belong to each class. This classification is not the only possible one; indeed it is not even the only one Maimonides himself proposed within his lifetime. Furthermore, although some individual laws "may be fancied . . . to have no utility or . . . to constitute a decree that cannot be comprehended by the intellect in any way" (III:35:538), Maimonides says that he will "explain the reasons for them and in what respect they are useful, making an exception only for those few whose purpose I have not grasped up to this time" (ibid.). The only remaining difference is that generalities seem to have utilities "about which there can be no doubt and to which there can be no objection" (III:27:510); whereas particulars, as is characteristic of our knowledge of historical and contingent matters, can vary in their probability and certainty. Thus for *all* laws, both in general and in detail, there are said to exist causes that differ, at most, in their epistemic status: in whether and how they are known.

Before turning to this epistemological interpretation of Maimonides' generality/particular thesis, there remains one last passage to be examined that has been claimed to support the ontological reading. Immediately following his statement that the "true reality of particulars of the commandments is illustrated by the sacrifices," Maimonides writes:

> Know that wisdom rendered it necessary—or, if you will, say that necessity occasioned—that there should be particulars for which no cause can be found; it was, as it were, impossible in regard to the Law that there should be nothing of this class in it. In such a case the impossibility is due to the circumstances that when you ask why a lamb should be prescribed and not a ram, the same question would have to be asked if a ram had been prescribed instead of a lamb. But one particular species had necessarily to be chosen. The same holds for your asking why seven lambs and not eight have been prescribed. For a similar question would have been put if eight or ten or twenty had been prescribed. However, one particular number had necessarily to be chosen. This resembles the nature of the possible, for it is certain that one of the possibilities will come to pass. And no question should be put why one particular possibility and not another comes to pass, for a similar question would become necessary if another possibility instead of this particular one had come to pass. (III:26:509)[20]

Note, to begin with, that this passage would not contradict Maimonides' original thesis that all laws are consequent upon wisdom—*if* it is *wisdom* that renders it necessary that there be particulars which have no causes (cf. III:15:459ff.; III:34:534). By the same token, the existence of such particulars would also not support the opposing view that some commandments are consequent on the divine will alone.

There is, however, one interpretation of this passage on which it does purport to show that particulars have no causes and instead are the products of arbitrary decisions of God's voluntary will. This interpretation was first offered by the medieval commentator Shem Tob ibn Shem Tob and, according to more recent scholars, the argument on this view is modelled after the classical problem of choice known as "Buridan's Ass," to which al-Ghazali alludes in his *Incoherence of the Philosophers*.[21] In opposition to the Aristotelians who held that all choices require a reason (including a preference) or "differentiating principle" that determines the alternative selected, al-Ghazali held that it is precisely the nature of the voluntary will to differentiate one thing from another, and so to choose one rather than the other, even where there exist no distinguishing grounds between the objects of choice. To use the standard example, suppose a thirsty man has before him two qualitatively indistinguishable glasses of wine. According to the Aristotelians, he will necessarily be unable to choose between them for lack of a distinguishing principle—and must remain forever thirsty. According to al-Ghazali, he will simply pick one, whichever it happens to be, without having any reason other than his will, whose nature it is to decide between such qualitatively indiscernable things. Similarly, to return to the example of chapter 26, the fact that Maimonides claims that we can always reverse the lamb/ram question is taken by Shem Tob to show that he believes that there is no reason, or differentiating principle, for choosing one over the other; hence, if God did command one and not the other, it must have been simply in virtue of an arbitrary decision of His will.

There are two serious difficulties with this interpretation. First, the fact that the question, Why a lamb and not a ram? can be reversed only shows that the two alternatives are symmetrical or mutually indifferent; that is, that we have equally good reasons for choosing one as we have for choosing the other. This situation is sufficient to give rise to the problem of choice raised by Buridan's Ass, but it does not yield the conclusion required by Maimonides: that neither alternative has any reason or that the choice in question is arbitrary—lacking all reason.[22] Second, one must at least wonder whether Maimonides could have plausibly held that choosing between a ram and a lamb or between different numbers of animals, is really analogous to the Buridan's Ass situation where we have two indistinguishable cups of wine. Of course, it is not necessary that there be no differences between the objects but only no *relevant* differences *relative to the chooser's beliefs*. But that there is no such difference in such cases for an omniscient divinity requires at the very least some additional argument.

There does seem to me to be, however, another possible indirect Ghazalian source for the argument in III:26, though its import is, again, epistemological rather than ontological. In considering the question of the eternity versus creation of the world, Maimonides repeatedly points out the failure of Aristotelian natural science to account for particular celestial phenomena. In words reminiscent of our passage in III:26, he argues, for example, that "we do not know what was His wisdom in making it necessary that the spheres should be nine—neither more nor less—and the number of the stars equal to what it is—neither more nor less—and that they should be neither bigger nor smaller than they are" (II:18:301–302). And as an apparent alternative to the Aristotelian God of necessity, he argues, therefore, for the existence of "One possessing purpose who chose freely and willed that all things should be as they are" (II:19:303), a conception of God that at first glance owes much to al-Ghazali. In fact, to describe this God and His mode of creation, Maimonides even takes over the Kalam terms *Particularizer* (*mukhassis*) and *particularization* (*takhsis*), terms closely connected to the mutakallimun conception of possibility according to which anything that can be imagined is possible and among these possible options there is never an intrinsic reason why one rather than another should exist. Therefore, what does exist in the particular way that it actually does can only be due to the free action of a Particularizer who willed it to exist as such.[23]

Yet, despite these apparent similarities, there is also good reason to doubt that Maimonides himself held to such a notion of a God. For the Kalam conception entails the utter negation of nature and natural causality while Maimonides not only holds to these in principle but even believes that Aristotelian natural science actually gives us a satisfactory causal explanation of sublunar phenomena. Furthermore, and of special importance to us, Maimonides explicitly tells us that what the Kalam means by "particularization" is not what he means (II:19:303). Although he posits the existence of a Particularizer to account for the celestial phenomena for which we have no adequate physical theory, the major function this posit serves—inasmuch as the will of this Particularizer follows from His wisdom—is to register the fact that there exist causes for these phenomena despite the limitations of human knowledge that may prevent us from knowing what they are. In other words, Maimonides' introduction of a Particularizer is simply a means of baptizing the distinction between the metaphysical and epistemological theses that all natural—including celestial—phenomena are caused.[24]

To return now to the passage in III:26, the moral I wish to draw should be clear. The reversability of the ram/lamb question, and its analogue in "the nature of the possible," suggests a Kalam conception of alternative possibilities each of which, *at least relative to human knowl-*

edge, could equally well have been actualized if not for the act of a Particularizer who chose one of them. But the Legislator who chooses one rather than another particular of the Law, like Maimonides' Particularizer in nature—and among the terms for *particular* used in III:26 is the very same Kalam term for *particularization* (*makhsus*) of Part II—is not one who chooses arbitrarily or by virtue of His will as *opposed* to His wisdom. Rather, for all these particulars, as for the particulars of all natural and celestial phenomena, there are causes determined by divine (i.e., natural) wisdom, though we may never know them. Here, again, the sole function of the argument is to register the distinction between the metaphysical thesis that there exist causes for all laws and the epistemological claim that they may nonetheless lie beyond the limits of human knowledge.[25]

For the remainder of this chapter, I will therefore take it as established that Maimonides' statements that some particulars of commandments "have" no causes should be understood only as the epistemological claim that they have no causes known to us. This brings us to our next question: What are Maimonides' grounds for this epistemological view? When he first introduces the *huqqim* in III:26, he distinguishes two reasons why the Sages believed that their causes may be "hidden from us": "the incapacity of our intellects" and "the deficiency of our knowledge" (507). We are now in a position to make these reasons more precise, beginning with the second.

As we have already mentioned, and will further see in the next section, Maimonides believes that the positive explanation of the *huqqim*, or of particulars of certain commandments, must take into account the idolatrous practices current among the ancient Sabians at the time of the Mosaic legislation. The first way, then, in which one can fail to know their reasons is by being ignorant of, or "deficient" in, this historical knowledge. This is the typical situation of the uneducated multitude. But because records about certain details of Sabian idolatry may also have been lost or destroyed, even the philosopher might find himself in a similar deficient state of knowledge. Thus Maimonides explicitly states on three occasions in the course of his actual exposition of *ta'amei ha-mitzvot* that he does not know the reasons for particular commandments and, in each of these instances, the explanation would appear to be the lack of available historical information (cf. III:45:578; III:46:591; III:47:597).

The second reason—"the incapacity of our intellects"—appears to hint at a still stronger constraint on *possible* human knowledge of causes for particulars. An elaboration of this theme is possibly to be found at the very conclusion of Maimonides' exposition of *ta'amei ha-mitzvot*, where he inserts a novel element into his account:

The fact that there are particulars the reason for which is hidden from me and the utility of which I do not understand, is due to the circumstance that things known by hearsay are not like things that one has seen. Hence, the extent of my knowledge of the ways of the Sabians drawn from books is not comparable to the knowledge of one who saw their practices with his eyes. (III:49:612)

And, again, in the next chapter, while explaining the details of scriptural narratives, which he describes as "mysteries of [sitrei] the Torah," Maimonides adds:

You should also understand that the status of things that are set down in writing is not the same as the status of happenings that one sees. For in happenings that one sees, there are particulars that bring about necessary consequences of great importance, which cannot be mentioned except in a prolix manner. Accordingly, when narrations concerning these happenings are considered, the individual who reflects thinks that such narrations are too long or repetitious. If, however, he had seen what is narrated, he would know the necessity of what is recounted. (III:50:615)

It is not obvious how much we should make of these passages. On the one hand, this source of ignorance is not simply a matter of contingent accident, for example, failure to possess the appropriate information because the records of Sabianism have been lost or destroyed. The limitation to which Maimonides points here applies to *every* individual's knowledge about *some* happenings in the past, no matter how complete his evidence, because, for each individual, there are certainly some events he never saw with his own eyes (say, before he was born) and which he can know only on the basis of some other individual's description, either oral or written. If we accept Maimonides' argument, no matter how rich and complete these descriptions may be, they must nonetheless fail to describe with accuracy some particular aspect of those past happenings without which some particular in the Law or in a scriptural narration cannot, in turn, be explained. Thus this brand of skepticism with respect to human knowledge of the past would seem to arise as a matter of *necessity* given such a theory of human knowledge and linguistic description.

On the other hand, Maimonides gives us almost no argument for this view of knowledge, keeping in mind that it is the correctness of all *possible* written and oral description that is in question. Much writing and hearsay is, of course, inaccurate and imprecise, but that truism obviously carries little weight in epistemology. One might detect a touch of verificationalism in Maimonides' position but, in short, he tells us too little in these brief remarks to support much of a conclusion. The one implication which is absolutely clear is that if we do not know the cause of some particular in the Law, it is not because there is no cause, but because of our knowledge.

IV

The *huqqim*, I have now argued, are no exception, according to Maimonides, to his general thesis that the particulars as well as generalities of commandments all have reasons, though we do not always know what they are. However, as I argued in section II, Maimonides also appears to believe that, while the *huqqim* have reasons, it would be better for some members of the community *not* to know them. To explain why, and its consequences for his general conception of *ta'amei ha-mitzvot*, I now wish to turn to Maimonides' own positive idea of a *hoq*, which is based, as we have already mentioned, on his use of historical or contextual explanations for certain commandments.

Beginning in chapter 29, Maimonides summarizes the "doctrines, opinions, practices, and cult of the Sabians" from which, he tells us, "the meaning of many of the laws . . . and their causes became known to [him]," including "the reasons for the commandments that are considered to be without cause" (III:29:518)—the *huqqim*. His use of this information about Sabian culture to explain various commandments as means of eradicating idolatry, "the first intention of the Law" (III:29:517), is well known. Here I will only discuss certain differences among these historical or contextual explanations of different types of laws that are specifically relevant to Maimonides' understanding of a *hoq*.

We can distinguish three different classes of commandments whose explanations utilize historical information about the Sabian context in which the Law was first commanded to Israel. The first class, which Maimonides introduces through an example of nonlegal scriptural exegesis—the interpretation of the particular blessings and curses of the covenant (III:30:522–23, III:37:543)—consists of all those commandments that came to refute what had been the idolatrous practices of the Sabians at that time. These commandments require us either (i) to perform the contrary of what the Sabians performed or (ii) to refrain from some action because it was one of their idolatrous practices or (iii) to perform it because they prohibited it. In each of these ways, "wrong opinions, which are diseases of the human soul, are cured by their contrary found at the other extreme" (III:46:582); and, on this medical model, Maimonides explains the classic Rabbinic example of a *hoq*, *sha'atnez* (mingled stuff), as well as a large and varied group of other laws, thus beginning to expand the class of *huqqim* beyond the traditional number.[26]

Why are these particular prohibitions and prescriptions called "*huqqim*"? According to their midrashic characterization, the *huqqim* are laws "criticized by the Gentiles." If the Gentiles symbolize the forces of idolatry, it is understandable why they oppose these laws designed to obliterate idolatry. Furthermore, to identify the scriptural prohibition against following the practices of the Sabians, Maimonides cites the verse "And you shall not walk in the customs of the nations [*huqqoth ha-goyim*]" (Lev. 20:23), which the Rabbis interpreted to refer to "Amorite usages," that is, "magical practises [that are] not required by reasoning concerning nature and [that] is turned into a glorification and a worship of the stars" (III:29:517; III:37:543), and which Maimonides, in turn, extends to all activities associated with idolatry. Philologically, the *huqqim* are so-called because they refute the *huqqoth ha-goyim*.[27]

In addition to this already broad class of commandments, Maimonides extends his characterization of a *hoq* to cover a still larger and more central portion of the Law. In this connection it is especially important that we find in the *Mishneh Torah* the two following *halakhic* decisions:

> All the [laws concerning the] sacrifices are in the category of *huqqim*. (*MT* "Me'ilah" viii, 8)

> It is plain and manifest that the laws of impurity and purity are decrees of Scripture and not matters about which the opinion of men [*da'ato shel 'adam*] could form a judgement; and behold they are included among the *huqqim*. (*MT* "Mikva'ot" xi, 12)[28]

Neither of these *halakhot*, to my knowledge, has a precedent in the Rabbinic literature; only in the *Guide* do we find their full explanation but there, on the other hand, neither is drawn as an explicit conclusion. We have here a further example of how the *Guide* serves as the *gemara* for the *Mishneh Torah* and the *Mishneh Torah* as an apodictic compendium of the often not openly drawn results of the *Guide*. To illustrate why Maimonides considers these two classes of commandments *huqqim*, I shall examine now the sacrificial commandments in some detail. The laws of purity and impurity I shall take up in turn in the next chapter.

As others have noted, Maimonides' explanation of the commandments of sacrifice found in the Mosaic legislation in terms of the prevalence of sacrificial worship in the idolatrous ancient world differs from his appeal to similar historical facts to explain the first class of *huqqim*. With the latter, the commandments are shown to be particularized so as to deny or uproot the specific idolatrous practices that historically existed; with the former, the commandments reflect an attempt to accommodate the worship of God as it was ideally intended with the historical circumstances, given certain necessities of human nature—man's resistance to radical changes, his reliance on habit, his need for gradual transitions.

What should also be emphasized is the difference between the *explananda*—what is being explained—in the two cases. With the first class of *huqqim*, what is explained is why the practice (e.g., *sha'atnez*) is commanded at all. But with the second class, it is obvious why, for example, sacrifices are commanded: to worship God. As Maimonides hints and Scripture explicitly states, sacrifice as a mode of divine worship was well entrenched before the Mosaic legislation and, more important, even before the first appearance of idolatry. What he wishes to explain in giving the reason for the Mosaic commandment of sacrifice is not what end its serves, but rather, given the first intention of the Law to efface idolatry and all practices associated with it, how God could nonetheless command Israel as part of the Mosaic legislation to offer, or continue to offer, sacrifices, also given their idolatrous identification at that time. It is not, then, because the reason for sacrifice is unknown that it needs explanation. What needs explanation is that sacrifice is commanded *despite* the fact that as a common mode of idolatrous worship its use is *inconsistent* with the first intention of the Law.[29] Sacrifice, in short, is *problematic*. And it is in answer to this problem that Maimonides proposes that the diety's "wily graciousness" and His "gracious ruse"—again drawing on the deep parallel between the divine commandments and natural acts—did not require the "rejection, abandonment, and abolition of all these kinds of worship" but instead "transferred" them to His worship while "restricting" their practice to specific places, times, and persons (III:32:526–28). In this way both the first intention of the Law—the effacement of idolatry and establishment of belief in the existence and unity of God—as well as its second intention—to respect the necessities of human nature—were simultaneously achieved. Sacrifices exhibit, in proper Talmudic fashion, the resolution and compromise of contrary and contradictory pressures, the ideals of the Law with the demands of human nature.

The *huqqim* exemplified by the sacrifices thus occupy a central place in Maimonides' theory of *ta'amei ha-mitzvot* because they provide a model of explanation for the commandments in general. This, we should emphasize, stands in contrast to all previous rabbinic accounts according to which the *huqqim* were isolated exceptions to the Law which lack reasons, either ontologically or epistemologically. According to Maimonides' model, each commandment can be analyzed as the 'product' of two 'vectors' denoting its first and second intentions. Depending on the relative contributions of the first and second intentions to the final shape of the commandment, the 'magnitudes' of the vectors will vary relative to each other.[30] For example, sacrifice and prayer share the same first intention (to worship the divinity), but the vector denoting its second intention will be greater in the case of sacrifice than in the case of prayer where the commandment "comes closer to the first intention" (III:32:529). By identifying these distinct intentions behind each commandment, one comes to apprehend the divine wisdom by means of which the fundamental principles of divine worship were realized within the constraints of nature. Furthermore, one also comes to appreciate better how in practice to engage in that worship, for example, how to avoid mistaking the second intention of a commandment for its first intention.[31]

This model of explanation, based on distinguishing first and second intentions underlying commandments, also creates a new challenge to the authority of the Law. If the particular form of a certain commandment is the product of realizing a first intention of the Law within the confines of nature at a given time according to its second intention, why shouldn't it be permissable, and even desirable, to attempt to realize that first intention in other ways when the original circumstances of nature shift or change? In particular, if the sacrifices and elements in the first class of *huqqim* were designed to deny, either directly or indirectly, the particular Sabian idolatrous practices current at the time of the Mosaic legislation, why should it nonetheless be obligatory to continue to perform these commandments when idolatry in general and these Sabian practices in particular have disappeared? Explanations like Maimonides' should at least make us ask why it must be true that "there never has been a Law and there never will be a Law except the one that is the law of Moses our Master" (II:39:379). In the next, and last, section of this chapter, I turn to Maimonides' response to this variety of antinomianism.[32]

V

In Part I we distinguished two different questions one might be asking in seeking *ta'amei ha-mitzvot*: the "commandment question" and the "performance question." With the *huqqim*, such as sacrifices, these two questions radically diverge: not only is the reason why Israel was originally commanded to offer sacrifices not a reason for *me* at *present* to perform that same commandment; assuming I recognize the idolatrous associations of all sacrifice, even in worship of God, knowledge of those historical reasons for the commandment would be reason for me now not to sacrifice.

In the case of the *huqqim*, it is *knowledge* of their reasons that creates, then, the potential for a new variety of antinomianism, new opportunities for the rejection of the Law. This form of antinomianism should be distinguished from a more general type, which Maimonides also counters in the *Guide* and which is directed against *all* inquiry into *ta'amei ha-mitzvot*, not specifically against study of the reasons for the *huqqim*:

> There is a group of human beings who consider it a grievous thing that causes should be given for any law; what would please them most is that the intellect would not find a meaning for the commandments and prohibitions . . . For they think that if those laws were useful in this existence and had been given to us for this or that reason, it would be as if they derived from the reflection and the understanding of some intelligent being. If, however, there is a thing for which the intellect could not find any meaning at all and that does not lead to something useful, it indubitably derives from God; for the reflection of man would not lead to such a thing. (III:31:523–24)

We might paraphrase this argument as follows. Any explanation of a commandment that purports to provide an independent reason why God legislated it is ipso facto a reason why a human legislator also should have instituted it—and a reason why we ought to perform it, *whether or not God commanded it*. So, by furnishing reasons to explain why God legislated the commandments, we have thereby explained *away* their status as the products of a divine author and, hence, impugned their divine authority. This Euthyphrolike argument has a counterpart in the explanation of natural phenomena. In III:25 Maimonides tells us that the Ash'arites deny that any particular natural phenomenon has an end (only) because they fear that, conceding that point, they will ultimately be forced to accept the eternity—or (causal) necessity—rather than divine creation of the world. With both the commandments and divine, or natural, acts, then, the Ash'arites argue that any attempt at their rational explanation must lead to the denial that they are the free creations or products of an omnipotent divinity.

Maimonides' defense of inquiry into *ta'amei ha-mitzvot* against this threat of antinomianism is twofold. First, he argues that the Ash'arite argument entails a conception of God that turns Him into an agent whose actions are futile or worse (III:25:504, III:31:524). Second, and more important, it assumes a conception of the Law that denies its essential scriptural characterization: that its "whole purpose consist[s] in what is useful for us" (III:31:524). The crux of this second response lies in Maimonides' own conception of what makes a law divine, a conception diametrically opposed to the Ash'arite's. For the Ash'arite, a law is divine because it is the product of the unlimited, voluntary will of God;

its divine authority lies in the identity of its divine legislator. For Maimonides, what makes a law divine is its content: that its ordinances aim at the theoretical and intellectual perfection of its citizens as well as their physical, moral, and political well-being. A law is not divine, on his view, *because* it was legislated by a diety; rather, it must have been legislated by God because its content is divine.[33] Hence, to assert, as Maimonides does, that the Mosaic Law in particular is divine entails that its commandments have not only ends but specific kinds of ends, those that enable the community to achieve its intellectual well-being, namely, the kind of environment that in turn enables its individual members to realize their highest intellectual perfections according to their respective capacities. From this point of view, belief in the divinity of the Law and inquiry into the reasons for its commandments are not, then, mutually exclusive but complementary. Indeed belief that the Law is divine *mandates* inquiry into ta'amei ha-mitzvot. On the one hand, the divinity of the Law is what guarantees the presupposition for all such inquiry that each commandment has a reason to be sought, regardless of whether we discover it and even despite the fact that we will inevitably be ignorant of some reasons because of the limitations of human knowledge. On the other hand, the *ta'amei ha-mitzvot* are, in turn, what confirm and validate the belief that the Law is divine; for only such inquiry can demonstrate that the Torah actually achieves those specific ends that render it divine. Contrary to the Ash'arite argument, then, inquiry into *ta'amei ha-mitzvot* should not lead to denial of the divinity of the Law and subversion of its authority; it is rather absolutely necessary in order to substantiate its divine character.

This argument is meant to counter a more general worry about antinomianism than that engendered specifically by the *huqqim*. Yet even here the *huqqim* have a central place in Maimonides' response, for their explanation involves perhaps the paradigmatic use of natural causes that are "useful for us . . . in this existence" (III:31:524) and, hence, provide Maimonides' best case against proponents of this Ash'arite argument. Also for this reason, Maimonides interjects this objection in chapter 31, not at the beginning of his discussion of ta'amei ha-mitzvot in chapter 26 where one would naturally expect to find it, but sandwiched in between his first application of the method of historical explanation—the exegesis of the particular blessings and curses in the covenant (chapter 30)—and his second application to the sacrifices (chapter 32). The role of the *huqqim* emerges in Maimonides' central prooftext in answer to the Ash'arites, Deut. 4:6. This verse states explicitly

> that even all the statutes [*huqqim*] will show to all the nations that they have been given with wisdom and understanding. Now if there is a

thing for which no reason is known and that does not either procure
something useful or ward off something harmful, why should one say
of one who believes in it or practices it that he is wise and understanding and of great worth? And why should the religious communities
think it a wonder? (III:31:524)

The force of this prooftext does not consist solely in the fact that the
huqqim are laws whose reasons are typically not known or which are
typically believed to have no reasons. Equally important is what Maimonides believes *is* their reason: namely, to bring Israel to deny idolatry.
The verse states that the "Nations"—the purveyors of idolatry and,
according to the *midrash*, the critics of the *huqqim*—will themselves recognize the "wisdom and understanding" of the *huqqim*; that is, they will
recognize the *truth* of the belief the *huqqim* communicate—that idolatry
is false—through the idolatry-looking means they employ to communicate it. The eschatological dimension of the verse should also not be
ignored. Idolatry is not overcome until *all* idolators renounce it and,
until such time, all such *huqqim* will have a reason—even if they have
ceased to serve such an end for the community of Israel proper. With an
eye toward the further type of antinomianism raised specifically by the
huqqim, Maimonides may also be cautioning us not to dismiss them too
quickly as historically anachronistic.[34]

Now, that Maimonides' use of historical explanations for the sacrifices encourages antinomianism has often been raised as an objection.
But it is such an obvious objection—the problem was already discussed
by his medieval commentators and critics, both Jewish and Christian—
that it is impossible to assume that Maimonides could not have been
aware of it himself.[35] In the remainder of this chapter, I shall show how
he not only anticipated the objection but responds to it in the *Guide*. His
response takes several forms, corresponding to his different audiences
and the different issues that this problem of authority raises.

To begin with, as I have hinted all along, Maimonides' concern that
antinomian consequences would result if the multitude were to know the
reasons for the *huqqim* is what motivates the oblique presentation he
adopts in chapter III:26. This stance toward the multitude does not,
however, solve the philosophical problem Maimonides has created, nor
will it satisfy the philosophers among his readers. Maimonides' response
to this audience, and to the philosophical problem of antinomianism
raised by the *huqqim*, has at least three distinct dimensions.[36]

The first aspect concerns the character of the Law: Why could the
Law not be constructed in such a way that it be sensitive to changing circumstances, to the different needs of different individuals, and to vary-
ing historical conditions? If the Mosaic Law in particular was originally

framed in view of the historical conditions that obtained at the time of
its legislation, why, once those historical conditions have passed, must
it remain forever the same? Why is it not possible to revise its commandments, or to substitute new commandments for those that have
outlived their original function? This question, together with a different
though formally similar issue, is directly raised by Maimonides in chapter III:34 and elaborated in a sister passage in chapter III:41. Just as the
Law, which is "a divine thing," is necessarily framed only "for the
majority of cases" and does not "pay attention to the isolated" individual—even if he is harmed by the Law or not personally perfected by it—
so

> In view of this consideration, it also will not be possible that the laws
> be dependent on changes in the circumstances of the individuals and of
> the times, as is the case with regard to medical treatment, which is par-
> ticularized for every individual in conformity with his present temper-
> ament. On the contrary, governance of the Law ought to be absolute
> and universal, including everyone, even if it is suitable only for certain
> individuals and not suitable for others; for it it were made to fit indi-
> viduals, the whole would be corrupted and *you would make out of it
> something that varies.* For this reason, matters that are primarily
> intended in the Law ought not to be dependent on time or place; but
> the decrees ought to be absolute and universal, according to what
> He . . . says: *As for the congregation, there shall be one statute
> [huqqah] for you.* [Num. 15:15] (III:34:534–35)[37]

Here Maimonides makes three claims: (1) The Law, unlike
medicine, cannot be made to fit every need of every individual in every
circumstance. (2) Precisely for this reason, the *first* intentions of the Law
("matters that are primarily intended") should be independent of time
and place; that is, they should be purposes that are appropriate ends to
seek in all circumstances, or reasons that are *beyond* the changing con-
tingencies of time and place. (3) However, the decrees or commandments themselves—in the language of the prooftext, the *huqqoth*, a
choice of expression that cannot be merely coincidental given Maimonides' general use of the term—are to be absolutely—that is, uncon-
ditionally—and universally—that is, without exception—binding
despite the fact that they are the products of *second* (in addition to first)
intentions that generally are appropriate only in some times and places
and take into account historical conditions that change.

The same theme is elaborated in III:41. There Maimonides argues
that specifically *because* God knew that commandments

> will need in every time and place . . . to be added to or subtracted from
> according to the diversity of places, happenings, and conjunctures of
> circumstances, He forbade adding to them or subtracting from

them . . . For this might have led to the corruption of the rules of the Law and to the belief that the latter did not come from God. (III:41:563)

Here Maimonides alludes to two reasons—also to be found in III:34—why the Law must remain the same despite changes in the contingent circumstances of individuals or the community: the first political or institutional, the second ontological. Politically or institutionally, a law that admits changes and exceptions to its rules as circumstances change will be "corrupted"; in attempting to give its due to every particular, the Law must lose its universality or nomicity, hence, its law-likeness. The deeper consideration, however, is the ontological one: the implication that, if it did allow such change, it would be believed that the Law did not "come from God." This issue draws on the deep parallel we have repeatedly seen between the Law and nature. "All things proceed from one deity and one agent and have been given from one shepherd" (III:34:534). So, to appreciate why it must be the case that the Law is framed only for the majority of cases and "is not perfectly achieved in every individual," *and* why this feature is no deficiency in the Law, Maimonides tells us to turn to the example of nature where we also discover that "natural things" only aim at the "general utility" despite the fact that it [the general utility] "nonetheless produces damages to individuals" (III:34:534). Analogously, just as nature—"the works of the deity" (II:28:335)—is perfect, with no excess or deficiency because of which it might ever be changed or might ever come to a temporal end, so the Law which is also "as perfect as it is possible to be within its species" (II:39:380) will never change or be nullified.[38]

Some further implications of this parallel should also be made explicit. When Maimonides claims (in II:28) that nature, or the world, will never change, he means that it is eternal *a parte post*, and a similar claim is intended for the Law (in II:39). But just as the eternity *a parte post* of the world does not exclude change *within* nature, and *in accordance with* its laws, so the claim that the Law will never be changed does not exclude—on the contrary, it allows for and even requires—change *within* the Law *according to the measures and means set up by the Law*. Drawing out this very implication, Maimonides argues in III:41 further that, precisely in view of the constancy or eternity of the Law, courts are permitted to enact innovative regulations [*takanot*] and temporary decisions [*hora'ot sha'ah*]. "Through this kind of governance the Law remains one, and one is governed in every time and with a view to every happening in accordance with that happening" (III:41:563). In sum, the analogy between nature and the Law not only picks out a common sense in which they are meant to be *eternal* but also common modes in which each admits *change*.[39]

In light of his use of the same argument from "perfection" for the eternity *a parte post* *both* of the world (in II:28) and of the Law (in II:39), we can better understand why Maimonides cites Ps. 148, 6 as prooftext for his claim that the heavens are eternal *a parte post* (though created). According to the verse, "the *statutes*, which He has laid down, will never be changed. For the word *statute* alludes [*remez*] to the *statutes of heaven and earth* (Jer. 33, 25) . . . However, he makes it clear that they are created" (II:28:335). On the external meaning of the verse, the word *statute*, the word Maimonides figuratively uses to *allude* to the heavens, *literally refers* to the legal entity. Thus he implies that the "statutes" of the Law—the *ḥuqqim*, for whom the problem of authority arises in particular—also will never depart. Recalling Maimonides' description of the two levels of parabolic interpretation, here we have a perfect example of a verse whose "external meaning contains wisdom that is useful in many respects, among which is the welfare of human societies" and whose "internal meaning . . . contains wisdom that is useful for beliefs concerned with the truth as it is" (I:Introduction:12). The external meaning of the verse is a claim about the Mosaic law governing the Jewish community, its internal meaning, a claim about the eternity *a parte post* of the physical world.

The second dimension of the problem of authority concerns the grounds of obligation to obey commandments when the reasons why they were originally legislated are no longer pertinent; the third concerns the reason an agent at present might use to justify their performance. Maimonides does not, to my knowledge, explicitly address either of these questions as they apply to the community as a whole. Instead he responds to similar questions that arise specifically for the *hakham*, the philosopher or "man of science," and leaves it to his reader to work out the corresponding answers for the questions that arise for the community. So, to take the first of these last two questions, Maimonides directly responds to the more specific question: Why *should*, and *must*, the philosopher at the highest stage of worship continue to observe all, or certain, commandments, one, when he can worship God through the higher form and, two, when he knows that certain commandments are even *opposed* to the requirements of that higher form of worship?[40]

Maimonides directs us to his response to this question by way of an apparently incidental analogy he interjects into his explanation of the commandment of sacrifice. To illustrate how difficult it would have been for the ancient Israelites to accept a Law absolutely abolishing sacrifice, given its entrenchment at that time and given "the nature of man, which always likes that to which it is accustomed," Maimonides suggests that

> At that time this would have been similar to the appearance of a
> prophet in these times who, calling upon the people to worship God,
> would say: "God has given you a Law forbidding you to pray to Him,
> to fast, to call upon Him for help in misfortune. Your worship should
> consist solely in meditation without any works at all." (III:32:526)

The point of this analogy is unmistakable: just as sacrifice was a divine
concession to achieve the first intention of the Law (to deny idolatry)
within the limits imposed by the second intention (to respect the necessities of human nature) and the historical circumstances, so the institution of verbal prayer is a similar accommodation, "closer to the first
intention and . . . necessary for its achievement" (III:32:529), but
nonetheless an ideally undesirable accommodation to certain other
necessities that remain "in these times." Sacrifice and verbal prayer, in
other words, differ only in *degree*, indicating more importantly that they
are one in *kind*: each, in its particular context, is a particular mode of
worship that is legislated only in light of certain exigencies of human
nature.[41]

The basis for this negative attitude toward verbal prayer is found in
Part I of the *Guide*. Because prayer utilizes affirmative attributes to
describe, refer to, and praise God, all of its predications either falsely
compare Him to created entities or contradict His Unity or imply a deficiency in Him. The content of verbal prayer thus contradicts, and
obstructs, our apprehension of God, to the limited extent to which it is
possible at all. At most we can describe Him using negative attributes—
though even that mode of expression is not free of all problems; but at
best "silence and limiting oneself to the apprehensions of the intellect are
more appropriate" (I:59:140; cf. I:57: 132–33).

But if this is so, if verbal prayer necessarily involves the utterance of
falsehoods about God, then why is it *commanded*? And why must those
who have attained a correct apprehension of possible human knowledge
of God and thus recognize that silent contemplation would be far
preferable to verbal prayer—why must they, according to the Law,
nonetheless continue to use verbal prayer? Maimonides' answer:

> if we were left only to our intellects we should never have mentioned
> these attributes or stated a thing appertaining to them. Yet the neces-
> sity to address men in such terms as would make them achieve some
> representation—in accordance with the dictum of the Sages: *The Torah
> speaks in the language of the sons of man*—obliged resort to predicat-
> ing of God their own perfections when speaking to them. It must then
> be our purpose to draw a line at using these expressions and not to
> apply them to Him except only in reading the Torah. However, as the
> men of the Great Synagogue, who were prophets, appeared in their
> turn and inserted the mention of these attributes in the prayer, it is our

purpose to pronounce only these attributes when saying our prayers. According to the spirit, this dictum makes it clear that, as it happened, two necessary obligations determined our naming these attributes in our prayers: one of them is that they occur in the Torah, and the other is that the prophets in question used them in the prayer they composed. (I:59:140)

Exactly like sacrifice, Maimonides tells us that it was only circumstantial necessity due specifically to the limited understanding and habits of the multitude—"the sons of man"—that led to the introduction, first in the Torah and later in prayer, of predications of affirmative attributes to God. However, once these divine attributes occurred in the Torah and once they were used by the prophets in their verbal prayers, these facts alone seem to have been sufficient to make it obligatory on everyone in the community, including the philosophers, to continue their use in verbal prayer—despite the fact that some of them also know better.

The crux of this defense of the obligatory use of affirmative attributes in reading the Torah and in verbal prayer—and, by implication, of the obligatoriness of the *huqqim*—is the assumption that we must distinguish between the reason why something was legislated and that which renders it necessary or obligatory. If we do distinguish the two, then even if the *explanation* of the legislation of a commandment reveals among its causes contextual factors which are no longer pertinent, its *necessity* or *obligatoriness*, given that it was commanded, might be claimed to stand on its own. To this extent we can attempt to 'insulate' the grounds of obligation to obey a commandment from the obsolescence threatened by context-restricted reasons because of which it was introduced.

This move does not, however, give *us* a reason why *we* should or must perform these practices and, unfortunately, we are told disappointingly little about positive grounds of obligation. Maimonides only states that they consist in the fact that (say) the attributes "occur in the Torah" or, more generally, as part of the Prophetic tradition. Perhaps the sacred character of these texts is meant to render whatever is found in them sacred and, therefore, in some sense, obligatory.[42] Or perhaps Maimonides' idea is that individual practices should not, and (in some cases) cannot, be justified or be shown to be obligatory each in isolation, taken one by one, but only derivatively as parts of the Torah or prophetic tradition as a whole, which itself, to borrow a phrase of W. V. O. Quine, faces the tribunal of justification as a single corporate body. Thus the grounds for one's obligation to obey the Torah are not the sum total of the isolable obligations of its component commandments, but the other way around: individual commandments are obligatory only insofar as they belong to the Law as a whole which distributes its holistic justification among its parts. And certain individual commandments that cannot be independently justified—and, indeed, by the dictates of reason, ought to be forbidden—might, then, acquire justification, or become obligatory, simply in virtue of entering into the Law, no matter how circuitous their route or that it was through a back door.

Whether or not either of these suggestions is what Maimonides intended, it is difficult to avoid the conclusion that he has created a problem for which he has no very satisfactory solution—and it seems equally difficult to believe that Maimonides himself did not realize this. For this reason, because he lacks an adequate answer in terms of grounds of obligation, I suggest that Maimonides himself shifts his attention in the chapters following the account of *ta'amei ha-mitzvot* to a different, third dimension of the problem of antinomianism: Do the *huqqim* serve a purpose *now* and, if so, what is it? Is there a reason an agent might use to justify their performance at present—what we called a "performance" reason? For an answer to these questions might serve in place of a general account of our obligations to perform commandments that were legislated for reasons that are now obsolete. Again, the focus for Maimonides' discussion of this issue is not a commandment like sacrifice, which raises the question for the community at large, but the very same examples just cited in chapter I:59—reading the Torah and prayer—which are problematic specifically for the philosopher.

Maimonides addresses this last question in chapters III:51–52, two chapters whose relation to the extended account of *ta'amei ha-mitzvot* in chapters III:26–50 is itself another of the puzzles of the *Guide*. After having concluded chapter III:49 with the statement that he has now given reasons for all commandments, Maimonides prefaces chapter III:51 with the announcement that

> This chapter that we bring now does not include additional matter over and above what is comprised in the other chapters of this Treatise. *It is only a kind of a conclusion*, at the same time explaining the worship as practiced by one who has apprehended the true realities peculiar only to Him after he has obtained an apprehension of what He is; and it also guides him toward achieving this worship, which is the end of man. (III:51:619; my emphasis)

Contrary to these explicit claims, however, a closer look shows that chapters III:51–52, far from serving as a conclusion to the earlier chapters and including no additional material, contradict Maimonides' earlier statements concerning the aims of the Law. In chapter 27, Maimonides explicitly states that the "Law as a whole aims at two objects: the welfare of the soul and the welfare of the body," both perfections of humankind in this existence, as he also emphasizes in chapter 31. In chapter 51, on the other hand, he tells us, first, that man's highest form of worship is to "set [his] thought to work on God alone after"—and only after—"[he has] achieved knowledge of Him" (III:51:620) and, second, since this highest form of worship is entirely contemplative, that "all the practices of the worship, such as reading the *Torah*, prayer, and the performance of the other commandments, have only the end of training you to occupy yourself with His commandments, . . . rather than with matters pertaining to this world" (III:51:622).

In a similar vein Maimonides concludes chapter 52 by emphasizing that "the purpose of all the actions prescribed by the Law" is that "by all the particulars of the actions and through their repetition . . . some excellent men obtain such training that they achieve human perfection, so that they fear, and are in dread and in awe of, God" (III:52:630). There are two significant differences between these portrayals of the Law. First, its aims in III:27 are squarely focussed on man and his perfection in this world; in III:51–52 they are entirely directed toward God and matters other than those of this world.[43] Second, in the earlier chapters each commandment and particular has its own specific reason or explanation, determined by its particular mix of first and second intentions; in III:51–52 all the commandments are reduced to one uniform purpose: to "train" man to "turn wholly toward God" (III:51:620) and to fear Him. On this latter account, one might even say, in contrast to what we argued is Maimonides' actual opinion in III:26, that particulars have no reasons or causes in the sense that all particulars indifferently serve one and the same function of "training," beyond which there are no further specific reasons for each particular that distinguish among them.

To resolve this apparent contradiction, it is necessary to remember that chapters III:26–49 are concerned with the aim of the Law for the entire community, the multitude and ordinary people as well as the philosophers and exceptional members, each according to his respective capacity; chapters 51–52, on the other hand, are concerned specifically with the worship appropriate for the person who has already "attained perfection in the divine science" and "apprehended the true realities."[44] This individual is instructed to engage in a purely meditative mode of divine worship because but not only because he is able to in virtue of the intellectual perfection he has achieved. This and more. As Maimonides shows in I:59, such a person will also recognize the problematic character of the "practices of worship," especially—and here Maimonides' choice of examples in III:51 cannot be simply coincidental—commandments on the order of reading the Torah and verbal prayer which make use of affirmative attributes to describe and praise God.[45] For the person at this highest stage of worship, the reasons for which these practices were originally legislated are not reasons he can use to justify his own performance of them. On the contrary, because these practices outwardly impute beliefs that contradict his apprehension—hence, his love—of God, the reasons for which they were originally commanded to the community may *now* be grounds for him in particular *not* to perform them. Consequently, for the individual at this highest level, the only mode of worship that is a genuine alternative is purely meditative.

But what purpose, then, do the "practices of worship" serve for this person at this highest stage? How is their performance related to the philosopher's mode of divine worship? The answer to this question is found, I suggest, in Maimonides' statement that chapters 51 and 52 are "a kind of *conclusion* to the other chapters" of the *Guide*. The reader to whom these two chapters are addressed has already, we are told, "apprehended God *and His acts* in accordance with what is required by the intellect" (III:51:620, my emphasis); in particular, then, he has apprehended the science of the divine acts legislating the commandments, the account of *ta'amei ha-mitzvot* found in chapters III:26–49. Knowing all of this, however, he will also have realized that what served as reasons for certain commandments for the community as a whole at the time of their original legislation cannot serve as *his* reasons for performing those same commandments in his present situation. He will know that for the community to whom these practices were originally legislated, they were an appropriate vehicle of divine worship in their historical context—that they served as a means toward a "good" for them given their circumstances "in this existence." But he will also know that for himself they serve no such purpose; for his present situation in "this existence" is not that to which these practices were originally attuned and in his present situation the appropriate vehicle of divine worship—the "good" he seeks—involves no such practices. On the other hand, precisely because these practices do him no "good" in his circumstances "in this existence"—and because he knows this—they are ideally suited for him to use instead as means to train himself to occupy himself with God's commandments as opposed to "matters pertaining to this world"—as opposed to what serves his desires and needs in this world. Hence, in virtue of knowing the reasons, or goods in this existence, because of which these practices were originally introduced, he can now utilize them in his present situation to turn away from concern with this world and toward God. He can exploit their present obsolescence by employing them as other-worldly training. It is in this sense that III:51–52 are a "kind of conclusion" to the earlier chapters of the *Guide*: knowing the content of the earlier chapters, especially on *ta'amei ha-mitzvot*, the philosopher will possess the "premises" from which he can now draw the "conclusion" that for him the commandments only serve the end of "training" Maimonides proposes in these last chapters.

The status of the *huqqim* with respect to the present community of Israel parallels this situation of "the practices of the worship" with respect to the *hakham* or philosopher. In knowing the reasons because of which the *huqqim* were originally legislated to Ancient Israel, the members of the present community know reasons they cannot now use to justify their own performance of the same commandments—and even suggest that they should not perform them. The conclusion Maimonides intends for them to draw from this is, I propose, the same conclusion he explicitly draws for the *hakham*: the community is also meant to reconceive their own reason for performing the *huqqim*: to make them into a means of "training," or preparing, themselves to turn wholly toward God and renounce every good in this existence, every matter other than Him.[46] Thus, the *huqqim* not only provide a model for the explanation of the legislation of the Mosaic commandments; they also enable those members of the community who know their reasons to glimpse the philosopher's reasons for performing the commandments at the highest stage of divine worship.

CHAPTER 3

Problematic Commandments II: Maimonides on Decrees of Scripture

Students of Maimonides, beginning with his medieval commentators Shem Tob ibn Shem Tob and Moses of Narbonne and, in recent years, Isadore Twersky and Jacob Levinger, have pointed to an apparent contradiction between two passages in the *Guide* and *Mishneh Torah*:[1]

> You must not allege as an objection against me the dictum of [the Sages], may their memory be blessed: He who says: Thy mercy extendeth to young birds [should be silenced]. For this is one of the two opinions mentioned by us—I mean the opinion of those who think that there is no reason for the Law except only the will [of God]—but as for us, we follow only the second opinion. (III:48:600)

> He who states in his supplications: "May He who had mercy on the nest of the bird and forbade taking the mother together with her children, or [He who] forbade slaughtering it and its young on the same day, have mercy on us," and similar statements, is silenced; for these commandments are a decree of Scripture [*gezerat ha-katuv*] and [their reasons] are not mercy [for the animals]; for if they were [legislated] because of mercy, [He] would not permit us slaughtering of animals at all. (*MT* "*Tefillah*" ix, 7)

In the passage from the *Guide*, the "second opinion" to which Maimonides refers is the second opinion described in the "disagreement" over the explanation of the Mosaic legislation that opens III:26. According to the first of those two opinions, the opinion of the Kalam, the commandments of a divine law are simply the product of the arbitrary uncaused divine will and have no reason independent of the fact that they are commanded by God. According to the second opinion, which Maimonides himself endorses,[2] the "Law is consequent upon wisdom and aims at some end" (507); that is, each of the commandments has a reason or utility because of which it was legislated. The commandment of *shiluah ha-ken* [the commandment to let go the mother bird from the nest when taking its young (Deut. 22:6–7)] must also, then, have a reason which, Maimonides says earlier in the same passage in III:48, is also the reason for the prohibition against slaughtering a mother and its young on the same day: "this being a precautionary measure in order to avoid slaughtering the young animal in front of its mother. For in these cases animals feel very great pain, there being no difference regarding this pain between man and the other animals" (III:48:599). Likewise with *shiluah ha-ken*: "The Law takes into consideration these pains . . . of beast and bird" (III:48:600). And in the same chapter, Maimonides explains yet a third commandment, the slaughter of animals for food, by a closely related reason. Given the necessity that "animals be killed" in order for man "to have good food . . . the aim was to kill them in the easiest manner, and it was forbidden to torment them through killing them in a reprehensible manner . . ." (III:48:599).[3] All of these statements suggest, in sum, that these commandments were legislated (1) for a reason and (2) for a reason that "takes into consideration" the pains of the animal victims.

In the passage from the *Mishneh Torah*, on the other hand, Maimonides appears to deny these two claims. First, he explicitly states that neither *shiluah ha-ken* nor the prohibition against slaughtering a mother and its young on the same day were legislated "because of mercy" for the animals; on the contrary, if mercy were a consideration, slaughtering of animals would be prohibited tout cour. Second, in apparent agreement with the first opinion in the *Guide* III:26, the view which he rejects there, Maimonides says in *MT* "*Tefillah*" that the Mosaic commandment of *shiluah ha-ken* is a 'decree of Scripture' [*gezerat ha-katuv*], using the Rabbinic phrase that would seem to mean that the commandment is one for which (to quote the *Guide*) "there is no reason . . . except only the will of God." Thus, on the first point as well, Maimonides appears to take a position in the *Mishneh Torah* that contradicts his later position in the *Guide*.

The *Mishneh Torah* is not the only Maimonidean text to contradict the *Guide* on this very topic. In two passages in the *Commentary* on the *Mishnah*, we find Maimonides giving what appears to be the same explanation as in the *Mishneh Torah*. Commenting on *Megillah* IV, 7, Maimonides writes that we silence the speaker because the Mosaic commandment of *shiluah ha-ken* "is not for the reason of divine mercy [*hemlah*] but a decree of Scripture [*gezerat ha-katuv*]." And in *Berakhot* V, 3, he offers the same explanation—adding the argument later to be found in the *Mishneh Torah* that if mercy were the reason, slaughtering would be absolutely forbidden—except that for the phrase "decree of Scripture," he substitutes Saadiah's classificatory term "a revelational commandment [*mitzvah shimm'it*] that has no reason." From here, then, there is also further proof that the meaning Maimonides attaches to the phrase "a decree of Scripture" [*gezerat ha-katuv*] is "a commandment that has no reason."

Granted now that there exist these contradictions within the Maimonidean corpus; what of them? Are they simply intertextual inconsistencies whose significance is limited to the particular commandments and laws they explicitly involve? Or do they bear on larger themes that are crucial for our general understanding of Maimonides? In particular, do they hint at deeper tensions—a "duality"—among Maimonides' works?

One classical reaction to these contradictions is that of Moses of Narbonne who concludes that Maimonides' true *halakhic* opinion is to be found in the *Guide*. Contrary both to the uncontested view of the *Mishnah* and to his decision in the *Mishneh Torah*, Narbonne claims that Maimonides really believes that we do *not* silence the speaker who says "Your mercy extendeth to young birds." This conclusion does not follow. For the alleged objection to which Maimonides responds in the *Guide* is not based on the *halakhic* decision of the *Mishnah* but on the explanation of that decision that claims that the commandment of *shiluah ha-ken* is an arbitrary decree of divine will. Maimonides may only be denying this interpretation of the mishnaic decision, not the decision itself. As we shall later see, there are other explanations for the mishnaic decision and, when Maimonides responds that "as for us, we follow only the second opinion," he may be indirectly pointing us to another of them.

A second, recent response to these contradictions is that of Jacob Levinger. Levinger argues that the contradiction over *shiluah ha-ken* is only one among a number of such contradictions between the *Mishneh Torah* and *Guide*—another concerns the Nazirite laws which are discussed in the same chapter III:48 of the *Guide*—and that Maimonides deliberately takes opposed positions in the two texts because they are primarily directed to two different audiences: the former to the multitude, the latter to the philosophical elite. In light of this difference between their primary intended audiences, Levinger claims that we often find in the *Guide* opinions that Maimonides cannot openly express in the *Mishneh Torah* for fear that they would harm the multitude.

Here is not the place for a thorough examination of this general conception of the "duality" of the Maimonidean corpus, but if it is correct—if Maimonides did hide certain reasons in the *Mishneh Torah* because they would harm the multitude—we are certainly entitled to ask what particular harm would result for the multitude from knowing the reason for *shiluah ha-ken*. To this Levinger responds with Maimonides' own closing statement at the end of the *Book of Commandments* where he describes the general danger of antinomianism that can arise from people's knowledge of the reasons for any of the commandments. Now, it is true that Maimonides does express this concern; but it should also be noted, first, that it does not prevent him from giving reasons for commandments in general *even* in the *Mishneh Torah* and, second, that this passage tells only half of the story: elsewhere Maimonides voices the opposite concern that lack of knowledge of reasons for commandments can equally well lead to antinomianism.[4] Thus the danger of antinomianism is unique neither to *knowing* the reason for a commandment nor to *shiluah ha-ken*. Furthermore, this argument is at best an argument for not *revealing* the reasons for commandments; it does not begin to explain why Maimonides should explicitly say, and in this particular example, that the commandment is a "decree of Scripture" [*gezerat ha-katuv*] if that means that it has no reason—a statement that contradicts other statements, not only in the *Guide*, but also *within* the *Mishneh Torah* that all commandments, whether or not we know them, have reasons.[5] In short, Levinger's interpretation fails to explain what harm would befall the multitude if they knew the reason for *shiluah ha-ken* in particular and why Maimonides specifically describes it, among all the commandments (knowledge of whose reasons, according to Levinger, would also be potentially harmful to the multitude), as a *gezerat ha-katuv*.

In my opinion also, larger issues hang on the interpretation of these individual passages in the *Mishneh Torah* and *Guide*. However, what their interpretation illustrates is not the independence of the two works but their interdependence. To begin with, it should be noted that, while the apparently conflicting passages concern a rather isolated Rabbinic law, its explanation has consequences for two major philosophical themes that are central to Maimonides' thought. The first is his view of the rationality of the Law and his conception of a divine legislator, the second his conception of divine providence. For if *shiluah ha-ken* is simply a decree with no reason, then it would appear, as the Kalam holds, that God (at least sometimes) acts arbitrarily and that (at least some of) the commandments may simply be the expression of His uncaused will. On the other hand, if He is perfectly rational and all commandments express His wisdom, then this commandment, like all others, must have some reason, whether or not we know what it is. From the parallel Maimonides draws between our passage in III:48 and the dispute of III:26, it is clear that this is the significance he himself attaches to his discussion of the Rabbinic dictum. But if this is the underlying significance of these apparent textual inconsistencies, then a genuine contradiction between the *Mishneh Torah* and *Guide* must also be a contradiction on this larger issue. In other words, there will really be a contradiction between these passages only if Maimonides takes the position in the *Mishneh Torah*, as opposed to his clear position in the *Guide*, that *shiluah ha-ken* truly has no reason, that it is an arbitrary, uncaused commandment of God's will. As I argued in chapter 2, it is not enough if we simply do not, or even could not, *know* its reason, for such an episte-mological claim would be compatible with the fully rational God of the *Guide*. It must be shown that in the *Mishneh Torah* Maimonides uses the phrase "decree of Scripture" [*gezerat ha-katuv*] to express the same strong view that he uses it to express in the *Commentary* on the *Mish-neh*, namely, that the commandment lacks all reason or is (metaphysi-cally) uncaused, not merely that it has no known reason.

Similarly for the second alleged point of contradiction: If the *Guide* and *Mishneh Torah* express truly opposing views of divine providence with respect to the individual members of species other than man, it must be shown that in the *Guide* Maimonides explains *shiluah ha-ken*, not merely by reference to considerations related to the pain and suffer-ing of the bird, but in terms of divine mercy *for* the bird.

Both of these claims—the claim that in the *Mishneh Torah* Mai-monides himself uses the phrase "decree of Scripture" [*gezerat ha-katuv*] in order to express the view that the commandment in question lacks all reason and the claim that in the *Guide* the reason for *shiluah ha-ken* is specifically mercy for the bird—have been taken for granted by previous Maimonidean commentators, such as Narbonne and Levinger, who claim that there exists a genuine contradiction between the *Guide* and *Mishneh Torah*, which they then attempt to resolve. What I shall argue is that a closer look suggests that neither of these assumptions appears to be true; hence, there is no contradiction that requires resolution. At the same time, Maimonides' use of the term *gezerat ha-katuv* does require some explanation and, like Levinger, I believe that he uses it in order to conceal something from a certain readership. What he wishes to conceal, however, is not that *shiluah ha-ken* has no reason but some-thing its reason implies.

The relation of the *Commentary* on the *Mishnah* to these two later works is more problematic, and there I see no choice but to admit a con-tradiction. Indeed Maimonides' general view of the *explanation* of the Law changes (or perhaps is clarified) from the *Commentary* to the *Mish-neh Torah*. As I argued in chapter 2, a similar shift occurs in Mai-monides' account of the *huqqim* which, as we shall see, Maimonides connects to the *gezerot ha-katuv*.[6] In *Eight Chapters* 6, he agrees with Saadiah's view that the *huqqim* are commandments that (metaphysi-cally) have no reason for their legislation independent of the fact that they are commanded by God. In the *Mishneh Torah*, however, he already holds that they are simply laws whose reason is not evident, obvious, or known to the multitude, and it is this epistemological inter-pretation that is vigorously defended in the *Guide* where it is explicitly opposed to the metaphysical claim of the Kalam that some laws have no reasons. For in the *Guide* Maimonides directly confronts the implications of these theses for the conception of God, which are only hinted at in the *Mishneh Torah*.[7] To be sure, it is not certain whether Maimonides changed his view of the *huqqim* from the *Commentary* to the later works or whether he simply came to see the significance of the difference between the metaphysical and epistemological interpretations and, consequently, clarified his position. In either case, inasmuch as there is this general shift in his thinking about the explanation of the *huqqim*, it is not surprising to find a similar shift with respect to *shiluah ha-ken* characterized as a *gezerat ha-katuv*.

Let me now turn to the two assumptions on which the alleged contradiction rests, beginning, briefly, with the second.

A decisive reason not to assume that Maimonides' reason for *shiluah ha-ken* (or the prohibition against killing a young animal in the presence of its mother) in *Guide* III:48 is God's mercy for the individual bird is that this contradicts his general view within the *Guide* (e.g., III:17)—for which he gives arguments he nowhere else challenges—that divine providence does not extend to the individual members of any (nonhuman) animal species. Echoing the argument of *MT "Tefillah"* that if mercy were a consideration, no slaughtering would ever be permitted, Maimonides writes instead that precisely because divine providence does not extend to the individual members of nonhuman species, "killing them and employing them usefully, as we wish, has been permitted and even enjoined" (III:17:472–73). The reason that all commandments require the humane or merciful treatment of animals is not, then, the welfare of the animals, but to "perfect *us* so that we should not acquire moral habits of cruelty and should not inflict pain gratuitously without any utility, but that we should intend to be kind and merciful even with a chance animal individual, except in case of need—*Because thy soul desireth to eat flesh* [Deut. 12, 20]—for we must not kill out of cruelty or for sport" (III:17:473–74; my emphasis). And this reason, in turn, is also the general reason Maimonides gives for the thirteenth class of commandments to which the commandments under discussion belong: all these commandments are intended "to put an end to the lusts and licentiousness manifested in seeking what is most pleasurable and to taking the desire for food and drink as an end" (III:35:537). For to take such "lusts and licentiousness" as ends leads to the very "cruelty and sport" these commandments are meant to prevent. This is not, of course, to deny what Maimonides states in III:48 about the feelings of animals; it is simply not *because* of those feelings, or *out of mercy for* the animals, that God commanded these laws. But because animals, as much as humans, have these feelings it is proper for *us* to exercise our moral habits in these circumstances. Thus, the reason for the commandment of *shiluah ha-ken* in the *Guide* is not a matter of mercy for the animals and, on this score, there need be no contradiction with the *Mishneh Torah*.[8]

Let me turn now to the second source of the alleged contradiction, Maimonides' use of the Rabbinic phrase "scriptural decree" [*gezerat ha-katuv*]. As we have emphasized, for there to be a substantive contradiction between the *Mishneh Torah* and *Guide*, it is essential that Maimonides use this phrase to mean nothing weaker than a commandment that is arbitrary, or has no reason. It is not enough for the phrase to refer merely to a commandment whose reason is either unknown or contrary to some piece of known reasoning. Whether or not all Talmudic uses of this phrase in fact had this sense is not certain, but various medieval Talmudists understood it that way and that, too, seems to have been the popular understanding of the term.[9] For Maimonides, however, the phrase is far from unequivocal; he seems to use it in different contexts in at least three different general senses. What is important for us is that, because it has these multiple meanings and serves as this multipurpose term, it is no longer absolutely necessary that it have the contradiction-raising sense of arbitrary in the *halakhah* of MT "*Tefillah*."[10] To document this claim, I will now simply review one by one the nine *halakhot* in which the expression occurs in the *Mishneh Torah*, concluding with that in "*Tefillah*."[11] I have divided the *halakhot* into roughly three groups corresponding to these three different general senses; those in the first two groups I will discuss only briefly, those in the last group at greater length.

A. In the two *halakhot* in this group, the phrase *gezerat ha-katuv* occurs in contexts and with senses that are unrelated to the question whether the law in question has or does not have a reason.

(1) MT "*Ishut*" xxv, 2: At first sight Maimonides seems to use *gezerat ha-katuv* here in contrast to the phrase *devarim shel ta'am*, which might be taken to imply that the former lacks a *ta'am* or reason.[12] In fact, however, Maimonides' use of the phrase *devarim shel ta'am*, which seems to be based on Talmudic usage, does not refer to matters of, or for, a reason but rather to matters that are reasonable or rational or logical using purely human reasoning (i.e., good sense), in contrast to laws that are scripturally derived.[13] In this *halakhah*, Maimonides justifies his view that the laws under discussion vary greatly from community to community, depending on local customs and practices, on the grounds that they are (simply) *devarim shel ta'am*, whereas scripturally derived laws—*gezerot ha-katuv*—ought to be universal and constant from circumstance to circumstance.[14] There is no implication here that a *gezerat ha-katuv* has no reason, or is arbitrary.

(2) *MT "Mamrim"* vi, 7: Here no commandment or law is said to be a *gezerat ha-katuv*. The issue rather are the limits of parental honor and respect: No matter what humiliation or pain someone's parent inflicts on him, the Law obligates him to "accept the *gezerat ha-katuv* [decree of Scripture, or here the King of Kings] in silence." That is, the phrase refers to authority that requires unconditional obedience; whether or not the authority has grounds or a reason is simply not raised.

B. In each of these *halakhot*, Maimonides calls a law a *gezerat ha-katuv*—despite the fact that it seems to have a reason (which Maimonides also sometimes suggests)—apparently for the reason that the law (also) *conflicts* with what reasoning would otherwise require of us.

(3) *MT "Mamrim"* vii, 11: Here Maimonides states, first, that it is a *gezerat ha-katuv* that "the stubborn and rebellious son" is stoned and, second, that this judgment does not apply to a daughter, for which he gives a reason—namely, that, unlike a man, she will not customarily [*she-'ein darkah*] continue to eat and drink in a manner that will lead to murder—as well as a scriptural prooftext—prima facie implying, then, that a *gezerat ha-katuv* may nonetheless have a reason.[15] However, this reason is not the only relevant reason one might adduce for or against including her under this commandment. In the Talmud, R. Simeon argues, to the contrary, that on grounds of sexual promiscuity a daughter ought to be included in this commandment just like the son (BT *Sanhedrin* 69b–70a). This suggests that what may render the commandment a *gezerat ha-katuv* is not that it has no reason but that certain reasoning, especially concerning the application and interpretation of the commandment, seems to be arbitrarily excluded simply because it is not mentioned or alluded to in Scripture. Here, for example, the only admissible criterion for judging whether someone falls under this commandment is the (scriptural) condition of "gluttony and drunkardness" (Deut. 21, 20)—which turns out to exclude the daughter—rather than, say, sexual promiscuity, which would have the consequence of including her. But obviously the fact that the law is, thus, contrary to certain reasoning does not show that it has no reason.

(4) *MT "Sanhedrin"* xviii, 6: Here also Maimonides describes a law (that no defendant in court is either put to death or lashed by his own confession but only by the testimony of two witnesses) as a *gezerat ha-katuv* only to follow up that statement with a reason for the law, albeit a psychological reason and one that really only applies to capital punishment.[16] Nonetheless it would appear, as in the previous *halakhah*, that *gezerot ha-katuv* in principle do have reasons.[17] Instead what makes the law a *gezerat ha-katuv* seems to be, again, the fact that certain rea-

soning—the type that lies behind the cases cited in the first part of the same *halakah* where the same procedural requirement of two witnesses is unnecessary—is simply excluded or overruled.

(5) *MT* "*'Edut*" xiii, 15: Here, again, Maimonides seems to call the scriptural disqualification of relatives as witnesses a *gezerat ha-katuv* primarily in order to exclude a natural reason for this law—the presumption that relatives are biased lovers/friends—rather than to deny that the law has any reason at all. He emphasizes that, by implication, the scriptural disqualification of relatives permits the testimony of friends and enemies, a still further affront to ordinary reasoning. So, even more than in previous cases, what makes this law a *gezerat ha-katuv* seems to be its inconsistency with ordinary reasoning or, if you will, Reason. But this does not, of course, show that the law in question has no reason.

(6) *MT* "*'Edut*" xviii, 3: Here Maimonides says that the fact that we always believe the second set of witnesses who challenge the testifiability of the first set of witnesses—(1) regardless of their respective numbers and (2) despite the fact that with all other cases of conflicting pairs of witnesses we dismiss both—is a *gezerat ha-katuv*. More perhaps than any of our previous examples, Maimonides' use of the phrase *gezerat ha-katuv* here, which he substitutes for the term *hiddush* in his Talmudic source, underscores the fact that the law in question is anomalous, strange, and exceptional.[18] But its uniqueness does not seem to lie in the fact that it simply may have no reason, but rather in that it contradicts other scriptural or rabbinic rules (e.g., the majority rule and the rule of evidence to reject both pairs of contradictory witnesses). Again, the function of characterizing a law as a *gezerat ha-katuv* seems to be, not to demonstrate its absolute arbitrariness, but to draw attention to its incompatibility with other laws, and indifference to conflicting reasons, which, in this case, are not based on general reason or good sense but are specific to the Torah. However, none of this shows that the law does not have a reason; we simply may not know what it is.[19]

C. In the *halakhot* in this third class, which includes our own case from *MT* "*Tefillah*," I will argue that Maimonides exploits the received or popular meaning of *gezerat ha-katuv* as a law that has no reason in order to conceal from certain elements in his audience some problematic implication of what he believes *is* the true reason for the law in question.

(7) *MT* "*Teshuvah*" iii, 4: In this *halakhah*, as well as in the next one to be discussed (*MT* "*Mikva'ot*" xi, 12), the phrase *gezerat ha-katuv* occurs as part of a formula in which the commandment is said to be a *gezerat ha-katuv*, but that there is a *remez*, an allusion of its reason or signifi-

cance, concealed in it.[20] Here, for example, the sounding of the *shofar* (ram's horn) on *Rosh HaShanah*, the New Year, is said to be a *gezerat ha-katuv* although it contains the *remez*: "Awaken, those of you are are asleep from your sleep; slumberers, arouse yourselves from your slumbering! Investigate your actions and return in repentance and remember your creator, those of you who forget the truth in the vanities of the times and go astray all year long."[21]

In the *Guide* III:43, a chapter concerned with the reasons for the festivals and their rituals, Maimonides gives the same reason for sounding the shofar on the New Year, referring the reader for elaboration to the *halakhah* in the *Mishneh Torah*. Now, however, he links this explanation to his general account of the New Year, which he also describes exclusively as "a day of repentance in which the attention of the people is called to their negligence." There is no mention of the other classic rabbinic reasons for the holiday and, in particular, that it marks the creation of the world.[22] Indeed the New Year is entirely subordinated to the fast of the Day of Atonement, *Yom Kippur*, the day primarily devoted to the theme of repentance. *Rosh HaShanah* assumes the status simply of "a preparation for and introduction to the Day of the Fast [of Atonement]. Accordingly, it is generally acccepted in the tradition of the religious community that the *ten days from New Year to the Day of Atonement* should be observed." It now seems, despite his statement that the "New Year lasts similarly [to the festival of Weeks] for one day," that in fact the New Year is just the first of a ten-day period that culminates with the Day of Atonement, a period entirely devoted to repentance.

The reason of repentance explains why something should be done to arouse people to repent. But it does not explain why specifically the *shofar* was chosen. Maimonides does not explicitly give a reason for this particular. Instead he goes on to discuss the festival of Tabernacles, including an explanation why the festival occurs in the fall, for which he says we find corroboration in Aristotle's statement that a festival during the season of leisure following the harvesting of the fruit was a "general practice of the religious communities in ancient times" (III:43:572). He concludes this discussion with a comment on an opinion inculcated by Tabernacles: that "this *too* is one of the pivots of the Law" (ibid., my emphasis). Now, taking off from the "too" of this remark, Moses of Narbonne claims that here Maimonides alludes to yet another—and, for our purposes, more interesting—"pivotal" principle of the Law which underlies his reference to Aristotle. According to Narbonne, this is the principle that the Law attempted to retain, and adapt for Israel, as many as possible ancient (cultic) practices so long as they did not smack of idolatry.[23] Among these ancient practices, given Maimonides' general explanation of the particular commandments of sacrifice and other cultic commandments in the Law, it would hardly be surprising for him to have a similar explanation of the sounding of the *shofar*. Indeed elsewhere he cites a Sabian text according to which "all the ancient sages have said and the prophets have commanded and prescribed to play on musical instruments before the statues during the festivals" (III:30:523). But this reason is exactly the type of historical explanation of the commandments Maimonides would also want to conceal from a general audience—and elsewhere does.[24] Calling it a *gezerat ha-katuv* serves exactly this function. As he writes in the *Letter on Astrology,* by reading texts of ancient idolatry, he learned "what the reason is for all those commandments that everyone comes to think of as having no reason at all other than the *decree of Scripture*" (my emphasis).[25]

There is also, I would suggest, a deeper connection between blowing the shofar, repentance, and the Sabian star worship that the Law aims to refute. According both to the *Guide* and the *Mishneh Torah,* the scriptural source for the commandment to call on God in times of need and calamity is the verse *"Then ye shall sound an alarm with the trumpets"* (Num. 10, 9).[26] Through this action, Maimonides argues, "the correct opinion is firmly established that [the deity] apprehends our situation," that He improves or ruins people's situations depending on how they act, and that what happens is not "mere chance," a view that Maimonides elsewhere identifies with Epicurians and "unbelievers in Israel" (III:17:465). What is wrong about agents thinking that calamities are matters of mere chance, he continues, is that this belief "contributes to necessitating their persistence in their corrupt opinons and unrighteous actions, so that they do not turn away from them" (III:36:540). The mirror image of this argument is his explanation of the importance of belief in the possibility of repentance. Every human, he observes, is bound to sin and err, either through ignorance or because he is "overcome by desire or anger" (ibid.). Unless people believed in the possibility of repentance, they would therefore think that their error could never be corrected; indeed they would "disobey even more because of the fact that no strategem remains at [their] disposal" (ibid.). That is, if not for belief in the possibility of repentance, people would be fatalists, thinking that their actions were determined and out of their control. Therefore, *both* the belief that what happens is only chance and the belief that what happens is fatalistically determined lead people to believe that they are not responsible for their actions. Both of these views are explicitly attributed by Maimonides to the Sabian idolatry that the Law aims to refute.[27] The false doctrine of fatalism is exactly the kind of consequence that follows from Sabian astrology and star worship. And belief that everything is chance is the view of those, according to Maimonides, who doubt God's existence, those who "have belied the Lord and said: *It is not He*" (Jer. 5, 12), a verse he also uses to describe the Sabians.[28] Thus, if blowing horns or the shofar as part of worship was originally a Sabian rite, the Law took a practice originally performed in service of fatalistic idolatry and transformed it into an act affirming human freedom and responsibility for one's actions.

As Maimonides elsewhere recognizes, however, it is only a fine line, if any, that divides the divine apprehension which is a precondition for the Law's conception of human responsibility and the astral determination that the same Law aims to refute.[29] Lacking a clear criterion to distinguish the two, he may not have the philosophical grounds to justify accepting the one thesis while denying the other. This, in turn, may have been a further reason for him to conceal the full explanation for the commandment of blowing the shofar although he nonetheless makes it a vehicle of repentance. By calling the commandment a *gezerat ha-katuv* and at the same time making its reason a *remez,* he simultaneously reveals and conceals its problematic reason.[30]

(8) *MT "Mikva'ot"* xi, 12: Like the previous *halakhah,* this one also follows the formula that the commandments in question are said to be *gezerot ha-katuv,* although a *remez* of their reason or significance can be found in them. But there are also significant differences between this use of *gezerat ha-katuv* and the previous occurrences we have examined. First, here it is an entire class of laws, all those discussed in the Book of Purity, that are called *gezerot ha-katuv.* Being a *gezerat ha-katuv* is now the rule rather than the exception.[31] Second, the fact that these laws are *gezerot ha-katuv* is explicitly linked to the claim that they are *huqqim,* those laws which in the Rabbinic tradition were claimed either to have no reason or to have a reason we do not and perhaps cannot know. This association is not, moreover, either accidental or incidental. In *MT "Temurah"* iv, 13 Maimonides also implies that the other major class of *huqqim,* the sacrifices, are *gezerot.* There he writes that "the statutes of the Law [*huqqei ha-Torah*] are all of them divine edicts [*gezerot*], as we have explained at the close of [*MT*] '*Me'ilah.*'" Now, at first sight, this phrase "the statutes of the Law" might be taken in a broad sense to refer generally to all commandments rather than some specific class. However, if we look at *MT "Me'ilah"* viii, 8, to which Maimonides cross-refers, we discover that it is the special class of *huqqim* (which he contrasts with the *mishpatim*) and not all commandments that is under discussion there. Moreover, he concludes that passage with the *pesaq:* "All sacrifices are included in the category of *huqqim.*" Hence, Maimonides' judgement in *MT "Temurah"* is clearly meant to imply that in particular the sacrifices, as *huqqim,* are *gezerot.*[32] And the fact that both classes of laws, those of sacrifice and of purity and impurity, are called

both *huqqim* and *gezerot* strongly suggests that there is a common explanation for the systematic usage of these terms.[33] In chapter 2 we discussed Maimonides' treatment of sacrifice as part of his general conception of a *hoq*; here I shall explain how this notion of a *hoq* bears on his use of *gezerat ha-katuv* with reference to the laws of purity and impurity.

To begin with, the *pesaq* that all the laws of purity and impurity, including the laws of immersion, are *huqqim*—like the analogous claim concerning the laws of sacrifice made in MT "*Me'ilah*" viii, 18—has no explicit precedent in rabbinic literature. For explanation and argument we must look to the *Guide* where, on the other hand, neither of these claims is drawn as an explicit conclusion. Here, then, we have yet another example of how the *Guide* serves as the *gemara* for the *Mishneh Torah,* and the *Mishneh Torah* as an apodictic compendium of the often not openly drawn results of the *Guide*.

In the *Guide*, Maimonides argues at length that the *huqqim* are no exception to his general thesis that all commandments have reasons; they are simply commandments whose reason or "utility is not clear to the multitude" (III:26:507). What the multitude fail to understand about the *huqqim* is twofold. First, their explanation—for example, Maimonides' explanation of sacrifices in light of the practices of Sabian idolatry—requires historical knowledge of the circumstances and culture in which they were initially legislated. Not only do the multitude typically lack this historical information; Maimonides also seems to suggest that they are better off not knowing it. Second, what requires explanation in the case of the *huqqim*—and this is especially true of the sacrifices—is not *why* they are commanded, but *how* they could be commanded given that they are *inconsistent* with the aims and presuppositions of the Law. In particular, how could sacrificial worship be commanded given (i) its close identification at that time with idolatry and (ii) the "first intention of the Law" to efface idolatry and everything associated with it? In a word, the legislation of the *huqqim* is *problematic*—and Maimonides' reasons for the *huqqim* are an attempt to solve such problems by appealing to a "divine ruse" or the deity's "wily graciousness," which seeks to achieve the "first intentions of the Law" within certain confines and limitations established by its "second intention," which is to respect the necessities of human nature and contingent circumstances.

Now, in the case of the laws of purity and impurity, what is the analogous problem? Maimonides begins by stating that "to the totality of purposes of the perfect Law there belong the abandonment, depreciation, and restraint" of desires, appetites, and lusts; the inculcation of gentleness, docility, and obedience; and the achievement of purity and sanctification; in short, "the purification of the actions and the purification of the heart from polluting opinions and polluting moral qualities" (III:33:532–3).[34] Given these aims, the particular commandments the Law prescribes are not easily understood. If "purification of the inner" is the aim, how is that achieved by the bulk of the laws of purity that are concerned instead with the "purification of the outer"? As Maimonides puts it even more bluntly in *MT* "*Mikva'ot*": "uncleanness" [*ha-tum'ah*] is not mud or filth which water can remove, but is a matter of scriptural decree and dependent on the intention of the heart." But if this is so, if "uncleanness" is not something water can remove, why *is* immersion obligatory? And why in general is the Law so concerned with all the details and varieties of bodily uncleanness when they do not directly contribute to sanctification or purification of the heart?

To solve this problem—How, *by* immersing oneself, does one affect the "intentions of his heart"?—Maimonides answers that there is in fact no *direct* connection between the two. It is not *through* immersion that one achieves purity. Rather, a first intention of the Law is to inculcate within people humility and obedient fear of God; for only these attitudes lead to performance of the commandments—the primary sense of "sanctification" [*qedushah*] and "purity" [*taharah*] (III:33:533)—and to avoidance of transgression of the commandments—the primary sense of "uncleanness [*tum'ah*]" (III:47:595).[35] Therefore, the Law legislated that Israel build a Sanctuary; because this, among other things, encourages these attitudes: "so that on seeing it, man should be affected by a sentiment of submission and servitude" (III:45:577) and, on visiting it, be affected "with a feeling of awe and of fear" (III:47:593). However, given human nature, Maimonides reminds us, the more contact one has with a venerated object, the less awe and fear it inspires. Therefore, exploiting the fact that in the Sabian context at that time it was "generally accepted and customary for unpleasant things [to be] imposed . . . in cases of [bodily] uncleanness" (III:47:594), the Torah forbade the [bodily] unclean to enter the Sanctuary and, the more frequent the kind of [bodily] uncleanliness, the more difficult it made its purification. In consequence, the familiarity that would breed nonchalance toward the Temple was kept to a minimum, the desired fear and humility inspired by the Sanctuary were inculcated, and, with these proper attitudes, the people were ultimately sanctified and purified through performance of the commandments—or so at least the Law intended. In sum, the laws of purity and impurity are the product of two intentions: operating within the bounds set by natural necessity as required by its "second intention," the Law adapts practices prevailing in its historical context of legislation in order to achieve its "first intention." This mode of legislation that characterizes the *huqqim* Maimonides calls a "divine ruse."[36]

But precisely *because* this type of reason for these commandments makes them into a "divine ruse," it is also likely to raise objections from the multitude. For if the relation between the actual detailed means afforded by these commandments and their ultimate end is so indirect, people will ask "how is it possible that none of [them] should be intended for its own sake, but for the sake of something else" (III:32:527)? And if their specific forms are simply a function of the idolatrous practices that obtained once, at the time of their original legislation, but no longer do, then people are likely to wonder why they must now continue to observe such obsolete rites. Therefore, their explanation might be better concealed from the community at large. And because of just these concerns that arise as a consequence of the explanation Maimonides gives in the *Guide*—not because they are arbitrary laws that have no reason—I also wish to suggest that here in *MT* *"Mikva'ot"* Maimonides calls the laws of purity and impurity *gezerot ha-katuv*. What makes them "matters about which human understanding is [not] capable of forming a judgment" is not that they lack a reason but that their reason is problematic.[37] And taking advantage of the popular meaning of *gezerot ha-katuv* Maimonides thereby attempts to dissuade a certain audience from prying into that reason.

(9) *MT* *"Tefillah"* xi, 7: Finally, we return to the original *halakhah* with which we began this chapter. Here the sense of *gezerat ha-katuv* is related to its sense in the previous *halakhah*, though *shiluah ha-ken* has a *moral* intention (rather than the eradication of idolatry or the attainment of purity) as the end that it realizes through indirect means. In this sense of the phrase Maimonides also writes in the *Guide*: "Know that certain commandments [*mitzvot*] also contain prescriptions that are intended to lead to the acquisition of a useful moral quality, even if they prescribe certain actions that are *deemed* to be merely *decreed by Scripture* [*gezerat ha-katuv*] and not to have a purpose" (III:38:550; my emphasis)[38] Now, *who* deems them to be merely *gezerot ha-katuv* and not to have a purpose? Maimonides does not say, but the obvious candidate is the multitude. And if Maimonides himself calls a commandment a *gezerat ha-katuv*, perhaps it is also because there is a reason, as with the *huqqim*, that he believes the multitude is better off not knowing.

But why should the reason for the commandment of *shiluah ha-ken*, if it is an instrument of moral education, be obscure to the ordinary person? What about its reason is problematic? For an answer, we must again turn to the *Guide*. Maimonides compares *shiluah ha-ken* to the prohibition against slaughtering a mother and its young on the same day. The latter, he explains, is a "precautionary measure in order to avoid slaughtering the young animal in front of its mother. For in these cases animals feel very great pain" (III:48:599). Analogously, Maimonides appears to regard *shiluah ha-ken* primarily as a precautionary measure.

> For in general the eggs over which the bird has sat and the young that need their mother are not fit to be eaten. If then the mother is let go and escapes of her own accord, she will not be pained by seeing that the young are taken away. In most cases this will lead to people leaving everything alone, for what may be taken is in most cases not fit to be eaten. If the Law takes into consideration these pains of the soul in the case of beast and birds, what will be the case with regard to the individuals of the human species as a whole? (III:48:600)

The reasoning of this passage is not entirely clear. If the ultimate aim is to teach us to spare the mother the pain of seeing her young taken away, then in situations where the young or eggs are inedible and will be left undisturbed, the Law should also not require us to send away the mother. To act otherwise would, on the contrary, be gratuitous cruelty. And because this is the actual situation "in general" and "in most cases," and the Law is framed for the majority of cases,[39] this should be the general law. Nonetheless the Torah simply commands us not to take the mother with her young and, on the contrary, commands us "to let the mother go and take only the young." Moreover, as is well known, the commandment of *shiluah ha-ken,* as interpreted by the Rabbis, is a negative ordinance "transformed" into a positive prescription [*la'av ha-nitak le'asei*]; similarly, Maimonides in MT "Shehittah" xiii, 2 states that the positive prescription serves to "correct" transgressions of the negative ordinance: if one has taken the mother, then we are obligated to send her away. In short, if the ultimate aim is to teach us to be merciful in every situation, the only way to explain the particular requirement of the Mosaic commandment as Maimonides describes it in the *Guide* is as a precautionary measure. Likewise, this precautionary character of the commandment is what Maimonides emphasizes in the closing homiletic moral he draws.[40]

The idea that the form of the commandment of *shiluah ha-ken* is shaped by precautionary considerations is not unproblematic. First of all, one might object, as with sacrifices and the laws of purity and impurity, that the commandment is not "intended for [its] own sake but for the sake of something else" (III:32:527). Second, and more important, Maimonides emphasizes that his "purpose [in the *Guide*] is to give reasons for the [biblical] texts and not for the pronouncements of the legal sciences" (III:41:558)—that is, for the Written Law and not for the Oral Law. However, the legislation of precautionary measures is one essential way by which he characterizes, and justifies, the rulings of the rabbis as a continuation of the Oral Law—in contrast to the prohibited activity of adding to or subtracting from the Written Law. On the one hand, Maimonides explains, God recognized that, because of changes in human circumstances, the Law will need to be changed in order to continue to apply. On the other hand, He recognized that continual changes would lead to the "corruption" of the Law and "the belief that the latter did not come from God" (III:41:563). Therefore, He permitted the Rabbis "to take *precautions* with a view to consolidating the ordinances of the Law by means of regulations in which they innovate with a view to repairing fissures, and to perpetuate these *precautionary* measures" (III:41:563; my emphasis). But if Maimonides' explanation of *shiluah ha-ken* is correct, we already find "precautionary" measures like those of the rabbis *within* the Written Law. That is, *within* the Written Law we find traces of the kind of changes of the Law that are reserved for the Oral Law. But this, in turn, undermines Maimonides' sharp distinction between the Written and Oral Laws, a distinction he emphasizes to defend the "fundamental principle of our Law that there will never be another Law . . . except the Law of *Moses our Master*" (II:39:379).[41] This implication of his explanation of *shiluah ha-ken* is what Maimonides wishes to conceal from the multitude. Hence, its description as a *gezerat ha-katuv*.

Now, whether or not all the details of this interpretation are correct, it is sufficient for my main argument that none of the occurrences of the phrase *gezerat ha-katuv* that we have examined *requires* the reading that some commandment is arbitrary with no reason. Of course, this still does not exclude the *possibility* that some occurrence of the phrase may nonetheless have that meaning, and I rather doubt that an impossibility proof to that effect could ever be given. I have, however, tried to present a number of reasons—for example, the analogous shift concerning *huqqim* from the *Commentary on the Mishnah* to the *Mishneh Torah* and *Guide* and Maimonides' general conception of a rational legislator—that legislate against such an interpretation. If for no better reason than charity in interpretation, we should not, then, read Maimonides in the contradiction-raising sense and, in particular, we need not saddle MT "*Tefillah*" xi, 7 with that troublesome interpretation.

One final question remains: Even allowing for the fact that he gives the phrase *gezerat ha-katuv* a different meaning and that he exploits its popular meaning for his own purposes, one might still wonder why Maimonides chooses to use a phrase that can so easily be read to mean that the commandments are arbitrary when that is so directly opposed to his own conception of the Law? Why does he see fit to adopt a misleading reason and terminology when, just as easily, he might have avoided even the appearance of contradiction by not citing the reason at all? Add to this the fact that Maimonides himself attests to the strangeness of his own statement when he cites this very opinion in the *Guide* as an *objection* to his explanation of *shilu'ah ha-ken*. To answer this question, we must look at Maimonides' Talmudic sources for his ruling.

A total of four reasons for the mishnaic decision to silence the speaker are proposed in the Babylonian and Palestinean Talmuds.[42] The reason Maimonides actually gives is the first of two cited in the Babylonian Talmud: the opinion of R. Jose bar Zebida who "makes God's commandments [the result of] His mercy when they are nothing but decrees [*gezerot*]." Odd as this choice may seem, it becomes more understandable when we survey the alternatives. For all the rest imply that what is wrong in praising God specifically for *shiluah ha-ken* is that in reality He has mercy on *all* individual creatures in all species. But this is an opinion about divine providence that Maimonides holds on philosophical grounds to be false; only R. Jose bar Zebida's opinion is consistent with Maimonides' philosophical view of divine providence. Of course, this would not alone have been sufficient reason to have chosen this statement. However, suppose Maimonides, though free in his choice among talmudic reasons and their interpretations, attempted to limit his range of *choices* to those suggested in the Talmud; given his view of the terminology of *gezerat ha-katuv* and his concern with the precautionary character of the explanation of *shiluah ha-ken*, the matter of providence may then have casted the deciding vote.[43] In the *Guide*, Maimonides could not cite this opinion without *openly* contradicting the thesis he defends there that all commandments have reasons. Therefore, after emphasizing the latter view, he leaves it to the discerning reader to understand that when he turns to the *Mishneh Torah* and finds his explanation of this *halakhah*, he must accordingly reinterpret the phrase *gezerat ha-katuv*.

As a closing note, it is tempting to speculate that the source of the objection that Maimonides raises in III:48 is his own statement in the *Mishneh Torah*—understood according to a more popular sense of *gezerat ha-katuv*. His response is an oblique instruction to the careful reader about how to read the *Mishneh Torah* and how to interpret that troublesome phrase. Not only need there be no contradiction between the two works. To understand either one, the attentive reader must carefully consult the other. *Complementarity* rather than *duality* may be the correct term to describe the relation between these two texts in the Maimonidean corpus.

CHAPTER 4

Maimonides and Nahmanides on the Interpretation of Parables and Explanation of Commandments

It has been common among scholars and lay readers to interpret Nahmanides primarily as a critic, even an opponent, of Maimonides.[1] For many readers, to paraphrase the *Guide*, the two Moses have no more in common than the name alone. There is, of course, some reality beneath this appearance. Despite the many references to Maimonides in his writings, the reader is usually left with the impression that Nahmanides cites the "Rav" primarily to disagree with him. However, a closer look reveals a more subtle, less polarized, relation between the two, as a number of more recent scholars have argued.[2] Nahmanides' stance toward his predecessor is also at times simply obscure. In some instances, as we shall see, the disagreement appears to be the result of misunderstanding, and perhaps even deliberate misrepresentation, of Maimonides' actual words by Nahmanides. In other instances, Nahmanides coopts the Maimonidean approach and takes it one step further than Maimonides himself did, even while he presents his interpretation as if it were in opposition to Maimonides'. In some of these cases, Nahmanides' view remains within the broadly philosophical framework in which Maimonides wrote. In other contexts, Nahmanides' dissatisfaction with Maimonides' philosophical solution to the problem at hand prompts his turn to kabbalah or leads him to transform a philosophical conception into a kabbalistic one. But in none of these cases is Nahmanides' stance toward Maimonides simply one of opposition.

In this chapter, I shall examine one instance of this complicated relation between Maimonides and Nahmanides: their respective conceptions of the project of *ta'amei ha-mitzvot*, the explanation of, or reasons for, the commandments of the Mosaic Law. Maimonides and Nahmanides were arguably the two greatest medieval exponents of *ta'amei ha-mitzvot*, and their disagreements over reasons for particular commandments are well known. However, despite these many differences between the contents of their reasons, the strong influence of Maimonides' method on Nahmanides' approach can be discerned at a deeper, formal level. Nahmanides, as is well known, typically offers multiple reasons for individual commandments, just as he frequently offers multiple interpretations of specific verses and texts. In the latter case, as Elliot Wolfson has recently observed, Nahmanides' model of interpretation is "highly reminiscent" of Maimonides' theory of multilevelled parabolic interpretation.[3] I shall argue that this resemblance runs very deep and, furthermore, that the Maimonidean conception of the multilevelled interpretation of parables, which he himself extended to the explanation of commandments, also underlies Nahmanides' approach to ta'amei ha-mitzvot.[4] First, I shall present Maimonides' own two-levelled account of external and internal reasons for the commandments, an explanation that emerges from his conception of a parable. Then, I shall show how Nahmanides adapts the same kind of schema for his account. Finally, I draw some implications from this account for Nahmanides' view of the obligatoriness of the commandments.

I

The largest self-contained bloc of Maimonides' *Guide* explicitly devoted to a single topic is chapters 26–49 of the third part, which lay out a systematic explanation of the reasons for the Mosaic commandments. The general outline of this account is well known; for our purposes I would emphasize three themes. First, in opposition to the Ash'arites, who claimed that all the commandments of a divine law are necessarily willed by the deity "without being intended toward any end at all" (III:26:506) and against the Mu'tazilites (including their Jewish followers, such as Saadiah), who claimed that this is true of only some divine laws, Maimonides argues that every commandment must serve an excellent end if only because it was legislated by the paradigm rational agent, the deity, who acts and commands only out of wisdom. Furthermore, in His legislation of the commandments, Maimonides argues that the deity acts, not for His own good or utility, but always for a utility or good for humankind, for human well-being.

Second, Maimonides attempts to show how each commandment is a means toward one of two general aims of "the Law as a whole," both of which are directed at the "welfare" of the general community. The first of these is what Maimonides calls the "welfare of the body," namely, the political and social well-being of the general community and the moral improvement of its individual members. The second, for which the first is itself a means, is the "welfare of the soul," by which Maimonides means the acquisition by the members of the community-at-large of "correct opinions corresponding to their respective capacity" (III:27:510). Maimonides goes on to distinguish these two kinds of communally oriented "welfare" from two corresponding kinds of individual "perfection," but he emphasizes that the Law is specifically directed at, and attuned to developing, the former rather than the latter.[5] That is, the Law is specifically addressed to the communal good, be it intellectual or social-political, rather than individual perfection.

Third, and probably most distinctive, Maimonides makes extensive use of historical-anthropological information about the pagan environment of ancient Israel in order to show how the particulars of many commandments—related to the Temple, sacrifice, purity and impurity, agriculture, and dress—were legislated to wean the people away from idolatry—either through counterpractices or through accommodation—and toward worship of one incorporeal deity. As I argued in chapter 2, this broad class of commandments, whose reasons cannot be known apart from historical knowledge of the circumstances of their legislation, constitutes Maimonides' reconstruction of the class of laws distinguished by the Rabbis as *huqqim*, commandments whose reasons are not known (or, as some held, are unknowable).[6] As qualified by Maimonides, the reasons for these commandments are not known *by the multitude*, namely, those who lack such historical knowledge. Furthermore, Maimonides also holds that these *huqqim* are laws whose reasons are best left unrevealed to the multitude—because knowledge of those reasons might easily lead to antinomianism. Thus, given his historical, context-dependent explanation for their legislation, the objection will undoubtedly be raised: Why, in different historical circumstances (say, already in Maimonides' twelfth-century Andalusia in which idolatry was no longer a live threat), should one nonetheless be obligated to perform these commandments? Lacking a good answer to this question, or at least a persuasive answer for the community-at-large, Maimonides suggests that the rabbis thought it best not even to suggest that there exist these problematic reasons for the commandments.[7]

The impact of Maimonides' naturalized, Aristotelian conception of the project of *ta'amei ha-mitzvot*, and especially his interpretation of the *huqqim*, was enormous. Among the Jewish philosophers, it provided the impetus for a continuing literature that carried on Maimonides' rationalist program of *ta'amei ha-mitzvot* while being at the same time largely critical of his more radical explanations.[8] Among the emerging kabbalists in Spain and Provence, Maimonides' naturalized account, which was ipso facto a devaluation of their older esoteric understanding of the commandments, precipitated both a vigorous polemical literature and a new genre of commentaries on the mystical significance of the commandments.[9] In chapter 6, I shall describe the influence, or effect, of

Maimonides' analysis of the *huqqim* on Nahmanides in particular. For now, I would emphasize that the possible antinomian implications of his naturalized account of the reasons for the commandments, and the questions these implications raise about the permissability of engaging in inquiry into *ta'amei ha-mitzvot*, were not lost on Maimonides himself. At the conclusion of the *Book of Commandments*, commenting on negative commandment 365 (based on Deut. 17:16–17), Maimonides cites the well-known example of Solomon who, knowing the reason for this prohibition, was thereby led to disregard and ultimately transgress it, thinking that he could achieve its purpose or end without the specific Mosaic commandment as a means. "For this reason"—concerned that the vulgar multitude would surely be led to such "enlightened antinomianism" if Solomon could not resist its temptation—Maimonides concludes: "the Exalted One has concealed (*histir*) the reasons [for the commandments]."[10] Of course, this danger did not in the least stop Maimonides from going ahead with his philosophical explanation of the commandments. But the danger was real and, as we shall see, it was not ignored by his contemporaries, including Nahmanides.

Although Maimonides' explanation of the commandments in *Guide* III:26–49 is his longest, most explicit, and best-known discussion of the subject, it is not his only account of *ta'amei ha-mitzvot*. In chapters 51–52 of the third part he presents, in very succinct form, a second general account that is eclipsed, or concealed, by the prominence of the earlier account. According to this second account, the "actions prescribed by the Law" (III:52:630) or "the practices of the worship, such as reading the Torah, prayer, and the performance of the other *commandments*" (III:51:622), "have only the end of training you to occupy yourself with [God's] commandments . . . rather than with matters pertaining to this world." In contrast to the first account, this explanation of the ends of the commandments is not based on the good or wellbeing of their agents, be it the welfare of their bodies or the welfare of their souls. Both of these kinds of goods fall under what Maimonides categorizes here as "matters pertaining to this world." Rather, the sole end of the commandments on this second account is "training," or discipline, designed to detach the agent from anything pertaining to this world, that is, any needs or desires that would concern one as a creature composed of matter as well as form. This account of the commandments, Maimonides tells us, is not for everyone; it is directed to the individual who has already "attained perfection in the divine science," indeed the "rank of the prophets" (III:51:620). It is only when this sort of person achieves this kind of detachment from the world, only when he disassociates himself from the impulses of his matter or body to the fullest extent possible, only when he empties his thought of all concern with the material world—it is only then that he can reach the state of an acquired intellect, fully and solely engaged in contemplation of the deity, or divine science, the state of a fully actualized intellect totally absorbed in apprehension of intelligibles.

It is perhaps worth adding that the claim, according to this second account, that the commandments were legislated to "train" people to be "occupied" only with the deity and with nothing other than Him is *not* to say that the commandments are simply the consequence of the divine will alone, the view of the Ash'arites.[11] For the kind of detachment and emptying that the commandments aim to achieve is not itself arbitrary or for no reason; it is a necessary condition for the person to achieve the perfection of an acquired intellect. However, according to this second account it is true that all the particular commandments have the *same* end or reason: detachment, emptying, occupying oneself only with that which is other than the world. Therefore "no cause will ever be found for the fact that one particular sacrifice consists in a lamb and another in a ram"; that is, no *differentiating* cause will be found for choosing one particular commandment rather than another; they "were all given merely for the sake of commanding something" (III:26:508). The grain of truth in the Kalam position is that there is no particular reason or end for each individual commandment, only one very general end that applies to all commandments and does not distinguish among them.

What, then, are the differences between these two accounts of *ta'amei ha-mitzvot*? Both accounts are concerned with the *reasons of the legislator*—that is, the reasons or explanation why particular commandments, or the Law as a whole, were legislated to Israel at the time of the Mosaic revelation—rather than with a reason for a *performer of the commandment*—a justifying reason or, more generally, a *motive* for a human agent at some particular time to perform that commandment, some end that would properly *motivate* one to do the act.[12] Both accounts also assume that the deity legislated the commandments for a reason, indeed an excellent reason. The main difference between the two accounts consists in the contents of their respective reasons. The reasons in the first account are anthropocentric—that is, oriented toward achieving human goods in this world. The reasons in the second account are theocentric, at least insofar as they are oriented toward denying everything other than the deity, everything of "this world." Furthermore, the commandments according to the first account are attuned to achieving goods for the community as a whole; according to the second account, the commandments enable individuals, indeed a very select group of individuals, to achieve perfection.

How, then, should we characterize the relation between the two different accounts of *ta'amei ha-mitzvot*? I propose that we understand it

on the model of the different levels of meaning Maimonides distinguishes in the interpretation of a parable. In the introduction to the
Guide, Maimonides tells us that one of the greatest sources of misunderstanding of prophetic texts, including the Torah, is the failure to recognize all of their meanings. In particular, the ordinary reader fails to
realize that these texts contain parables "not explicitly identified there
as such" (I:Intro.:6). He fails to realize that these texts possess, in addition to their "vulgar" meaning—the meaning of their words, as the vulgar multitude (I:Intro.:9) exclusively understands them—two other
kinds or "levels" of meaning, what Maimonides calls their "external"
and "internal" meanings.[13] In contrast to the vulgar meaning of scriptural verses, which (at least sometimes) expresses beliefs that no reasonable person should hold (e.g., the corporeality of God or the belief that
the highest perfection is moral rather than intellectual), both the external and internal parabolic meanings of the text express beliefs grounded
in wisdom. The difference between the external and internal meanings
of a parable is, as Maimonides explains in his interpretation of the rabbinic parable of "apples of gold in settings of silver," that the external
meaning "contains wisdom that is useful in many respects, among
which is the welfare of human societies" whereas its internal meaning
"contains wisdom that is useful for beliefs concerned with the truth as
it is" (I:Intro.:12). That is, the external meaning of a parable communicates the beliefs necessary for welfare of a community; its internal meaning communicates beliefs necessary for apprehension of the truth (to the
degree to which and in the form in which it can be achieved), beliefs
concerning the apprehension of physics and metaphysics. But this distinction, I should immediately add, is not a distinction simply between
the theoretical and practical. Maimonides emphasizes that the welfare of
the community is both "of the body" and "of the soul" (III:27:510–12),
both moral/political *and* intellectual. However, both the contents of the
beliefs and the character of apprehension necessary and appropriate for
communal welfare are not, or not always, what is necessary for individual intellectual perfection. The contents are not always "the truth as it
is" and the grounds of apprehension may be tradition or authority
rather than demonstration. On the other hand, the content of the internal meaning, "wisdom that is useful for beliefs concerned with the truth
as it is," may also not always be "the truth as it is" about physical or
metaphysical reality (if, for example, those truths lie beyond the limits
of human apprehension) and it may involve practical wisdom concerning the kind of training that is necessary to achieve the highest kind of
apprehension within the limits of human capacity. We shall meet one
example of this training in chapter 5.

Nonetheless the difference between the external and internal meanings of a parable is a function entirely of their *contents*. It is not a difference in their respective intended audiences or in their literary forms of presentation, such as whether the meaning is revealed or concealed, explicit or simply implied, intended for a select school or closed group or for the public at large. Of course, Maimonides also employs (as he states in the introduction) various devices (deliberate contradictions, allusions, chapter headings, scrambling of passages, and the literary figure of the parable) to conceal the contents of some of his claims and interpretations. However, these means of concealment are *in addition to* his distinction between the external and internal meanings of parables, a distinction based on content. Rather than force Maimonides' hermeneutics into a dualistic schema like the exoteric/esoteric dichotomy, it would be more correct to view it as the product of a coordinate system with two axes, one for differences in content like the distinction between parabolic external and internal meaning, the other for differences in literary presentation that would differentiate concealed/secret and revealed/public information. Thus, not only its internal meaning but sometimes the external meaning of a parable, or parabolic passage, may be subject to literary concealment. The internal as well as external meanings of other parabolic passages may be openly, explicitly stated. Hence, the different possible combinations of these two interpretive axes allow for a much more subtle interplay of contents and forms of interpretation than can be achieved by the exoteric/esoteric dichotomy—which, to make matters worse, simply conflates differences of content with differences of form.

There is a second difference I should mention between the external/internal parabolic meaning distinction and the exoteric/esoteric distinction. The esoteric meaning of a text, in the received view, is typically presented as the "real" meaning of the text, the author's intended meaning, the meaning that expresses what the author himself believes. The exoteric meaning is the interpretation presented "merely" for public consumption, for the multitude or community-at-large, what must be said out of political, religious, or social necessity. The distinction I believe Maimonides draws between the external and internal meanings of a parable does not carry this contrast: both external and internal meanings are meanings expressed by or "contained" in the text. Both were intended by the author. The text, in other words, is genuinely polysemous, or systematically ambiguous. Both meanings express kinds of wisdom the author himself believes, intends to convey, and qua wisdom believes ought to be believed by his reader.

To be sure, apart from their external and internal parabolic meanings, texts also have their "vulgar" meaning, the meanings of their words. In some cases the vulgar meaning expresses the external or internal parabolic meaning; the words mean just what the text says, in whole or part. In other cases (say, where it describes God corporeally), it expresses neither kind of wisdom; instead it expresses harmful falsehoods that are the very opposite of wisdom, falsehoods that the author does not believe and that he does not believe should be believed by any reasonable person—although it was absolutely necessary, or unavoidable, to use such language in its original context of utterance.[14] And in yet other cases, the "vulgar" meaning is innocuous: what it expresses is neither wisdom that ought to believed nor falsehood that it is harmful to believe. At bottom, I would say that Maimonides is simply uninterested in such meaning, the meanings of words. He is concerned with what we ought to believe, and "belief is not the notion that is uttered but the notion that is represented in the soul" (I:50:111). The vulgar meaning of the text aside, it is among the things that ought to be believed, and that the author intends to express, that Maimonides distinguishes the external and internal meanings of parables. Neither one of these to the exclusion of the other could be called the esoteric as opposed to exoteric meaning of the text.

Now, corresponding to this distinction between the external and internal meanings of a parable, Maimonides also distinguishes two analogous levels or kinds of *reasons* for commandments.[15] The first kind of reason is concerned with wisdom appropriate for communal welfare, both moral/political and intellectual; the second with beliefs concerned with individual apprehension (within the limits of human capacity) of physical and metaphysical truth. With the commandments, however, Maimonides engages in this sort of parabolic interpretation, or explanation, with both microscopic and macroscopic units. At the microscopic level, he doubly explains certain individual commandments, or attributes to them two reasons, corresponding to the two parabolic levels of meaning. These particular commandments all appear to be concerned with the body: for example, the commandment to bury one's excrement (Deut. 23:14; see III:41, 43), the commandment of circumcision (III:49), and the commandment to rest one's body, or refrain from work, on the Sabbath (II:31).[16] Maimonides' worry that the focus on the body of these commandments will disengage the person from full, undivided concentration on the deity—who is separate from all matter—appears to be what motivates him to interpret these commandments as parables.

At the macroscopic level, Maimonides explains the totality of the Law—"the practices of the worship, such as reading the Torah, prayer, and the performance of the other commandments"—on the same two-levelled parabolic model. In III:26–49 (or, in summary, in III:27–28), the reasons given for the commandments of the Law as a whole all serve the "welfare of human society," including the welfare both of the body and the soul—that is, political and social goods for the community and the inculcation of correct opinions by its members according to their respective capacities. Thus, the commandments explicitly cited as examples in the passage just quoted are said to "bring about useful opinions," that is, "beliefs concerning [God] as is necessary for *everyone* professing the Law" (III:44:574). These opinions and beliefs are not, to be sure, intellectually apprehended by everyone who is thereby led to profess them. And the way in which the commandments "bring about" these beliefs is not a way in which those who thereby hold them could be said to *know* them or to achieve intellectual perfection. Rather, the belief achieved in this way creates a community of a certain caliber that aims at the "welfare of the soul" as well as the "welfare of the body," the kind of community Maimonides says is created by a divine law.[17] Hence, in this first general explanation, the commandments serve to communicate "wisdom that is useful in many respects, among which is the welfare of human societies" (I:Intro.:12). In short, this description is exactly how Maimonides characterizes the external meaning of a parable.

In III:51–52, on the other hand, the reason given for the commandments—to train oneself to be occupied with [God's] commandments rather than with matters pertaining to this world—corresponds to the internal meaning of a parable. Here the substantive content of occupying oneself with the divine is primarily negative: one occupies oneself *with* God by detaching oneself *from* this world, from pursuit of material needs and desires. This, in turn, is a precondition for being an acquired intellect, an intellect engaged fully and exclusively in contemplation of truth within the limitations imposed by human capacities. Thus, the reason for the commandments on this second account is analogous to Maimonides' characterization of the internal meaning of a parable: "wisdom that is useful for beliefs concerned with the truth as it is" (ibid.). The commandments do not, strictly speaking, *contain* wisdom concerned with knowledge of physics and metaphysics. But by enabling one to engage in intellectual apprehension to the greatest possible degree without the interference of the body, their performance *enables* one to be engaged in apprehension of truth to the highest possible degree compatible with human capacities.

In sum, the general structure under which we might subsume Maimonides' two different explanations of the commandments, in III:26–49 and in III:51–52, seems to fit exactly the two-levelled structure of his idea of parabolic interpretation. As with the two meanings of parabolic texts, the commandments have both of these reasons and were legislated to achieve both of these different kinds of ends. At the external level, their reasons are oriented toward anthropocentric communal well-being; at the internal level, toward the theocentric (intellectual) perfection of individuals who are capable of such perfection.[18]

II

With the Maimonidean background in hand, I now turn to Nahmanides' conception of *ta'amei ha-mitzvot*, which he lays out almost entirely in his commentary on Deut. 22:6 ("*Ki Yikareh Kan Tzippur Lefanekha,*" C 448–51). His choice of this verse, and the commandment of *shiluah ha-ken,* as the locus for his most extensive discussion of this topic is entirely determined by its Maimonidean prehistory. Indeed Nahmanides opens his discussion by taking issue with Maimonides on two separate issues connected to this verse. Both of these disagreements are striking as much for what they omit as for what they say.

Nahmanides' first criticism of Maimonides is focused on the specific reason for the commandment of *shiluah ha-ken,* the commandment to send away the mother bird from the nest before taking her young. Nahmanides proposes two alternative explanations of his own: (1) The commandment is a means of moral education or character training: to instil in humans the trait of mercy rather than cruelty, even toward animals. (2) It inculcates belief in the doctrine of creation, by forbidding an act that, were one to perform it, could be construed "as if the [the human agent] had destroyed a whole species," a consequence that, in turn, would contradict the account of creation in Genesis according to which species were created with "the power to reproduce: that they might exist in perpetuity [*a parte post*] so long as God wills the existence of the world."[19] By keeping the prohibition, the agent tacitly acknowledges the presupposed belief. Details aside, these two reasons are reminiscent of Maimonides' two aims for "the Law as a whole . . . the welfare of the soul and the welfare of the body" (III:27:510), the two aims that guide his first account of *ta'amei ha-mitzvot* in III:26–49. The only difference is that Nahmanides seems to interpret the Maimonidean dictum to mean that *each* commandment serves *both* of these ends.

Now, after stating these two reasons for *shiluah ha-ken,* Nahmanides contrasts them with Maimonides' explanation in *Guide* III:48. Although Nahmanides correctly says that Maimonides' reason for this commandment is the same as his reason for the prohibition against slaughtering an animal "and its young on the same day" (Lev. 22:28), the specific reason for these two laws that Nahmanides attributes to Maimonides is incorrect. According to Nahmanides, Maimonides' reason for both is divine mercy for the parent animal or bird, whose love and concern for its young is based in the imagination (translated *koah ha-mahashavah* in Al-Harizi's translation of the *Guide*, the text used by Nahmanides)[20] rather than intellect and, therefore, is no different from that of humans for their young.

However, as we saw in the previous chapter, this reason—divine mercy for the animal or bird—is not Maimonides' true explanation for these commandments. Most important, it explicitly contradicts his theory of providence according to which divine providence does not extend to the individuals of species other than the human (III:17:471–74). Maimonides' actual view is the same as Nahmanides': the commandment is meant to inculcate in *us* humans the appropriate moral character trait. Of course, to educate someone to act mercifully, one teaches the person to do so in circumstances that call for mercy. But it does not follow that the legislator's reason for commanding *us* to be merciful in such circumstances, say, that of *shiluah ha-ken*, was *his* (or God's) mercy for the bird.

Nahmanides' misrepresentation, or misunderstanding, of Maimonides' reason in the *Guide* is complicated by an objection he raises against it. If the reason for *shiluah ha-ken* were mercy for the bird, as he alleges Maimonides holds, then all slaughter of animals for consumption as food ought to be prohibited. Now, as Nahmanides undoubtedly knew, this is an argument given by Maimonides himself in both his *Commentary on the Mishnah* and the *Mishneh Torah*. In the course of explaining the mishnaic decision to silence the one who says in his supplications, "May He who had mercy on the nest of the bird have mercy on us," Maimonides states: "these commandments are a decree of Scripture [*gezerat ha-katuv*] and [their reasons] are not mercy [for the creatures]; for if they were [legislated] because of mercy, [He] would not permit any slaughtering" (*MT* "*Tefillah*" ix, 7). Therefore, Nahmanides' view on this question is in fact the true Maimonidean opinion, whereas his grounds for rejecting the position that he (mis)represents as Maimonides' is Maimonides' own argument in the *Mishneh Torah* for rejecting that very view.

This is not the only puzzling feature of Nahmanides' discussion. A second problem arises in the course of his own positive account of *ta'amei ha-mitzvot* that, in turn, is built on a second criticism of Maimonides. Let me first describe the context for this second puzzle.

After discussing the specific reason for the commandment of *shiluah ha-ken*, Nahmanides cites two rabbinic passages quoted by Maimonides in the *Guide* that suggest that the commandments of the Law were willed by God for no reason at all, a view that would evidently undermine all inquiry into *ta'amei ha-mitzvot*. The first of these passages is quoted by Maimonides immediately following his own explanation of

shiluah ha-ken in the *Guide*. He then adds that he should not be criticized for disagreeing with the rabbinic opinion, mentioned above,
according to which "We silence he who says: Thy Mercy extends to
young birds, and so on" (*Berakhoth* V, 3). "For this is one of the two
opinions mentioned by us—I mean the opinion of those who think that
there is no reason for the Law except only the will [of God]—but as for
us, we follow only the second opinion" (III:48:600).[21] Here Maimonides
is referring back to his main discussion in the *Guide* III:26 where, as we
mentioned earlier, he rejects the Ash'arite (as well as Mu'tazilite) view
and argues that all commandments have reasons, the "second opinion"
he mentions here.

The second passage cited by Nahmanides is the well-known
midrash in *Bereshith Rabbah* quoted by Maimonides in *Guide*
III:26:508:

> What does it matter to the Holy One . . . that animals are slaughtered
> by cutting their neck in front or in the back? Say therefore that the
> commandments were only given in order to purify the people [*letzaref
> et ha-bri'ot*]. For it is said: The word of the Lord is purified [*tzerufah*].

It is, you will recall, in the wake of this *midrash* that Maimonides makes
his (apparent) qualification that only the generalities of commandments
and not their particulars have reasons, a qualification he claims is illustrated by the case of sacrifices—for which he then goes on to give his
detailed historical reasons! However, as we mentioned earlier, these
innovative explanations are Maimonides' most controversial *ta'amei ha-
mitzvot* and, because of their potential antinomian consequences (which
he anticipates in his *Book of Commandments*), he may also have
thought it best to conceal them. Nahmanides entirely omits this qualification in the Maimonidean position, as well as Maimonides' reinterpretation of the above midrash to suit his own theory of *ta'amei ha-
mitzvot*.[22] However, it is impossible not to read his citation of these
problematic passages—loci classici for those who opposed inquiry into
ta'amei ha-mitzvot precisely because of its dangers—and his vigorous
reaffirmation of Maimonides' view that every commandment has a reason as a reassertion of the legitimacy and indeed obligatoriness of
inquiry into reasons for the commandments *even* in the face of its antinomian dangers.[23]

Furthermore, Nahmanides' general conception of the project of
ta'amei ha-mitzvot follows Maimonides closely. For both, to say that
every commandment has a reason (*ta'am*) is to say that none was *legislated* simply in virtue of divine will, *hefetz ha-boreh*, the kind of voluntaristic will that Maimonides associates with the Kalam. For Nahmanides as for Maimonides, then, the project of *ta'amei ha-mitzvot* is

concerned with the reasons of the legislator, not reasons for the per-former.[24] Following Maimonides' use of the term *gezerah* ("decree") in III:38:550, Nahmanides also explains that it refers not to that which is arbitrary or without reason (as many thought) but to all commandments and especially to those whose good is not *immediately* recognizable to the *multitude*—for example, commandments whose purpose is moral discipline or character training, even when this is not readily apparent.[25] Also like Maimonides, Nahmanides emphasizes that each of these *ta'amim* is a "benefit (*to'elet*) and for the welfare of man (*tikun le'adam*)."[26] Indeed, because he does not make Maimonides' explicit qualification that only the generalities of commandments have reasons, and because he argues explicitly that the goods are only for humans— and not for other nonhuman creations or creatures—Nahmanides seems to take the Maimonidean approach one step further than Maimonides himself did.[27]

At the same time, and perhaps to counterbalance his strong advo-cacy of the project, Nahmanides emphasizes the antiquity of *ta'amei ha-mitzvot*—that the reasons for the most obscure commandments were revealed to the ancient sages, Moses, Solomon, and R. Aqiba. Here he paints a much more conservative picture of the enterprise of *ta'amei ha-mitzvot* than Maimonides, and one that would legislate against the inno-vative, naturalistic extremes of the *Guide*. In Nahmanides' conception, knowledge of the true reasons for the commandments must be by way of a tradition received from these earlier sages to whom they were divinely revealed.[28] As he concludes, we do not know the reasons for cer-tain commandments, not because they have no reasons or because of the nature of the reasons, but because of "blindness in our intellects"— blindness that prevents the reasons from being revealed to us or discov-ered through our autonomous intellects, as they were revealed to or known by the ancient sages of Israel.[29]

Now, having defended the legitimacy of inquiry into reasons for the commandments while restricting the kinds of reasons one might dis-cover, Nahmanides next says that Maimonides misinterprets the pas-sages quoted previously which "he finds so difficult." Maimonides took them to be saying that the commandments have no reasons. Nah-manides wants to discredit this view entirely, so much so that he is unwilling even to allow for a minority rabbinic opinion supporting it. Instead, he argues, these passages advocate the different claim that the goods, or utilities, because of which the commandments were legislated *by* God are never goods or utilities *for* God; they are goods only for their human agents. Notwithstanding the *peshat*, the literal, plain, or external meaning of Scripture, God receives no benefit from the Temple cande-labrum as if He "needed" (*sheyitztareikh*) its light, nor does he "need" the sacrifices for food or the incense for its fragrance.[30] Even the many commandments that serve to commemorate God's miraculous acts are not of value for or benefit to Him; rather they enable "us to know the truth and to be worthy of it." And the meaning of the *Bereshith Rabbah* statement that the commandments "purify" us is not, as Maimonides suggests, that they discipline people simply to obey the divine will; instead it means that the commandments cleanse humanity of ill traits and evil beliefs as one purifies a crude metal of its impurities. Here, then, Nahmanides appears to take a very strong line—more so than Maimonides—on the anthropocentric, even antitheocentric, character of the commandments.

It may not be entirely clear why Nahmanides argues this point at such great length nor whom he is arguing against. However, what is strangest about Nahmanides' vigorous refutation of this view is that he does not even allude to the fact that he himself elsewhere endorses a position at least superficially like it. In his commentary on Exodus 29:46, following a hint by Abraham Ibn Ezra, Nahmanides refers to the "great secret" (*sod gadol*) that *hashekhinah beyisrael tzorekh gevoha velo tzorekh hedyot*, that the Shekhinah—by which he seems to mean all aspects of divine worship, and specifically the commandments, which cause the Divine Presence to dwell within Israel—satisfy "higher [i.e., divine] needs" (*tzorekh gevoha*) and not, as the literal meaning of Scripture (*peshat hadavar*) suggests, "ordinary [i.e., profane or human] needs" (*tzorekh hedyot*). The idea to which Nahmanides is referring here is a motif that becomes central to later kabbalistic theories of *ta'amei ha-mitzvot:* that the human performance of the commandments serves to satisfy, complete, or perfect the deity or divine nature. As Moses de Leon describes this process of *hit'orerut* (arousal, awakening), "the event above [in the sefirotic realm] is 'stirred up' or 'aroused' by the event below."[31] The commandments in this view are essentially theurgic in function. They were legislated to "satisfy" divine "needs," divine needs that can only be fulfilled by humans performing the commandments.

This theurgic explanation of the commandments is, of course, entirely foreign to the philosophical tradition and especially to Maimonides. However, what is more significant is that we now face in Nahmanides' writings, as in the *Guide*, two contrasting accounts of the reasons for the commandments, one highly anthropocentric, the other radically theocentric. According to the first account, which Nahmanides advances in his commentary on Deut. 22:6, the commandments were legislated to serve human needs and ends, explicitly not divine needs and purposes. According to the second account, hinted at in the commentary on Exodus 29:46, they do just the opposite: the commandments fulfill divine rather than human needs. What, then, is the relation between these two mutually incompatible explanations?

To resolve this contradiction in Nahmanides' writing, I wish to propose that the relation between his two almost diametrically opposed accounts of the reasons for the commandments—the one oriented toward human needs and ends, the other toward divine needs—is modelled by Nahmanides after Maimonides' idea of parabolic interpretation in general and, more specifically, after his "parabolic"—that is, two-levelled—explanation of commandments. Although their accounts differ on the specific reasons they give for commandments, especially at the internal level, they both hold that the commandments should be explained on the two-levelled model of parables, that they have both internal and external reasons (in addition to their literal, or vulgar, meaning, the meanings of their words). Nahmanides' account of *ta'amei ha-mitzvot* in Deut. 22:6 provides the external reasons for the commandments according to which they communicate or serve the ends of their human performers, social, moral, and intellectual. The account hinted at in his commentary on Exodus 29:46 provides the internal reason for the commandments—a theocentric account concerned with the truth or "according to the way of truth," as Nahmanides standardly refers to his kabbalistic traditions.

Nahmanides' general adoption, or adaptation, of the Maimonidean parabolic model of interpretation can be seen most clearly in the introduction to his "Sermon on the Words of Kohelet." There he introduces his hermeneutical theory with Proverbs 1:6, the same verse with which Maimonides opens his discussion of the multiple levels of meaning of parables in the introduction to the *Guide*:

> And it is said: He instructed the people (Eccles. 12:9). For the parable (*mashal*) that Solomon spoke [served] to symbolize (*lermoz*) good character traits concerning one's behavior in this world and to symbolize the matter of the World to Come. And it symbolizes the higher [or divine] wisdoms [or sciences], concerning the [Account of the] Chariot, and the secrets (*sitrei*) of the Torah. Therefore he cautioned them to understand his words, and it is said: To understand a proverb (*mashal*) and a figure (*melitzah*); the words of the wise and their riddles (*hidatam*). That is to say, they will understand the parable (*mashal*) and they will understand the figure (*melitzah*) which is the literal sense (*peshat*). And they will understand that which is wisdom (*hakhmah*) and riddle (*hidah*), that is to say, the secret (*sod*) which it is forbidden to explain. And this is as the matter of the chapter "A capable wife who can find" (Prov. 31:10). For the figure (*melitzah*), which according to its literal meaning (*peshuto*) is true, teaches knowledge concerning the good diligent wife, who acts with good ethics in her work and with her husband and all the members of her household and with the

poor. And [the chapter] symbolizes (*termoz*) the act (or performance) of the Torah (*ma'aseih Torah*) with her husband, the teacher who engages in it [i.e., the Torah] for its own sake (*leshmah*) and with her sons the students and with the poor, i.e., the multitude (*hamon*). And it symbolizes the attribute called '*Atarah* and her actions in the governance of the world.[32]

Like Maimonides, Nahmanides here distinguishes three levels of meaning in the interpretation of a parable (*mashal*): (1) the *melitzah* (the external figure of speech), which he identifies with its *peshat*, its literal, plain sense—in the example of Prov. 31:10, the meaning according to which "the capable wife" signifies the knowledge of the diligent wife; (2) *hakhmah*, a kind of practical or moral wisdom, in this example, the wisdom concerned with performance of the Torah and its teaching; and (3) *hidah* (riddle), which he identifies with the *sod*, the kabbalistic significance of the verse—here the meaning that signifies the attribute '*Atarah*—which must be concealed and cannot be publically revealed.[33] The first meaning of the verse—the *melitzah*, that is, when the verse is taken simply as a *melitzah*—corresponds to Maimonides' vulgar (nonparabolic, external) meaning of the passage, its interpretation according to the meanings of its words as they are understood by the vulgar or ordinary reader for whom such passages are not even recognized to be parables but instead literally true narratives. This kind of meaning Nahmanides also labels *peshat*, adopting traditional terminology. The second and third of Nahmanides' meanings—the *hakhmah* and *hidah* contained in the verse—correspond respectively to Maimonides' two levels of external and internal meaning for the passage when it is recognized as a parable. *Hakhmah*, like Maimonides' external (parabolic) meaning, communicates wisdom concerning the welfare of the community, the kind of wisdom associated with the teaching of the Law, or Torah, both practical and intellectual.[34] *Hidah*, or *sod*, like Maimonides' internal meaning, is concerned with metaphysics or divine science, be it philosophic or theosophic.

Of course, Maimonides and Nahmanides respectively assign different contents to the corresponding levels of meaning. Where, for example, Nahmanides takes the innermost meaning, the *hidah* or *sod*, of the phrase "capable wife" of Prov. 31:10 to be referring to the divine attribute '*Atarah*, Maimonides interprets it as referring in its internal meaning to matter (III:8:433). However, what I wish to emphasize is, first, the common triadic *structures* of their two interpretive models: multilevelled writing with two kinds of parabolic meanings in addition to a nonparabolic external or literal meaning, the meaning of the words used. Second, both see the parabolic model of multilevelled interpretation extending from texts to commandments. Indeed Nahmanides continues the passage quoted above by explicitly applying his interpretive model to the commandments, which he says have both a literal meaning and an interpretation (*kepeshutah ukemidrashah*).[35] Third, for both thinkers the difference between the two parabolic reasons for the commandments is that one (the external meaning/reason) explains them in terms of human-oriented ends whereas the other (the internal meaning/reason) makes them instruments directed exclusively at the deity, either exercises designed to detach the person from everything other than God or theurgic acts that affect Him through concentration on His attributes.

There is, however, one significant difference between Maimonides' and Nahmanides' respective views about the "structure" of explanation of the commandments. As we saw in the first section, Maimonides takes both the external and internal *parabolic* meanings/reasons to be ones that the author/legislator intended. Both are meanings of the text/commandment, "contained" in them. However, the same cannot be said for the external *nonparabolic* meaning, the vulgar meaning of the text. Although this is the (literal, historical, philological, narrative) meaning of the *words* used—the *peshat*, if you will—Maimonides does not believe that this meaning must express the author's intention or opinion or what he wishes his reader to believe. It does not follow, in other words, that the *peshat* is in any way *meant* by the text or its author. In some passages (for example, the corporeal descriptions of God) the vulgar meaning, to the contrary, expresses something the author definitely does *not* intend his audience to believe (although there is, of course, a story why this language was nonetheless adopted). And even when the vulgar meaning is not wrong or corrupt, Maimonides is simply uninterested in this level or kind of meaning; what he "aims at" and "investigates" is "what we should believe" and not "what we should say" (I:50:111).

Nahmanides, on the other hand, *is* deeply interested in the literal meaning of the nonparabolic external utterance, its meaning as a *melitzah* or its *peshat*. Like Maimonides, he takes the interpretations of verses that constitute their *hakhmah* and *hidah/sod*—the practical and theoretical, or theosophical, truths they convey—as genuine meanings of the verses, as authorially intended meanings. But for Nahmanides, unlike Maimonides, these interpretations are always *in addition to* the literal meanings of their words, their *peshat*. All of these meanings—*melitzah/peshat* as well as *hakhmah* and *hidah*—are "borne by the words of the text" (*yisbol hakatuv et hakol*), and "included in its language" (*kulam belashon hakatuv nikhlalim*).[36] Similarly for the corresponding kinds of reasons for commandments. Thus, although Nahmanides emphasizes the multiple parabolic meanings of the text, or multiple parabolic reasons of the commandments, in no way in his view does this displace, dislodge, or demote the place of *peshat*, the meanings of the words. In some cases, the *peshat* parallels the *hakhmah* or *hidah*, in other cases they may even be identified.[37] In either case, the two parabolic levels of meaning tend to enrich Nahmanides' notion of *peshat*. As he emphasizes in his notes on Maimonides' *Book of Commandments*, even in purely legal contexts the biblical text never loses its literal sense—*'ain mikra' yotzei' midei peshuto*—in the presence of a rabbinic derived interpretation. Rather "the scriptural text has its [nonliteral] interpretation (*midrash*) together with its *peshat*; it does not exclude either of them; but the text bears (*yisbol*) all of them and both of them are true."[38]

Nahmanides' restoration of cognitive value to *peshat* in the aftermath of its Maimonidean devaluation is, I would suggest, one of his most important and original contributions to medieval scriptural exegesis. Indeed many of the sharpest differences between Maimonides and Nahmanides in their approaches both to *parshanut* and to *ta'amei ha-mitzvot* derive not from the philosophical vs. kabbalistic divide at the level of their respective internal meanings and reasons, but from their opposing attitudes toward *peshat*.[39] For Maimonides, the *peshat*, or vulgar external meaning of Scripture, adds up to "many layers of rind," which have so obscured the "great roots of knowledge" that lie at the "core" of the Torah that people have "thought that beneath them there was no core whatever" (I:71:176). For Nahmanides, in contrast, "all the [rabbinic] interpretations are included in the language of the text . . . because the Book of the Law of God is complete (*sefer Torat ha-Shem temimah*), it has no letter that is either excessive or lacking, everything in it was written in wisdom."[40]

The value and exegetical importance Nahmanides places on *peshat* in general may also help to solve one of the puzzling characteristics, mentioned earlier, in Nahmanides' commentary on Deut. 22:6: why he goes to such great lengths to show that the utilities or benefits of commandments are never for God. The key word in his discussion is, I would suggest, *peshat*: God does not need the light of the Temple candelabrum or the food of the sacrifices and the fragrance of the incense, Nahmanides argues, "even though it would so appear from the literal meaning of the verses" (*kinir'eh mipeshutaihem*). As we have seen, Nahmanides does hold that the commandments, according to their parabolic internal meaning, "satisfy divine needs." But what he is intent on showing is that, despite the theurgic function of the commandments and despite the generally authoritative status of *peshat*, the way in which the commandments act on the deity is *not* according to the literal meaning of the text: that the candelabrum fulfills a divine need for light, sacrifices a divine need for nourishment, and so on.[41] In this exception to his rule, *peshat* is not a good guide to discovering or understanding the theosophical significance of the commandments.

Finally, I would like to conclude with some brief comments on two aspects of Nahmanides' view of the obligatoriness of the commandments on which his multilevelled parabolic conception of *ta'amei ha-mitzvot* may throw some light.

A frequently recognized problem for naturalistic explanations of the commandments like Maimonides' and Nahmanides'—a problem that may also motivate one kind of philosophical antinomianism—is that they render the commandments at best reasonable; they do not justify their obligatoriness. Even if they show that the commandments are sufficient to achieve certain ends, rarely if ever do they show that the particular commandments are necessary for those ends. In light of this problem, it is significant that Nahmanides locates the ground for the obligatoriness of the commandments at their internal theocentric level of explanation rather than at the level of their external naturalistic reasons. Thus, at the end of his commentary on Lev. 19:2, Nahmanides writes: "You should not serve God in order to receive a reward (*'al menat lekabeil peras*) because His simple will (*retzono hapashut*) is [the] proper [reason to serve Him] and is what obligates [us to serve Him] (*hu' hara'ui vehamechayeiv*)."[42] Now, Nahmanides' notion of divine will is not the Kalam notion of an arbitrary, or absolutely unconstrained, voluntaristic divine will that legislates for no reason or utility. However, as with his internal reason for the commandments—*tzorekh gevoha*—this account makes their obligatoriness not only theocentric but dependent on a deity with quasi-personal characteristics: an active (though incomposite) will as well as passive needs that are satisfied by human acts. However reasonable it would be to perform the commandments because of the human goods for which they are means, it is only this divine will, manifest in the Mosaic legislation at Sinai, that renders the commandments obligatory. On his parabolic model, that is to say that the necessity of the Law is a function of its internal rather than external significance.[43]

A second Nahmanidean doctrine may also be related to this idea of the theocentric grounds for the obligatoriness of the commandments. This is the opinion, apparently unique to Nahmanides, that *all* commandments—even those that are "obligations of the body" (*hovot ha-guf*) such as wearing phylacteries and fixing the *mezuzah* as opposed to "obligations of the land" (*hovot ha-karka'*)—are to be *principally* performed only by those who dwell in the land of God (*ki 'ikar kol ha-mitzvot leyoshvim be-'eretz ha-shem*). This is, to be sure, not a halakhically normative claim. Outside the land of Israel, Nahmanides continues, these laws must still be observed with the same strictness in order that they will not be "novel to us" (*hadashim 'aleinu*) when we return to the land of Israel.[44] However, their performance in the diaspora is, in some sense, only to keep us "in practice" for their true observance in the land of Israel. Now, as long as we focus on the anthropocentric reasons for the commandments at their parabolic external level of explanation—the human goods for which they are means—it is difficult to see why there should be this difference between the land of Israel and other lands in evaluating the nature and domain of our obligation to perform the commandments. It is only when we turn to their parabolic internal explanation, their theocentric reason, that Nahmanides' distinction begins to make sense. The land of Israel, he argues, is under the direct, immediate governance of the deity, a governance not mediated by other celestial powers who have been "assigned" to the other lands and peoples and through whom, and only through whom, these others are governed. Hence, if the grounds for the obligatoriness of the commandments derive from their theurgic function as acts that satisfy *tzorekh gevoha*, the needs of the deity, then their principal, or primary, performance may only be in the land of Israel, which is directly governed by the deity whose needs they satisfy. Outside the land of Israel, they still serve as means to achieve the human goods that constitute their parabolic external reasons, their *hakhmah*, but their performance is only derivative from—at most training or practice for—their internal theurgic purpose. Only within the land of Israel do the commandments fulfill *both* of their parabolic *ta'amei ha-mitzvot*, internal as well as external reasons. Hence, only within the land of Israel do the commandments achieve their principal (*iqar*) performance.

CHAPTER 5

Maimonides on the
Parable of Circumcision

Maimonides' account of *ta'amei ha-mitzvot* in the *Guide of the Perplexed* is best known for its historical-anthropological explanation of the many rituals concerned with sacrifices, the Temple, and purity and impurity. As we have seen in chapters 1 and 2, all these commandments are said to have been legislated to counteract the idolatrous practices that prevailed among the nations in whose midst the ancient Israelites lived. But for the very reason that Maimonides applies this mode of explanation so systematically and so thoroughly to so wide a range of commandments, it is all the more striking when he does not employ it. One exception is the commandment of circumcision which Maimonides addresses in chapter III:49, the last of his chapters on reasons for the Mosaic Law.

Maimonides' explanation of circumcision is also anomalous for two other reasons. First, as a rule, Maimonides gives one and only one reason or utility for each commandment. For circumcision, he gives two. Moreover, he concludes the first of these by calling it "the strongest of the reasons for circumcision," and then adds about the second that it is "also a strong reason, as strong as the first . . . ; perhaps . . . even stronger than the first" (III:49:610). Why these two reasons? And why these obviously confusing, apparently contradictory descriptions of their relative strengths?

There is also a second anomaly in Maimonides' explanation of circumcision. His classification of the commandments in the *Guide* generally matches his classification in his legal code, the *Mishneh Torah*; here it does not. In the *Mishneh Torah*, the laws governing circumcision fall in the *Book of Love*, along with the laws of prayers, blessings, *mezuzah*, and the writing of the scrolls of the Torah and *tefillin*. In the *Guide*, Maimonides places circumcision in the fourteenth class of commandments, which contains the laws found in the *Mishneh Torah* in the *Book of Women* and in the "Laws concerning Prohibited Sexual Relations." Why these different classifications in the two works? Furthermore, in the introductory chapter to his explanation of the Law in the *Guide* (III:35)

Maimonides goes out of his way to tell us twice—once in his description of the ninth class of commandments and again in his account of the fourteenth class—that he has changed his classification of circumcision. Why does he direct so much attention on the change of category?

My immediate aim in this chapter is to resolve these anomalies about Maimonides' explanation of circumcision. However, the real interest of this account is broader than the circumscribed limits of this one commandment. Maimonides' explanation of this commandment, I will suggest, exemplifies the mode of parabolic interpretation we introduced in chapter 4, a mode of interpretation that he employs not only for the narrative portions of Scripture but also for the commandments and especially for those commandments that appear to be concerned specifically with the human body. The problem these commandments raise for Maimonides, which he then attempts to solve through parabolic interpretation, concerns the role of the body, or the performance of the commandments, in the achievement of human perfection and the highest form of divine worship, states that Maimonides takes to be essentially intellectual. The problem is not only that the commandments and body do not themselves constitute or belong to this final state. Because of the deep tension in Maimonides' thinking in the *Guide* between form and matter, or the intellect and body, the real problem is whether, and to what extent, the body or the performance of the actions of the Law prevent or hinder the achievement of intellectual perfection.

I

Maimonides' first reason for circumcision, which is of one kind with the other commandments with which it is classified in chapter III:49, is to bring about "a decrease in sexual intercourse and a weakening of the organ in question" (III:49:609). And this, Maimonides emphasizes, is aimed at "perfecting what is defective morally" and not, as "has been thought," at "perfecting what is defective congenitally" (ibid.). Here Maimonides is rejecting an explanation of circumcision that is found first in the rabbinic midrash *Tanhuma* (*Tazri'a* 5) and then in Saadiah's *'Emunot VeDe'ot*. In this earlier explanation, the foreskin is naturally superfluous and, because "the perfect thing is one that suffers from neither superfluity nor deficiency," by cutting off this unnecessary part of the body "what is left is in a state of perfection."[1] Maimonides has two reasons for rejecting this interpretation. First, disputing Saadiah's factual assumption, he explicitly asserts as a matter of common knowledge that the foreskin *is* "useful" for the member and, therefore, hardly superfluous (III:49:609). But second, and more important, throughout the *Guide* Maimonides denies the implication that any natural thing *could* be imperfect. By what standard of perfection? All natural things, which he identifies with the works of the deity, "are most perfect, and with regard to them there is no *possibility* of an excess or a deficiency" (III:28:335; my emphasis). That is, all natural things are perfect in being equibalanced.[2] But if the natural state of the male organ is already perfect, no commandment could have been legislated to improve on it.

Yet, this natural perfection of the uncircumcised male organ is also the very condition for its moral imperfection. When left in its natural condition, the uncircumcised male organ is a source of "violent concupiscence and lust that goes beyond what is needed" (ibid.)—that is, beyond the needs of its natural function, procreation. For the same organ that ensures the survival of the species is also "the faculty of sexual excitement" (ibid.), the source of "abominations" and the part of the person associated with the sense that, Maimonides invokes Aristotle to testify, is "a disgrace to us" (III:49:608). Therefore the natural perfection of the uncircumcised male organ is precisely what makes possible the person's moral imperfection, the bodily desires and acts that the Law opposes.[3]

It is this moral defectiveness of the uncircumcised male organ that, according to Maimonides, the act of circumcision is meant to perfect. But if its natural perfection is its uncircumcised state, how can circumcision morally perfect the person without making him naturally *im*perfect? We now seem to have a genuine tension between one's natural and moral perfection. How does circumcision resolve this?

In his last remark on circumcision, Maimonides contrasts it with the prohibition (in Lev. 22:24) against mutilating the sexual organs of male animals which, he says, "is based on the principle of *righteous statutes and judgments* [Deut. 4:8], I mean the principle of keeping the mean in all matters; sexual intercourse should neither be excessively indulged, as we have mentioned, nor wholly abolished . . . Accordingly this organ is weakened by means of circumcision, but not extirpated through excision. What is natural is left according to nature, but measures are taken against excess" (III:49:611). Here Maimonides proposes that mutilation of sexual organs is prohibited because it is an extreme that extirpates, or completely eliminates, sexual intercourse. Circumcision, in contrast, is prescribed because it corresponds to the mean, an intermediate state; it prevents excessive indulgence in sex without eliminating it entirely and without demanding complete abstinence.

In referring here to the ethical mean, Maimonides surely assumes that his reader is familiar with his account of the principle in his earlier ethical writings, *Shemonah Perakim* and *MT* "*Hilkhot De'ot.*"[4] However, there is all the difference between Maimonides' conception of the mean in these ethical writings and here in the *Guide*. In the ethical writings, Maimonides, following Aristotle and Al-Farabi, takes the mean to be the criterion of the virtuous characteristic of the soul, or habit, and only indirectly of the virtuous action. Extremes, both positive and negative, are deplored, and the intermediate characteristic is (almost) always sought. Indeed Maimonides says that the one who always "aims at the mean . . . is in the highest of human ranks."[5] To be sure, he recognizes that the commandments of the Torah do not always cleave to the mean, but where and when they deviate toward one or the other extreme it is only for the sake of curing a prior predeliction in the other direction, "to discipline the powers of the body." For the healthy individual, the "goal of the Law is for [him] to be natural by following the middle way" (ibid.).

This is not Maimonides' perspective toward the principle of the mean in this discussion of circumcision or, more generally, in the *Guide*. As he makes clear in chapter III:8, perhaps his most elaborate presentation of this position, the ideal state with respect to bodily desires and activities, like sex, is not an intermediate state of balance but a state in which we either have no such desires or only the absolute minimum.[6] Maimonides' argument for this position rests on his view that the true end of humanity is to be a fully actualized intellect (or, as he sometimes calls it, an acquired intellect) constantly and exclusively engaged in the apprehension of intelligible truths. But because one's matter, the body, its needs, desires, and faculties such as the imagination, only obstruct the achievement of this goal, "all the impulses of matter are shameful and ugly things, deficiencies imposed by necessity" (III:8:434; see also III:51:620–27). With the sexual and other bodily impulses, what we should therefore seek is not the moderate but "the indispensable," "to reduce [these impulses] to the extent to which this is possible." On the same note, the aim of the commandments and prohibitions concerning sexual unions is not balance but to "make sexual intercourse rarer and to instilling disgust for it so that it should be sought only very seldom" (III:49:606). Here, unlike *Shemonah Perakim*, nature is not a standard to be sought; rather "the thing that is natural should be abhorred except for necessity" (p. 606) and, without "measures," it is clearly implied that the natural naturally inclines toward excess. As an illustration of his ideal type, Maimonides directs us to the figure of Abraham, the biblical originator of circumcision, who will play a central role in the second reason for the commandment. Here, however, Abraham specifically exemplifies the "chastity" for which he is "celebrated" (III:49:609), by which Maimonides means not just modest behavior but—as in his prooftext, the rabbinic exegesis of Gen. 12:11, according to which Abraham did not even notice Sarah's beauty until he descended to

Egypt—the absence of all sexual impulses.[7] That is, an extreme, not the mean, is Maimonides' ideal according to this first reason for circumcision: the individual who has no *need* of circumcision in order to restrain his sexual impulses, who by nature is indifferent or oblivious to his bodily impulses, who has sublimated these desires to a point far beyond the "weakening" accomplished by circumcision.

But if the complete denial, or elimination, of bodily impulses is Maimonides' ideal, he also recognizes that it is only an ideal and not a real possibility for (most) humans. Just as one's matter can never be entirely eliminated in the quest for intellectual perfection—for wherever there is form, there must be matter (III:8)—so the male organ cannot be "extirpated through excision" (III:49:611) without excluding the possibility of human reproduction and, hence, the existence of the human species. Instead of denial by amputation, the effect of circumcision is an *accommodation* of the ideal with the necessities of reality.[8] "What is natural is left according to nature, but measures are taken against excess" (ibid.)—and not only natural necessity is respected since the Law itself commands man to "be fruitful and multiply." In sum, circumcision does not realize the highest aim but only the best that can be done given the fact that we are creatures of matter; it does not bring the person to the likes of Abraham but only to the best general state for humankind in general.[9] Rather than being a golden standard, the mean exemplified by circumcision attempts to resolve by compromise the tension between the natural perfection and moral imperfection of uncircumcised man.[10]

II

Whereas Maimonides' first explanation of circumcision is a kind of ethical perfection of the individual, his second reason for the commandment focuses on the community rather than individual and on its theoretical, or intellectual, as well as practical good.

> According to me circumcision has another very important meaning, namely, that all people professing this opinion—that is, those who believe in the unity of God—should have a bodily sign uniting them so that one who does not belong to them should not be able to claim that he was one of them, while being a stranger. For he would do this in order to profit by them to deceive the people who profess this religion. Now a man does not perform this act upon himself or upon a son of his unless it be in consequence of a genuine belief. For it is not like an incision in the leg or a burn in the arm, but is a very, very hard thing.
>
> It is also well known what degree of mutual love and mutual help exists between people who all bear the same sign, which forms for them a sort of covenant and alliance. Circumcision is a covenant made

by Abraham our Father with a view to the belief in the unity of God. Thus everyone who is circumcised joins Abraham's covenant. This covenant imposes the obligation to believe in the unity of God: *To be a God unto thee and to thy seed after thee* (Gen. 17:7). This is also a strong reason, as strong as the first, which may be adduced to account for circumcision; perhaps it is even stronger than the first. (III:49:609–10)

According to this explanation, circumcision serves two functions. First, the mark differentiates those within the community or religion who profess the unity of God from those outside who do not share this belief. Second, it creates the distinctive sense of community among its members that constitutes the Abrahamic covenant. Let me take up these two functions in turn.

As a means of communal differentiation, the sign of circumcision works in two directions. In the passage just quoted, it excludes foreigners who claim to belong to or who attempt to join the community for some improper ulterior motive, say, to marry Jewish women or to profit financially. Now, the suspicion that the would-be convert has an ulterior motive for wanting to become a Jew is frequent in the literature, and insofar as the first step in the procedure leading to conversion is always to eliminate such a motive, one might even say that there is a presumption of one.[11] However, already by the Rabbinic period, the court eliminated a prospective convert's ulterior purpose by verbal examination. In our passage Maimonides seems to be proposing that in ancient Israel this may have been a function of the act of circumcision itself: the very requirement that the would-be-convert must undergo circumcision—or its anticipation insofar as it was imagined to be "a very, very hard thing"—was meant to filter out the insincere and improperly motivated.[12] But on this view circumcision would not be a *part* of the conversion ritual so much as a *preliminary* to it.[13]

Circumcision may also function to differentiate members of the community in the other direction: not by preventing outsiders from improperly joining but by keeping members of the community from *exiting*. This role of circumcision emerges elsewhere in Maimonides' writing, in both the *Guide* and the *Mishneh Torah* in the course of explaining the scriptural prohibition that "No uncircumcised [male] shall eat of the [paschal lamb]" (Exod. 12:48). In the *Guide*, Maimonides reports in the name of the Sages that the reason for this injunction was that "during their long stay in Egypt" the Israelites had ceased circumcising themselves "with a view to assimilating themselves to the Egyptians" (*Exod. Rabbah*, XIX, cited in III:46:585); therefore, when the Law prescribed both the Passover sacrifice and the necessary condition that the individual and his family offering the sacrifice must be circumcised, all the Israelites circumcised themselves—"and *the blood of circumcision* mingled with *the blood of the paschal lamb* because of the great number of men who had just undergone circumcision . . ." (ibid.). Now, this powerful image may suggest in addition that the mass circumcision in Egypt, like a sacrifice, was meant to atone for the Israelites' failure to circumcise themselves during the interim. However, the primary point of the passage is that, because the mark of circumcision makes an individual physically distinguishable as a member of the Jewish community, it thereby prevents him from assimilating, from abandoning his communal identity. During the Hellenistic period, as is well known, individuals deliberately attempted to circumvent this differentiating effect of circumcision by stretching their foreskin, a fact to which the Talmud (JT *Pe'ah* 1.1) alludes and to which Maimonides also refers in the *Mishneh Torah.*[14] In this passage, Maimonides reads this differentiating function of circumcision already into its Mosaic legislation in Egypt. The ancient Israelites in Egypt were the first Hellenized Jews.[15] Therefore, at the first critical juncture in their national differentiation from the Egyptians among whom they had heretofore attempted to efface their identity, the Israelites were made to be circumcised precisely to ensure that, once distinct, they remained that way.

In the *Mishneh Torah* Maimonides makes a similar point but with a different emphasis.[16] Here he explains that the origin of the requirement that Gentiles undergo circumcision for conversion to Judaism is that the ancient Israelites entered the divine covenant through circumcision, a fact he infers from the same biblical injunction of Exod. 12:48. In this context, he takes the Passover sacrifice to exemplify the "new" Mosaic covenant, and circumcision serves not as a precondition for the sacrifice but as part of the process of entry into, or conversion to, that covenant. But here, too, Maimonides implies that the "new" covenant, and circumcision as part of a rite of passage into that new covenant, were necessary precisely because the Israelites had assimilated with the Egyptians. "*Moses* circumcised [the Israelites] because they had all, with the exception of the Tribe of Levi, abrogated [*bitlu*] the covenant of circumcision [*brit milah*] in Egypt" (my emphasis).[17] Here circumcision is not just one among other particular commandments the Israelites had ceased to perform. By ceasing circumcision, the Israelites annulled or abolished a *covenant*: they surrendered their identity as a distinct community. And having abrogated the previous Abrahamic covenant through assimilation, nothing less than a new covenant fathered by Moses was necessary. Hence, Maimonides emphasizes that it was Moses who circumcised the nation, just as the obligation of circumcision falls on the father of the uncircumcised infant according to Mosaic law.[18]

In the original passage in III:49, it is not the community as defined by the Mosaic Law that is differentiated by the mark of circumcision but the community described as "Abraham's covenant," all "those who believe in the Unity of God," a group that would seem to be more inclusive. Furthermore, as a "bodily sign" the mark of circumcision "unites" all those who believe in the unity of God precisely because it "imposes [on them] the obligation to" adopt that belief. And, finally, its differentiating function is subordinated to its other main function—to bring about "mutual love and mutual help" among members of the community whereby it "forms for them a sort of covenant or alliance." Indeed, because Maimonides uses the phrase "mutual love and mutual help" to characterize friendship throughout the chapter (see, e.g., III:49:601), one might say that the leading purpose of circumcision is to create a general bond of friendship among those who undergo it. But in order better to understand how it does this, it will help first to examine the role of friendship in the explanation of another commandment in the same class, the prohibition of harlotry.

Maimonides' first reason for the prohibition of harlotry (Deut. 23:18) is in order to preserve clear "lines of ancestry" (III:49:602) and not, surprisingly, sexual restraint (which is its second reason). This may strike us as odd inasmuch as harlotry is Maimonides' prototype for the pursuit of sexual satisfaction as an end in itself and its prohibition is the first commandment Maimonides addresses in the fourteenth class whose general reason is to "bring about a decrease of sexual intercourse . . . as far as possible" (III:35:538). As it turns out, however, these reasons are not unrelated. Knowledge of one's ancestry is necessary, Maimonides argues, because the family, or tribe, realizes the mutual love, support, and "fraternal sentiments" that characterize friendship in "their perfect form" (III:49:602); only by knowing one's lines of ancestry will one acquire these attitudes that are "the greatest purpose of the Law" (III:49:602). But what most undermines these sentiments of friendship is the unlimited pursuit of sexual desire, exemplified by harlotry, that destroys the fabric of the family. Therefore, Maimonides presents these two—the family as a model of friendship and harlotry as a model of sexual indulgence—as if they were contradictory alternatives. Commandments that deny the one he takes ipso facto to affirm the other and vice versa. For this reason, Maimonides opens this chapter devoted to diminishing sexual desire with an explanation oriented toward strengthening its complement, the ideal of friendship. What he sees as the true alternative to a life governed by impulses of matter is not a life of ascetic denial but one directed at the love characteristic of friendship.

The same type of explanation applies to circumcision. According to its first reason, the commandment diminishes the desire for and pleasure of sexual intercourse; according to its second, it creates a community of people giving mutual love and help to each other, namely, friendship. Here also, because Maimonides imagines the way of life that aims at sexual satisfaction as the rival to that which aims at friendship, he presents these two purposes of circumcision as complementary halves. The ritual of circumcision makes possible a community founded on friendship *by* diminishing the sexual impulses of its individual members.

There is also a second connection for Maimonides between friendship, which achieves its most perfect form in the family, and the covenant of circumcision. When he describes the community circumscribed by circumcision and distinguished by its belief in the unity of God as "Abraham's covenant," Maimonides' choice of Abraham—rather than Israel or Moses—is determined by more than the fact according to the Torah that Abraham was the first to perform circumcision. For Abraham was also the ancestor of Ishmael, or the nation of Islam. And in the Islamicate world in which he lived, Maimonides obviously knew that Jews were far from being the only, or the largest, group observing the rite of circumcision. Furthermore, elsewhere in his writings Maimonides unequivocally states that Muslims (in contrast to Christians) are pure monotheists who believe in the unity of God.[19] Thus the followers of Islam satisfy all three of Maimonides' criteria for membership in the covenant he describes as "Abraham's covenant," a term which is not, then, meant to be coextensive with any other term specifically for the Jews, such as "the people of Israel" or "the Mosaic covenant." And not only are the Abrahamic and Mosaic covenants extensionally different; what they "mean," the obligations they respectively demand, are also different.[20] Hence, in this explanation of the commandment, circumcision does not function to differentiate the Jews from other communities; instead it cuts across traditional national and religious divisions to unite all those who are circumcised and monotheists within a new covenant. However, this new covenant, outwardly marked by circumcision and inwardly by belief, is not opposed to or even separate from natural groupings like the family; it would be more correct to say that it selects one set of ancestral relations over others. It cancels, or plays down, the role of the more immediate ancestors—Israel and Ishmael—in order to unite all their descendents directly under Abraham, the remote ancestor. Similarly, the "degree of mutual love and mutual help that exists among those people who bear the sign of circumcision" should not be viewed entirely apart from Maimonides' conception of the degree of mutual love and help which is to be found in a family united under a common ancestor. On the contrary, because the artificial mark of circumcision coincides with the natural line of Abrahamic ancestry, the two complement and mutually reinforce one another.

We see a similar attempt to elevate circumcision from the status of a single Mosaic commandment to that of an essential criterion of an autonomous Abrahamic covenant in the *Mishneh Torah*. At the very end of the "Laws of Circumcision," Maimonides praises the significance of circumcision "in connection with [which], thirteen covenants were made with Abraham the Patriarch" in contrast, he adds, to the commandments of the Mosaic Law described in Scripture in connection with only three covenants.[21] There, too, he contrasts the two figures of Abraham and Moses with respect to their performance of circumcision. Abraham, "perfected" by circumcision, is presented in the strongest positive light; Moses, who failed to circumcise his own sons and was almost struck down for it on his return to Egypt, is cited, negatively, as an example of the severity of transgressing the commandment. Here, in other words, circumcision, as the identifying commandment of the Abrahamic covenant, is presented as if it were the equal of the entire Mosaic Law.

Of course, in using circumcision to reinterpret the notion of covenantal community to include Muslims, Maimonides is well aware of the fact that he is opposing the received Rabbinic position concerning the status of circumcision among Gentiles. In the *Mishneh Torah*, he therefore goes to considerable lengths in order to justify the legal consequences of his new conception of the Abrahamic covenant. He writes as follows:

> Circumcision was commanded to Abraham and his descendants only; as it is said "*You and your offspring to come*" (Gen. 17:9). The offspring of Ishmael are excluded, as it said: "*For it is through Isaac that offspring shall be continued for you*" (Gen. 21:12), and Esau is excluded because Isaac said to Jacob: "*May He grant the blessing of Abraham to you and your offspring*," from which we can infer that he alone is the descendant of Abraham who upholds his law [*dato*] and his righteous way. And they are the ones who are obligated to be circumcised.
>
> The sages said: The sons of Keturah who are the descendants of Abraham who came after Ishmael and Isaac are obligated to be circumcised. However, because the descendants of Ishmael have today become intermingled [*hit'arvu*][22] with the descendants of Keturah, all of them are obligated to be circumcised on the eighth day, even though they are not executed for it [i.e., for failing to do so]. (*MT* "*Melakhim*" x, 7–8)

Maimonides' reasoning in these two *halakhot* is a tour de force. In the first, he presents the received Rabbinic position which legally excludes Ishmaelite, or Muslim, circumcision.[23] The one novel point Maimonides adds to the talmudic discussion is his "inference" that authentic Abrahamic lineage is to be determined only in terms of the person's faithfulness to Abraham's way of life. In its immediate context, this criterion is clearly used to exclude Christianity, or Esau. However, in light of what we have already seen in the *Guide*, it might also be understood by implication to include Islam, which does uphold Abraham's monotheism. In any case, having explicitly excluded the Ishmaelites, or Muslims, from the obligation of circumcision in the first *halakhah*, Maimonides overturns this decision in the second. What in the Talmud is merely an individual opinion he now cites as the view of "the sages" in general that, because the descendants of Keturah, the second wife of Abraham (Gen. 25:2), are obligated to be circumcised and because the Ishmaelites have assimilated with them over time—with the result that we cannot now distinguish Ishmaelites from Keturites—all Ishmaelites are now also obligated to be circumcised, and on the eighth day.[24] To be sure, he recognizes that there is no legal force to this obligation. But what stands out in these passages is Maimonides' drive to find some legal strategem to legitimate Ishmaelite, or Muslim, circumcision. He cannot simply equate the Muslim practice with the Mosaic commandment without openly contradicting the rabbinic tradition. He must also preserve a distinction among the descendants of Abraham between Ishmael, the Muslims, and Esau, the Christians. Therefore, he invents a new invisible legal category of Abrahamic descendants, the children of Keturah, whose only function in practice is to ground the unenforcible "obligation," or legitimacy, of Moslem circumcision as a religious commandment of Abrahamic origin associated with belief in the unity of God.[25] With this legal fiction, Maimonides institutionalizes in the Mosaic Law as codified in the *Mishneh Torah* the idea conceived in the *Guide* of an Abrahamic covenant to which everyone circumcised belongs, including Moslems.[26]

To summarize, we have now seen two important ways in which Maimonides develops his notion of the Abrahamic covenant in terms of his idea of familial friendship or love. In one other respect, however, he distinguishes the love engendered by circumcision from the love found among family members and, in particular, parental love. This is a difference between them as kinds of love that are, furthermore, potentially in conflict or competition: for the one to be realized, the other must be suppressed or, at least, circumvented.

This difference, and tension, between the two kinds of love can be glimpsed first in Maimonides' explanation of the particular requirement that circumcision be performed on the eighth day after birth. For a start, this condition needs special explanation because it prima facie conflicts with Maimonides' claim that the covenant into which one enters by circumcision "imposes the obligation to believe in the unity of God." If circumcision signals such an obligation, the proper time for the ritual should be adulthood when the person has the mature intellectual faculties to acknowledge it.[27] Therefore, to explain away this discrepancy, Maimonides offers "three wise reasons," the third of which concerns us. According to this reason, the Law commands circumcision when the child is a newborn because "the imaginative form that compels the parents to love it" is not yet so "consolidated" at that age that it would induce them not to perform the circumcision. In other words, because parents' love is a function not of their faculty of reason but of their imaginative faculty, which "increases through habitual contact and grows with the growth of the child, . . . if [the child] were left uncircumcised for two or three years, this would necessitate the abandonment of circumcision because of the father's love and affection for it" (III:49:610).[28] Here, then, the Law recognizes that its aim—the covenantal love brought about through circumcision—may be resisted by the imagination-based love of the parent; out of love, the father may refuse to circumcise his child. In reaction, the Law does not attempt to deny or eliminate that parental love; once again, "what is natural is left according to nature." Instead the commandment is designed to exploit the imaginative faculty when it is at its weakest. By requiring circumcision in the first days of the child's life, the Law attempts to anticipate and circumvent the developed parental love that would exclude the covenantal love created by circumcision. As God, in His "wily graciousness and wisdom" (III:32:524ff.), indirectly led the Israelites through the land of the Philistines and did not directly take them into Canaan, so here the Law reflects a "wise reason" (p. 610) by reining in the imagination and cutting off its power of resistance before it matures.

This tension between the parents' love for their child and the love of the covenant created by circumcision is based on a yet deeper difference between them. Whereas the love of the parent is based in the imagination, the mutual love engendered by circumcision has its basis in the intellect. To be more exact, both what constitutes the ground of the Abrahamic covenant and what makes it a divine covenant is the content of the intellectually cognizable belief shared by the community that it communicates.

In order to appreciate this intellectual character of the Abrahamic covenant, it should be noted, to begin with, that nowhere does Maimonides describe Abraham's covenant as a covenant *with* God or *between* humans (or a nation) *and* God. Instead he says that the "mutual love and mutual help [which] exists *between people* who all bear the same sign . . . forms *for them* a sort of covenant and alliance" (III:49:610, my emphasis). In other words, the covenant is a relation entirely among humans. This characterization is a direct consequence of

Maimonides' metaphysics. For a covenant between God and man would entail the existence of a relation between God and creatures—and this Maimonides has already demonstrated to be impossible because relations hold only among members of the same species and there is no species common to God and anything else (I:52:116–18). Instead the Abrahamic covenant is an entirely natural, human relation constituted by the sentiments of mutual love and mutual help that exist among all the people who bear the sign of circumcision.

What, then, makes this covenant divine? Not the identity of one of its partners but rather its content: the fact that the covenant of circumcision was instituted "with a view to the belief in the unity of God" and that it "imposes the obligation to believe in the unity of God: *to be a God unto thee and to thy seed after thee* [Gen. 17:7]" (III:49:610). Here, it should be noted, Maimonides quotes only the second half of the biblical verse. He omits its first half in which God describes "My covenant between Me and you and your offspring to come," and he omits it, I would suggest, because it expresses the very kind of objectionable metaphysical relation he has demonstrated to be impossible. Instead of interpreting, then, the second half of the verse as expressing God's half of the pact, Maimonides takes it as expressing the content of the belief that makes the covenant divine.

In this interpretation, the covenant of circumcision follows the example of the Mosaic Law as a whole. For what distinguishes the Law according to Maimonides, and what makes it a *divine* law, is that it aims not merely at what he calls the "soundness of the circumstances pertaining to the body" but also at the "soundness of belief" or "correct opinions with regard to God."[29] Now, these "sound beliefs" and "correct opinions" that the divine law communicates are not what Maimonides elsewhere in the *Guide* describes as the "perfection of the soul," or "having an intellect in actu"—that is, apprehension of intelligibles or knowledge through demonstration (III:27:511). This perfection is achieved only through full intellectual apprehension of everything that can be known, it contains only intelligibilia but no "actions or moral qualities," and it "is the only cause of permanent preservation"—immortality. The sound beliefs that constitute the "welfare of the soul" are rather beliefs held on the basis of tradition or authority, beliefs that the Law does not present in a scientific, demonstrative form but only "in a summary way" and sometimes in the form of parables (III:27:510). Rather than conferring perfection themselves, these sound beliefs create an ideal environment for the intellectual community in which the capable individual can achieve perfection.[30] And this goal, Maimonides argues, is what makes the law that inculcates these beliefs divine.

Similar remarks hold for the divine covenant, or community, created among all the individuals who undergo the experience of circumcision. The bodily act of circumcision "imposes" the intellectual obligation to believe in the unity of God, but simply believing this does not yield intellectual perfection. What circumcision does bring about is a community all of whose members share (at least) this one obligatory belief that, for those who can engage in demonstration and scientific inquiry, can then be transformed into the kind of apprehension that does constitute intellectual perfection. So, although the performance of circumcision does not itself lead to intellectual perfection or "permanent preservation," it does create a covenant, or community, whose end is not merely the moral or political well-being of its members, the soundness of their bodies, but also their intellectual well-being, the soundness of their beliefs. And, as in the case of law, such a covenant, or community, is therefore divine.

One question remains unanswered throughout this account. Suppose that all individuals who are circumcised mutually love and help each other and, thereby, form a covenant among themselves. And suppose also that this covenant requires of its members that they believe in the unity of God. Still, one wants to know, exactly what is the connection between circumcision and belief in the unity of God? The former is clearly meant to be an outward bodily sign of the inner state of the believer, but why this sign—this act and mark on this part of the body— for this particular belief? Of all the parts of Maimonides' story, this is certainly the most enigmatic, if only because he tells us *nothing* explicit in answer to the question. It is not difficult, of course, to imagine various ways in which the highly suggestive act and sign of circumcision might be taken to symbolize this belief as well as countless other themes of the Law.[31] But the plain fact is that Maimonides makes no attempt to read any such symbolism into this ritual—or indeed any other commandment or sacred object or act. On the contrary, the reader senses genuine antipathy on his part to all such hermeneutics.[32]

Rather than look for ways in which circumcision might be taken to *symbolize* belief in the unity of God, let me suggest two other possible nonsymbolic connections. The first of these is by way of the fact that circumcision is *Abraham's* covenant—that is, because of the identity of its progenitor, Abraham, who is portrayed not only as the first person to practice circumcision but also, in Maimonides' writings, as "the first to make known the belief in Unity" (III:24:502). In both the *Mishneh Torah* and the *Guide*, he is described as the first philosopher who "claimed . . . that speculation and reasoning had come to him indicating to him that the world as a whole has a deity" and that He is one, knowledge which he then conveyed to the people "through speculation and instruction" (I:63:152–53).[33] Of course, Maimonides' emphasis that

Abraham himself came to these truths through his own speculative reasoning, rather than through divine revelation, is not only meant to inform us of a contingent fact about how *he* happened to discover them. As he explains elsewhere, demonstrative intellectual apprehension of these two propositions—the existence and unity of the Deity—is equal in epistemic status to their knowledge by way of prophetic revelation.[34] Therefore, Abraham's speculative knowledge of these truths is equivalent to, though autonomous of, their prophetic knowledge by way of the later Mosaic revelation, and to describe belief in them as an obligation of the Abrahamic covenant is to ground that obligation in the intellect independently of prophetic revelation, a ground shared by all rational creatures and not only the particular members of the Mosaic covenant.[35]

This relation between circumcision and belief in the unity of God by way of the figure of Abraham explains why *we* might draw such a connection. It does not explain why Abraham himself, as it were, would have taken circumcision "to be a covenant . . . with a view to the belief in the unity of God." Let me, therefore, offer a second conjecture about their relation. In a number of passages in the *Guide*, though not in III:49, Maimonides refers not to the "Unity of God" but to the "Unity of the Name of God."[36] The source of this description is unquestionably Gen. 21:33. This verse serves, first, as Maimonides' invocation at the beginning of each of the three books of the *Guide* and indeed of almost all of his other writings, both legal and popular.[37] Second, Maimonides also uses the verse to describe Abraham who, he says, arrived at his belief in the unity of God by speculation, which he then proclaimed "in the Name of the Lord, God of the world" (II:13:282; cf. also II:30:358 and III:29:516). Similarly, he describes the Patriarchs as having given their lives to "spread the doctrine of *the unity of the Name* in the world and to guide people to love Him" (III:51:624). Now, commenting on the verse Ps. 91:7–8, Maimonides states that "the meaning of *knowledge of the Name* is: apprehension of Him" (III:51:627). In other words, he *identifies* knowledge of God and of His name where, by the latter, Maimonides tells us in I:61, he means not just any description or singular term for the deity but specifically the underived and simple Tetragrammaton, which indicates God's absolutely simple and incomposite essence, His necessary existence in virtue of Himself. Only the Tetragrammaton, the name that is truly one, simple, and incomposite, names the One.[38] So, in contexts (like the passage just quoted) in which the unity of God is at issue, one can equally well speak of the unity of His Name. The one can stand in place of, or represent, the other.

Now, this connection between the unity of God and that of His name is significant in our present context because, according to various *midrashim* with which Maimonides was almost certainly familiar, the mark of circumcision is itself correlated with the divine name. Most notably, in the *Midrash Tanhuma*, God is said to "have placed His name on [the people of] Israel in order that they may enter the Garden of Eden. And what is the name and the seal that He placed on them? It is [the name] *Shaddai*. The *shin* He placed on the nose, the *dalet* in the hand, and *yod* on the [place of] circumcision."[39] Although this passage emphasizes the name *Shaddai*, which God is said to have sealed on the people of Israel, it is clear that the real point of the "seal," the mark that ensures entry into the Garden of Eden, is the imprinting of the letter *yod* on the male organ, for the letter *yod* is itself an abbreviation of the name of God—the Tetragrammaton.[40] That is, the mark of circumcision is an inscription of the Tetragrammaton on the human body. Now, as we have seen, for Maimonides the significance of the Name of God, that is, what makes it the *name of God,* is not a function of the word as such but of the notion it signifies, namely, His essence, which is His unity (I:62:150ff.). What I would therefore propose is that, if Maimonides indeed used this *midrash* as a source, he may well have interpreted the connection it draws between the mark of circumcision and the Name of God, not as a connection with the word, but as a connection with the notion it signifies, the essence or unity of the deity. Like the way, according to the *midrash*, in which God places, or inscribes, His name on the place of—and through the act of—circumcision, so Maimonides says that by the act of circumcision belief in the unity of God, the notion signified by the divine name, is "imposed," or placed, on the person. The mark of circumcision does not symbolize the belief but, like a legal seal, it represents the covenant that is the source of the obligation to believe in the unity of God.

III

With this explication of Maimonides' two reasons in the *Guide* for the commandment of circumcision, we can now return to our opening questions: Why these two reasons? Why the openly contradictory and confusing remarks about their relative strengths as reasons? And why the different classifications of the commandment in the *Guide* and *Mishneh Torah*? I shall take up these questions in turn.[41]

The presentation of multiple reasons for commandments is not characteristic of Maimonides' general approach to explaining the Law in the *Guide*, but, as we already saw in chapter 4, it is characteristic of his general method of interpretation of prophetic works. In the introduction to the *Guide*, he tells us that the greatest source of misunderstanding of prophetic texts is the failure to recognize all of their meanings. In particular, the ordinary reader fails to realize that these texts contain parables "not explicitly identified there as such" (I:Intro.:6), and that these parables possess, in addition to what we might call their "vulgar" meaning, two other kinds of meaning, an external and an internal meaning. In contrast to the vulgar meaning of scriptural verses, which expresses beliefs *no one* should reasonably hold, beliefs like the corporeality of God, both the external and internal meanings express kinds of wisdom—that is, beliefs that *should* be adopted. The difference between them is a function entirely of their content. As Maimonides explains in his interpretation of the Rabbinic parable of "apples of gold in settings of silver" (I:Intro.:11), the external meaning of a parable "contains wisdom that is useful in many respects, among which is the welfare of human societies," whereas its internal meaning "contains wisdom that is useful for beliefs concerned with the truth as it is" (ibid.:12). That is, the external meaning of a parable communicates the beliefs necessary for or pertinent to the twofold welfare of a community-at-large, both moral or political and intellectual, whereas its internal meaning communicates wisdom "useful for," or pertinent to, beliefs about true reality (even if the beliefs are not themselves truths), the kinds of beliefs that contribute to or enable the grasp of truth within the limits of human capacity. And because the apprehension of intelligible truth constitutes individual intellectual perfection for Maimonides, the internal meaning of a parable is also generally directed toward the individual rather than the community.

Just as Maimonides proposes that these two levels of meanings—in addition to their vulgar meaning—characterize textual parables, so I want to propose that, in addition to their vulgar reason, he recognizes two additional levels of *reasons* for certain commandments—we might call them *parabolic commandments*—including circumcision.[42] Thus the vulgar reason for the commandment of circumcision is to perfect a natural or congenital defect of the male organ—and this, as we saw, is a reason Maimonides rejects as an explanation for why the commandment was legislated. However, in addition he proposes parabolic external and internal reasons for the commandment. And true to the puzzle-like form of the *Guide*, he shifts their order of presentation, putting the internal reason first, the external reason second.

The first explanation that circumcision perfects the individual by restraining, weakening, and diminishing his capacity for sexual desire is its *internal* reason. Although the commandment does not itself contain a truth or a belief about true reality, it contains wisdom that is "useful for" beliefs concerning true reality. For in order to achieve and reflect on such beliefs to the highest degree, one must actualize one's intellect and devote oneself as fully, exclusively, and undividedly as possible to apprehension of intelligible truth; one must attempt to become (as close as one can) an acquired intellect separate from the organic body (I:72:193). And to achieve this state, one must minimize and diminish one's bodily needs and desires to the highest degree possible. To be sure, one can never entirely *eliminate* one's body. This is not only practically but metaphysically impossible: there is no form, or actualized intellect, without matter, or body (III:8:431f.). However, Maimonides conceives of circumcision as a model of the kind of *accommodation* that ought to be pursued in which the ideal state of pure intellectual apprehension is tempered to allow for the minimal bodily needs and desires that are naturally necessary.

The second of Maimonides' positive reasons for circumcision—that it fosters the creation of a divine community all of whose members accept the "obligation" to believe in the Unity of God—is its *external* reason: the commandment serves both to communicate to the community a belief that is necessary for its intellectual welfare and to bond together its members through the covenantal love engendered by their shared participation in the rite of circumcision. Thus it contributes to creation of a community that aims at the theoretical as well as practical welfare of its citizens, both the welfare of its soul and the welfare of its body (III:27:510–11). In sum, Maimonides' multilevelled explanation of the commandment of circumcision perfectly fits his model of parabolic multiple meanings.

Seeing Maimonides' two reasons as a two-layered parabolic explanation of circumcision may also throw some light on his confusing remarks about the relative importances and strengths of the two reasons. For his description of the relative values of the external and internal meanings of a parable in terms of the figure of "apples of gold in settings of silver" suffers from a similar equivocation. First he tells us that "the external meaning ought to be as beautiful as silver, while its internal meaning ought to be more beautiful," like gold to silver. But then he adds that the external meaning should give some indication to the observer of what is to be found in the internal meaning, suggesting that it already itself contains some gold. When seen from a distance, it looks like an apple of silver, already valuable; but when seen from up close and scrutinized with great attention, it becomes clear that it is of gold. Similarly, Maimonides initially states that his first reason for circumcision, its internal reason, is "the strongest of [its] reasons" because that reason is connected to the ultimate intellectual perfection of the individual. But he concludes with the statement that the second reason, its external reason, may indeed be as strong and even stronger than the first. This, I would suggest, is because the second reason bears on the political and intellectual welfare of the community, and the command-

ments of the Mosaic Law, according to Maimonides' general characterization of their purpose in III:27–28, aim at the welfare of the general
community rather than the perfection of its individual members. Hence,
this reason, rather than the first, more clearly fits the general conception
of the Law which governs the account of *ta'amei ha-mitzvot* in chapters
III:26–49.[43] In short, the first reason may be gold but the second is pure
silver.

Finally, let me turn to the problem of classification. Why does Maimonides classify the commandment of circumcision in the *Mishneh
Torah* in the *Book of Love*, rather than among the "Laws concerning
Prohibited Sexual Relations" in the *Book of Women* among whose laws
he classifies it in the *Guide*? Maimonides' commentators have not been
the only ones who have found the reason for this change obscure. Maimonides himself acknowledges its irregularity in his introduction to the
Mishneh Torah where he finds it necessary to comment on his classification of this commandment, hence, in need of some special justification. The reason he offers is that he includes it in the *Book of Love*
among the "commandments that are constantly performed and that we
are commanded to perform in order to love God and to keep Him reg-
ularly in mind" because circumcision is "a mark in their flesh to remember God at all times even when the person is not wearing phylacteries or
fringes." Other interpreters of Maimonides have focused on the themes
of regularity and constancy that enter into this explanation.[44] But this is
not all these commandments have in common. They all also bring the
members of the community to recognize that the highest, ultimate purpose of the Law is to create a community that values above everything
else love of God—that is, knowledge of God—and that shares the correct opinions that constitute that shared body of knowledge.[45] But this,
in turn, is precisely the function of circumcision according to Maimonides' second, external reason: to create a community founded on
love among its members, all of whom believe in the unity of the deity.
Hence, because of the belief in the unity of God that it "obligates" the
members of its covenant to accept, and the intellectual welfare it thereby
achieves—because of its external reason—Maimonides classifies circumcision in the *Book of Love* in the *Mishneh Torah*.

There is a second related reason. According to Maimonides, the
external aim of the Mosaic Law, its aim as a body of law directed to the
whole community, is communal welfare, both moral/political and intellectual, that is, "the multitude's acquiring correct opinions corresponding to their respective capacity," some of which opinions, furthermore,
are "set forth in parables" (III:27:510). And chief among these correct
opinions is belief in the unity of God (I:35:79–81). But if the *Mishneh
Torah* is a codification of the Mosaic Law (according to the Rabbinic

tradition), then its classification and systemization of the commandments ought to be set by the aims of the Law it codifies. The first book
of the *Mishneh Torah,* the *Book of Knowledge,* lays out the correct
opinions that all members of the community ought to believe. The second book, the *Book of Love,* lays out those commandments that inculcate in the community both belief in those opinions and belief in the idea
of a community with that aim. According to Maimonides' external reason for circumcision as an instrument of communal welfare, it is a commandment of precisely that kind. Therefore, he classifies it in the *Book
of Love* in his *Code.*

In the *Guide,* however, Maimonides' classification of circumcision
among the laws of prohibited sexual relations would seem to correspond to his first reason: that circumcision restrains one's sexual
appetite as a necessary accommodation to achieve intellectual perfection. Hence, its classification in the *Guide* follows its parabolic internal
reason, the wisdom it contains "that is useful for beliefs concerned with
the truth as it is." This is not surprising given the general character of
the *Guide* as a guide to individual perfection of the highest intellectual
kind. Although Maimonides comments earlier that he "shall give reasons for the [biblical] text according to its external meaning"
(III:41:567)—by which, I would argue, he means not the vulgar meaning of the biblical text but its parabolic external meaning—he may also
intend to direct our attention to the significance of their internal meanings through the *classification* of parabolic commandments with multiple reasons such as circumcision. Circumcision is also among the very
last commandments Maimonides treats in his first account of *ta'amei
ha-mitzvot* in III:26–49, which offers an external explanation for the
Mosaic Law in toto; hence, its position, with its external and internal
reasons, at the end of that exposition serves as a bridge to the second
account of *ta'amei ha-mitzvot* sketched in III:51–52, which lays out the
internal reason for the Law as a whole.

In claiming that the classifications of the commandment of circumcision in the *Mishneh Torah* and in the *Guide* are determined by their
respective kinds of parabolic reasons, one external, the other internal, I
want to emphasize that I am not making a claim about the audiences to
which the two works are respectively addressed. In saying that the *Mishneh Torah* is the codification of a law whose aim is communal welfare,
I am not saying that it is a book written for the community-at-large, let
alone the common run of men. Nor am I saying that the *Guide,* insofar
as its aim is to express wisdom concerned with the truth and its apprehension, is a work directed only at the philosophical elite.[46] This position is much too simple and crude. *Both* the external and internal meanings of Scripture, or reasons for its commandments, are kinds of wisdom

(in contrast to their vulgar meaning/reason) and, thus, the subject matter of philosophy. And neither of these kinds of wisdom corresponds to any particular class of audience. For all I know, the *Mishneh Torah* (in part or whole) may be aimed at individuals who see themselves as responsible for the welfare of the community and the *Guide* may be aimed (in part or whole) at the wider membership of the community without whose support individual members capable of perfection could not achieve it (II:40:381–84). The real moral of my story, as we have repeatedly witnessed in chapters 2 and 3, is not the duality but unity of Maimonides' corpus of writings, the degree to which his two greatest treatises (in contrast to his running commentaries) complement each other and the extent to which especially the *Mishneh Torah* depends for its full understanding on the argumentation provided in the *Guide*.

Given our analysis of the relation between Maimonides' two reasons for circumcision, it follows that he explains, or interprets, this commandment as a philosophical parable. But that does not mean that the commandment has any less *halakhic* significance. To explain a commandment as a parable is not to explain away its legal necessity or obligatoriness. What Maimonides' shift to the parabolic mode of interpretation does reflect is his attitude toward the body or, more generally, matter, which is an ineliminable obstruction both to concentration on and apprehension of God. Not only has one's body no active role to play at the highest level of divine worship; the very fact that one is a creature of matter, that one has a body with its needs and desires, may indeed prevent one from attaining such heights. Therefore, any verse or, even more so, commandment concerned specifically with the body or a bodily function—such as sexual intercourse, eating, or defecation—is necessarily problematic for Maimonides. Performance of all such commandments focused on the body lead one away from rather than toward the deity. With each of these commandments, Maimonides therefore attempts to show that within its bodily subject matter there exists a more abstract form (or forms), an object of the intellect, expressing the practical and theoretical perfections of humanity. The aim of the philosophical interpretation of Scripture, and the explanation of its commandments, is to strip off its outermost matter to reveal this inner form.

CHAPTER 6

Problematic Commandments III: Maimonides and Nahmanides on the Huqqim, Astrology, and Idolatry

I

In a well-known passage at the beginning of the *Guide*, Maimonides reports an "objection" raised by a "learned man" (*rajul 'ulumiyy*) concerning the biblical episode depicted in Genesis 2.[1] According to the learned man, the external meaning (*zahir*) of the biblical text states that Adam is rewarded for disobeying God: as a consequence of eating the forbidden fruit of the tree of knowledge, he acquires his greatest perfection, an intellect. He concludes his objection with a striking comparison: "This is like the story told by somebody that a certain man from among the people disobeyed and committed great crimes, and in consequence was made to undergo a metamorphosis, becoming a star in heaven" (I:2:23–24). Maimonides adds this mythical analogy to the objection not simply in order that the learned man can dismiss the Torah as a Hollywood star story that crime pays. Although it is quite unclear to what story in particular he intends to refer—perhaps, as Munk suggested, it alludes to the story of Nimrod[2]—the informed reader of the *Guide*, the reader who knows what lies ahead in chapters 29 and 37 of the third part, should be reminded of the detailed descriptions in those later chapters of the ancient Sabians, their star worship and astrologically oriented culture, including their fantastic fables about Adam, stories Maimonides says the Sabians concocted after the Torah had become "generally known . . . and they had heard the external meaning of the Account of the Beginning, taking the whole of it according to its external meaning" (III:29:520). It is the external meaning of the Torah itself, Maimonides is suggesting, that was a source of these radically false myths connected to star worship.

The learned man's mistake, according to Maimonides, is *not* that he understands the "external meaning" of the biblical text to express this star-cultic myth about reward and punishment. His mistake is that he takes its external meaning to be the *only* meaning of the biblical text. He ignores two additional and more important meanings of Scripture: a second meaning that Maimonides amphibolously also calls its "external meaning" and a third meaning he calls its "internal meaning" (*batin*) (I:Introduction:11–12).[3] I'll return in a moment to the difference between these two kinds of meanings, a distinction that also applies to Maimonides' reasons for commandments. The correct approach to the biblical text according to Maimonides is neither to *ignore* the Sabian myths nor to accept them as the *content* of Scripture, what the author intends to convey. Instead they should be recognized as the *context* in which Scripture must be interpreted and the Mosaic commandments explained. The first intention of the Law, Maimonides argues, is to bring its readers to "reject" idolatry, of which one of the two major kinds is Sabian star worship and its underlying belief in astrology and the causal influences of the stars on human action and character formation.[4] But unless one knows in detail the nature of this beast—the particulars of the Sabian culture—one cannot understand how the Law tames it. Knowing the idolatrous Sabian context in which the Mosaic Law was legislated—and which is reflected in the learned man's external meaning—is therefore essential to understanding why it forbids or commands this or that particular ritual.

Maimonides was, as far as we know, the first figure within the rabbinic tradition, from the classical period through the Geonim and from among the medieval philosophers, to explicitly acknowledge the formative role of pagan myth on the rituals and commandments of the Mosaic Law.[5] In particular, he employs it to explain systematically the class of laws known in the rabbinic tradition as the *huqqim* (literally: statutes)—for example, the prohibitions on cooking meat in milk, wearing *sha'atnez* (garments woven of wool and linen), or engaging in incestuous sexual relations, and prescriptions like sending forth the goat to *azazel* or burning the red heifer. Although some rabbinic statements hint at a pagan connection, they are at best allusive and implied.[6] Thus the classic rabbinic statement on the *huqqim* characterizes them as "Statutes that I have prescribed for you (*huqqim shehaqqaqti likha*), about which you have not permission to think (*leharher*), which Satan denounces (*meqattereq*) and the Gentiles refute (*hagoyim mishivin aleihem*): namely, eating pig, wearing *sha'atnez*, removing the sandal in the levirate ritual, the purification of the individual stricken with the plague of *tzara'at*, and the scapegoat sent out of the camp" (BT *Yoma* 67b).[7] This description, with its typological figures Satan and the Gentiles, may be pregnant with suggestions but it is hardly an admission of paternity.

The boldness and originality of Maimonides' position should therefore not be underestimated. But the significance of Sabianism for Maimonides was not simply historical. Apart from pseudo-Aristotelian magical texts that circulated in medieval Arabic and purported Sabian texts like Ibn Wahshiyya's *Nabatean Agriculture*—a work Maimonides quotes with great enthusiasm—Sabianism was not entirely dead in Maimonides' own day. A community that was known as "Sabian" existed in Harran, the biblical birthplace of the patriarch Abraham, and also in Baghdad at least as late as the tenth century.[8] Exactly what the name "Sabian" meant at this time, and the exact identity of the community in Harran, remains a matter of scholarly debate. However, the available evidence, based on reports by Ibn Abi Usaybi'a, al-Kindi, and especially al-Mas'udi, strongly suggests that the building identified as the Sabian place of meeting, which was also known as a temple, was in fact a Platonic or Neoplatonic academy, which served as a haven for the exiles of Athens after Justinian closed the School of Athens in 529. This academy, and the community surrounding it, was pagan throughout its history and, unfortunately, its philosophical activities were generally not distinguished from the popular Harranian religious practices in which its members engaged.[9] This identification, or confusion, as we shall see, is especially evident in Maimonides' descriptions of Sabianism which mix ingredients of Neoplatonism, astrology, and popular religion. Still more generally, Maimonides also appropriates the term "Sabianism" to refer to the wide range of myths and false doctrines that he believes lay at the roots of ancient Sabianism. He argues that these Sabian myths, entrenched by habit, familiarity, and the power of the written word, have come to have a life of their own and that they are still very much alive in the imagination of the twelfth century: especially in the form of belief in astrology, theurgy, and the efficacy of astrological and astral-magical practices. By uncovering the ancient Sabian myths that explain the Mosaic legislation of the *huqqim*, Maimonides believes that he is thereby exposing a major myth of his own day—astrology and the culture surrounding it—and thus a primary form of idolatry that the Law is still engaged in battling.

Maimonides' account that the *huqqim* were legislated in order to negate the idolatrous myths of the Sabians rests on his doctrine that astrology is false, vain, and nothing more than pagan superstition.[10] However, Maimonides' unqualified rejection of astrology was far from universally shared in his own time. Although some of the most important influences on Maimonides—Saadiah and Bahya ibn Paquda among the Jews and most of the eastern Muslim philosophers including Al-Farabi and Ibn Sina—also denounced astrology, it had strong supporters in the West, including Andalusians like Abraham ibn Ezra and Catalonians like Abraham bar Hiyya.[11] Moreover, however unscientific astrology may seem to us nowadays, it had an undeniably firm foot to stand on in Aristotelean natural philosophy, in Galenic medical theory, and in the theory of climatology. Indeed it is arguably a natural development of these almost universally accepted medieval theories.[12] And despite the authority of Maimonides, astrology also continued to draw many adherents in the post-Maimonidean thirteenth-century world of Christian Spain and Provence. Among these nach-Maimonidean figures, the most prominent perhaps was the other Moses of medieval rabbinic Judaism, the RaMBaN, Moses Nahmanides, in whose commentaries on the Torah and *derashot* we find the first systematic theory of the commandments to compete with Maimonides'. Nahmanides, in opposition to Maimonides, holds that astrology and astral causation are true. And whereas Maimonides explains the *huqqim* as commandments legislated in order to deny and to wean the people away from the mythic astrological beliefs and practices of their Sabian environment, Nahmanides explains the very same rituals in terms of the truth of the same astrological and astral doctrines: as commandments designed to acknowledge the roles of actual astrological powers within the constraints of the Law.

This path from Maimonides to Nahmanides is not a single straight line. Nahmanides' relation to Maimonides is much more subtle, ambivalent, and tense than the received view that sharply opposes him to Maimonides tout cour.[13] The latter view may be encouraged by some of Nahmanides' own remarks in which he appears to go out of his way to represent himself as Maimonides' opponent—but this, I shall suggest, may be due to different considerations. Furthermore, in addition to Maimonides, there were independent Andalusian and Catalonian traditions from which Nahmanides draws in his use of astrological themes to explain the reasons of commandments, especially the writings of Judah Ha-Levi and Abraham ibn Ezra, the second of whom he explicitly acknowledges.[14] Nonetheless I want to argue that Maimonides' explanation of the *huqqim,* based on his view that astrology and astral causation are false, shapes the particular ways in which Nahmanides uses the same astral notions—which he takes to be true—to explain the very same laws. It has been claimed that the reaction to Maimonides' philosophy among its later critics, especially but not exclusively the kabbalists, had the effect of "crystallizing" the pieces of the various amorphous traditions they already possessed.[15] This is, I think, an especially apt way to describe the formative role of Maimonides on Nahmanides' account of the *huqqim.* Indeed if we can describe Maimonides' explanation of the *huqqim* as a critique of astrology, Nahmanides' account of the same commandments might be read as a vigorous anti-Maimonidean *defense* of the veracity of astrology.

II

The *huqqim* stand out against the background of two claims shared by Maimonides and Nahmanides concerning *ta'amei ha-mitzvot*, the general explanation of the commandments. In order to place their real disagreement into relief, I shall begin by summarizing this common ground.

First, both Maimonides and Nahmanides hold that *all* commandments, without exception, were legislated for some reason or purpose and, furthermore, that one ought to engage in inquiry into *ta'amei ha-mitzvot*.[16] Maimonides argues for this position at length—in opposition to the Mu'tazilites and Ash'arites—and, as I argued in chapter 2, he holds this, despite some deliberately misleading remarks, both for the general classes of commandments and for the particular commandments in each class.[17] Nahmanides shares this Maimonidean view, but the opposing view that some or all commandments are arbitrary, divinely willed commands does not seem to have been a live philosophical position by his time, although he attacks (mainly by way of prooftexts) *parshanim* in Ashkenaz who seem to be of a like opinion.

The second claim derives from Maimonides' theory of parables, the model of interpretation of scriptural passages that, as we saw in earlier chapters, he also applies to *ta'amei ha-mitzvot*. On this approach, a correct understanding of scriptural texts requires that the reader recognize that they contain parables "not explicitly identified there as such" (I:Intro.:6). What Maimonides means by this is that these texts possess more than the learned man's kind of external meaning, what he sometimes calls their "vulgar" meaning, i.e., the meaning of the words or, roughly speaking, what other Andalusian exegetes called *peshat*. Maimonides calls this meaning "vulgar" because this is how the texts are *exclusively* understood by the vulgar multitude—a multitude that includes the learned man. The vulgar meaning expresses beliefs that no reasonable person should hold—like divine corporeality or the Sabian myths about the causal powers of stars.[18] But in addition to their vulgar meaning or *peshat*, Maimonides locates two other levels of meaning in these texts when they are correctly identified as parables, what he calls their (parabolic) "external" and "internal" meanings. In contrast to the vulgar meaning, both the external and internal parabolic meanings of the text express beliefs grounded in wisdom that the author himself believes and intends for his reader to believe. The sole difference between the external and internal meanings of a parable, which emerges in Maimonides' famous interpretation of the parable of "apples of gold in settings of silver," consists in their respective kinds of content. The external meaning "contains wisdom that is useful in many respects, among which is the welfare of human societies"—that is, beliefs that (at least some of which) contribute to the welfare of a community, both political-social and intellectual. The internal meaning "contains wisdom that is useful for beliefs concerned with the truth as it is" (I:Introduction:12)—that is, wisdom that is useful for beliefs concerning physics and metaphysics, those subjects that bear on the intellectual perfection of the individual.

It should be emphasized that this difference between the external and internal meanings of a parable is a function entirely of their *contents*. Both external and internal meanings are meant by or "contained" in the text. Both meanings express kinds of wisdom the author himself believes, intends to convey, and qua wisdom believes ought to be believed by his reader. The difference between external and internal meanings is not a difference between their respective intended audiences or between their literary forms of presentation—for example, whether the meaning is revealed or concealed, explicit or simply implied, intended for a select school or closed group or for the public at large. Of course, Maimonides also employs various devices (deliberate contradictions, allusions, chapter headings, scrambling of passages) to conceal the contents of some of his interpretations. However, these means of concealment are "perpendicular" to his distinction between the contents of external and internal meanings. That is, unlike a dualistic schema like the exoteric/esoteric, it would be more correct to view Maimonides' theory of interpretation as the product of a coordinate system, with one axis for differences in content like the distinction between parabolic external and internal meaning and the other axis for differences in literary presentation that would differentiate concealed/secret and revealed/public information. As a consequence, not only its internal meaning but sometimes the external meaning of a parable, or parabolic text, may be subject to literary concealment—and, indeed, the *huqqim*, I'll argue, are an example of this sort.

Corresponding to this distinction between the external and internal meanings of a parable, Maimonides also distinguishes two analogous levels of reasons or purposes to explain why the commandments were legislated.[19] As we have seen in earlier chapters, he engages in this kind of parabolic explanation of commandments both with the unit of the individual commandment—such as circumcision, the Sabbath, and the commandment to cover one's excrement in the battle camp—and with the unit of the Law as a whole or with large blocks of commandments. There is, however, only one passage in the *Guide* where Maimonides explicitly describes his explanatory approach to ta'amei ha-mitzvot as parabolic. But it is a significant example. In the course of explaining the reason for the scapegoat sent forth on the Day of Atonement—not accidentally, one of the classic examples of a *hoq*—he says that no one ever thought that sins could literally be transferred from one body to another; instead *"all these actions* are parables serving to bring forth a form in the soul" (III:46:591; my emphasis).[20] I shall return to discuss the specific parabolic explanation Maimonides goes on to give in this context, but the fact that he instructs us to take the scapegoat as representative of "all these actions," a deliberately vague but open-ended description, is his signal to us how to proceed in our inquiry into *ta'amei ha-mitzvot.*

The external reason for the totality of commandments is what we are given in Part III, chapters 26–49, Maimonides' longest and most sustained treatment of *ta'amei ha-mitzvot* in the *Guide.* All the reasons given in those chapters are concerned with communal wisdom: they explain how the Law is directed at the moral, political, and social well-being of the community, what he calls the "welfare of the body," *and* at inculcating in members "correct opinions corresponding to their respective capacity" (III:27:510), what he calls the "welfare of the soul." These opinions and beliefs are not intellectually apprehended through the performance of the commandments in a way by which those who profess them could be said to *know* them or to achieve intellectual perfection. Rather, the point is to create a community of a certain caliber that aims at the "welfare of the soul" as well as "of the body," the kind of community Maimonides says is created by a divine law.[21]

In Part III, chapters 51–52, Maimonides gives a second, entirely different kind of explanation for the commandments as a totality: they were legislated in order for the individual to train himself to be occupied with God rather than with matters pertaining to this world, that is, rather than with the kinds of goods that constitute the welfare of the body and soul. This second kind of reason corresponds to the internal meaning of a parable; it contains wisdom that is *useful* for beliefs concerned with the truth because occupying oneself *with* God *by* directing oneself away *from* this world—away from pursuit of material needs and desires and, I would add, from one's imagination—is a precondition for becoming or acquiring (and then sustaining) an acquired intellect, an intellect separated from matter, engaged fully and exclusively in contemplation of truths. To be sure, commandments do not, strictly speaking, *contain* beliefs concerned with the truth—that is, physical and metaphysical science. But their performance *enables* the individual to be engaged in apprehension of these truths in their highest form.

As we saw in chapter 4, Nahmanides follows both Maimonides' general idea of two-levelled parabolic interpretation and, more specifically, his application of this approach to the explanation of commandments. Although he differs in the contents of the specific reasons he assigns, he agrees that the commandments have both external and internal reasons. At the level of external reasons their major difference is that Nachmanides has a much more positive and richer conception of *peshat*, the meanings of words, than does Maimonides. Moreover, for Nachmanides, unlike Maimonides, both the practical and theoretical, or theosophical, truths conveyed by Scripture are always *in addition to* the literal meanings of their words, their *peshat*; they never displace it. At the level of internal reasons for the commandments, Nahmanides proposes, in place of Maimonides' wisdom concerned with knowledge of physics and metaphysics, a theocentric, theurgic account. On this view, *hashekhinah beyisra'el tzorekh gavoha velo tzorekh hedyot*: the Shechinah—by which he seems to mean all aspects of divine worship, for example, the commandments, which cause the Divine Presence to dwell within Israel—satisfies "higher [i.e., divine] needs" (*tzorekh gevoha*) and not, as the literal word of Scripture (*peshat hadavar*) suggests, "ordinary [i.e., profane or human] needs" (*tzorekh hedyot*).[22] That is, the human performance of the commandments serves to satisfy, complete, or perfect the deity or divine nature. However, apart from these differences in content, the *structure* of Nahmanides' two levels of reasons closely follows Maimonides.'

In sum, both Maimonides and Nahmanides hold that all commandments in all their particulars have reasons or causes, indeed, two reasons, one external—related to the welfare of human communal life— and one internal, related to individual intellectual perfection or theosophy and theurgy. It is against this backdrop that the *huqqim* come on stage—precisely because, on their received rabbinic understanding, they are said not to have reasons, even external reasons. Indeed it is primarily at the level of their external reasons that the *huqqim* are singled out by Maimonides and Nahmanides, although, as I shall argue, they also hint at a serious problem for the internal purpose of the Law, be it theoretical perfection or theurgy. I'll turn first to Maimonides' and then to Nahmanides' attempts to solve this problem posed by the *huqqim*.

III

Maimonides' "solution" to the problem of *huqqim* proceeds in a number of clearly delineated steps. First, he reinterprets the tannaitic passage quoted earlier (BT *Yoma* 67b) that literally states that the *huqqim* are "prescribed" (*shehaqqaqti*) or "decrees" (*gezerot*), expressions that were standardly understood to mean that they have no cause or reason. Maimonides instead states that they mean that the *huqqim* have no *known* cause or reason, thereby trading the objectionable metaphysical thesis for an epistemic claim about the "incapacity of our intellects or the deficiency of our knowledge" (III:26:507). Second, he answers the implicit question—Not known *by whom?*—by adding that the *huqqim* are "those commandments . . . whose utility is not clear *to the multitude*" (III:26:507, my emphasis). That is, the *huqqim* are commandments, knowledge of whose reasons was or is not evident to the ordinary member of the community. Third, he turns to the question his own interpretation now raises: Why should the reasons for these commandments be hidden from the ordinary person? The answer to this question will take us to the heart of our topic, but notice already how Maimonides has reconfigured the notion of a *hoq*: it is not a commandment that either lacks a reason or of whose reason we are ignorant simpliciter; rather the *huqqim* are commandments whose reasons are known by some but concealed from others, suggesting that there is some difficulty their reasons pose for some audiences. That is, *huqqim* are not arbitrary or mysterious but *problematic* commandments.[23]

Maimonides does not explicitly tell us what is problematic about the reasons for the *huqqim*. Instead he leads us through a series of examples calculated to elicit a certain conclusion. These examples are also significant insofar as they reveal a third major shift in his reinterpretation of the idea of a *hoq*. The tannaitic statement in BT *Yoma* 67b, you will recall, consists of a general characterization of a *hoq* followed by an enumeration of a few particular commandments: *sha'atnez*, the scapegoat, the prohibition against eating pig, the levirate marriage, and the purification rite of the leper. What exactly is the function of this list of commandments? Is it meant to be illustrative: a sequence of examples representative of larger (and perhaps even open) classes of commandments? Or is it meant to be exclusive and exhaustive—that is, an extensional definition of the *huqqim*: the *huqqim* simply are A, B, C, and D. On this second view, the *huqqim* would also clearly be understood as exceptions to the general rule of commandments which do have (known) reasons.

To the best of my knowledge, every figure in the history of Jewish thought with one exception has taken the *huqqim* in the second way: as a short exclusive list of exceptional commandments. The one exception is, of course, Maimonides. Following the passage in which he introduces the *huqqim* (III:26), he launches into a lengthy and deliberately obscure discussion (which I discussed at length in chapter 2) in which he claims that particulars (unlike generalities) of the Law have either no reasons or no known reasons, at the conclusion of which he says that the true reality of "particulars of commandments is illustrated by the sacrifices" (III:26:509). Earlier in the same chapter, while giving examples of *huqqim,* he shifts from *sha'atnez* to agricultural laws such as the interdictions against the first products of trees (*'orlah*) and against sowing the vineyard with diverse seeds (*kil'ayim*). These cases suggest that all agricultural laws like these are *huqqim*. And in the *Mishneh Torah*, he explicitly makes two broad generalizations, the arguments for which are only later spelled out in the *Guide*:

> All the sacrifices are in the category of *huqqim*. (*MT* "*Me'ilah*" viii, 8)

> It is plain and manifest that the laws of impurity and purity are decrees of Scripture . . . and behold they are included among the *huqqim*. (*MT* "*Mikva'ot*" xi, 12)

In short, the *huqqim* for Maimonides are not just a handful of curious exceptions but a broad and central portion of the Mosaic law, all the laws of sacrifice—or, as we shall later see, at least of burnt offerings—purity and impurity, and agriculture.

The one thing all these various classes of commandments have in common is that they are all explained in the *Guide* in light of the historical context in which the Mosaic Law was legislated, the Sabian culture centered on star worship. As Maimonides says, "the meaning of many of the laws became clear to me and their causes became known to me through my study of the doctrines, opinions, practices, and cult of the Sabians, as you will hear when I explain the reasons for the commandments that are considered to be without cause" (III:29:518).[24] Hence, if the *huqqim* are problematic, and if there is one problem common to all the *huqqim* that made it necessary for the author of the Torah and for the rabbis to conceal their reasons, the most plausible place to look for an explanation would be in their Sabian context of legislation.

The crux of Sabianism, according to Maimonides, is the identification of the deity with the stars, especially the sun and moon.[25] On the most philosophically sophisticated versions of Sabianism, Maimonides says, it was "imagined" that God is the spirit of the sphere, and the sphere the body of the deity. Since God is eternal, this is an argument for the eternity, hence, infinite duration, of the world. But it also follows that the deity, as the spirit of the sphere, is itself either a body or a force within a body, hence, finite. Therefore, God must be both finite and infinite. Already the patriarch Abraham, the first philosopher to refute Sabianism, realized that this is absurd (i.e., literally a reductio), but, for Maimonides, this is also the least and least harmful of the falsehoods of Sabianism. Because they also believed that the stars and sun govern the upper and lower worlds and that there are astral causal powers whereby the stars harm or help humans, the Sabians erected temples, set up statues, and planted trees—Asherot—which they worshipped and, in turn, to which "the forces of the planets *overflowed*" whereby people were given "prophetic revelations . . . that made known to [them] what was useful to them" (III:29:516ff.) And from this, Maimonides continues, the Sabians themselves attempted to influence the stars and developed into soothsayers, enchanters, sorcerers, necromancers, charmers, fire-passers (performers of the *molekh* rite)—practitioners of theurgic magic of every sort. Thus, the Sabian context for the Mosaic legislation was a pagan culture of star-worship built on, or presupposing, astrology which led in practice directly to magic. This is not only the way in which Maimonides believes idolatry and magic historically evolved, as he sketches it at the beginning of *MT 'Avodah Zarah.* The three are also one interconnected conceptual and psychological complex.[26] "The intent of the whole Law . . . is to put an end to idolatry, to efface its traces, and to bring about a state of affairs in which it would not be imagined that any star harms or helps in anything pertaining to the circumstances of human individuals" (III:29:542); that is, idolatry will not be eliminated unless astrology is not even imagined to be effective because "astrology leads to star worship." But for astrology to be eliminated, "it follows necessarily that all magicians must be killed" (ibid.) because these two go hand in hand: "in all magical operations it is indispensable that the stars should be observed" (ibid.). And, finally, people will cease to perform magic only when they cease to engage in practices that do not turn on reason or scientific demonstration and instead exploit "occult properties" and "astrological notions." For these will-nilly "turn into a glorification and a worship of the stars" (ibid.). Thus there is an inseparable connection between astrology, star worship, and magic. Following Lev. 20:25, Maimonides calls this whole complex, or form of life, *huqqoth ha-goyim,* the customs of the nations. The Mosaic *huqqim* are so-called because they refute or negate the *huqqoth ha-goyim.*

The *huqqim* negate the *huqqoth ha-goyim* in two ways. Some *huqqim* such as *sha'atnez,* the interdictions on first products of trees or grafting, and all prohibitions against magic either prohibit an action that the Sabians performed, command an act they forbade, or command us to do the opposite of what they did.[27] Other *huqqim,* most famously, all the commandments concerning sacrifice (or at least the burnt offerings), the temple cult, and purity, do not aim to directly *abolish* the Sabian practices but, at least as a first step, to *transfer* them to worship of the deity while "restricting" and moderating their performance. Because of human nature, or psychology, the power of habit, and human natural resistance to radical change, Maimonides argues that the Israelites at the time of the Mosaic legislation could not have tolerated an immediate, total prohibition on sacrifice. Therefore the deity in His "wily graciousness" *accommodated* the first intention of the Law, the elimination of idolatry, to its second intention, respect for the necessities of human nature. The product of this accommodation, as we saw in chapters 2 and

3, are the Mosaic laws of sacrifice, the temple cult, and purity.

It should be emphasized that this explanation that the *huqqim* were legislated in order to refute the *huqqoth ha-goyim*—the Sabian triad of astrology, star worship, and magic—is entirely at the level of their (parabolic) *external* reasons, the ways in which they contribute to the political-social and theoretical "welfare" of the community, including the inculcation of "correct opinions" for the community at large (III:27:510). Idolatry, astrology, and magic must be eliminated or overcome in order to achieve the kind of society in which capable individuals can achieve (intellectual) perfection. However, the *huqqim themselves* in this function do not enable the individual to achieve intellectual perfection or knowledge of truth. Hence, this reason for legislating the *huqqim* cannot count as their internal reason.

Yet, even though this explanation of the *huqqim* is only at the external level, knowledge of it must nonetheless be concealed from the multitude—those who must be weaned away from Sabian star worship, astrology, and magic. For the *huqqim* can be effective on this explanation only if the community at large imagines that the one deity also wants people to sacrifice to Him, or only if they imagine that their actions have some theurgic power. Because the power of Sabianism largely lies in its hold on the imagination, or psychology, of its practitioners, the *huqqim* most play along with the people's imaginations in order to release their poor souls, or intellects, from their bonds. If they were told why they were *really* being commanded to perform these acts—not because they are, as they imagine, good for them but in order to enable them to withdraw from their harmful addiction—the acts would not have the same psychological potency. The *huqqim* would be self-defeating.

This is one reason why the reasons for the *huqqim* must be concealed, but there are, I think, two deeper connections between Maimonides' Sabian explanation and the need for its concealment. Prima facie the reason just given explains only why Moses did not reveal the reason for the *huqqim* to the ancient Israelites. It does not explain why the rabbis continued to conceal the reasons for the *huqqim* or why Maimonides, as I have tried to suggest in my remarks about his treatment of the particulars of the Law, also presents his account of the *huqqim* in, if not a concealed, an at least far from explicit manner. One possible explanation for these later instances of concealment is antinomianism. For if these commandments were legislated in response to a particular Sabian context that existed in the ancient past, that furnishes no reason for people *now* to perform them. So, because *knowledge* of the Sabian explanation for the original legislation of the Mosaic commandments would create the potential for contemporary antinomianism, the rabbis and Maimonides do not explicitly reveal it.[28]

A second possible explanation is also related to antinomianism, but not because Sabianism was something of the distant past. This reason stems from the fact that Maimonides, I want to suggest, believed that an important vestige of Sabianism survived in his own time and remained to be overcome in the same way that Moses had to fight to overcome ancient Sabianism.

Who were these contemporary Sabians? Maimonides refers to "remnants" of the Sabians that survive "in the extremities of the earth," the Turks in the North and the Hindus in the South (III:29:515). But because of their remoteness, it is difficult to believe that these groups would have been a live concern to Maimonides. However, throughout his account Maimonides inserts allusions and reminders that *we*—or his immediate readers—are not entirely untouched by the influence of Sabianism, especially its root docrine and branches, namely, astrology and magic.[29] Some examples:

(1) After describing fables about Adam, *asherot* in Nineveh, and a quarrel between two bushes over their magical powers, Maimonides concludes:

> This is a long fable, from which, if you examine it, you may draw inferences concerning the intellect[30] and the sciences of the people of those times. Such were the *Sages of Babylon* that are referred to in those dark times. For these were the religious beliefs upon which they were brought up. If the belief in the existence of the deity were not generally accepted at present to such an extent in the religious communities, *our days in these times* would be even darker than that epoch. However their darkness is of different kinds. (III:29:519; my emphasis)

It is not entirely clear why Maimonides says that things would be even "darker" now than in the past, but he seems to have in mind various kinds of occult or superstitious practices that were widely accepted in his contemporary religious community—for example, the use of talismans and other theurgic activities to which he refers elsewhere in the passage (III:29:518).[31]

(2) After describing the Sabian fables about Adam purportedly inspired by the external meaning of the Torah, Maimonides tells his reader, with not a little irony, that "a man like you does not have to have his attention drawn to this point—as you have already acquired such sciences as will *prevent your mind from becoming attached* to the fables of the Sabians and the ravings of the Chasdeans and the Chaldeans who are devoid of all science that is truly a science—I have warned against this in order to safeguard others, *for the multitude frequently incline to regarding fables as the truth*" (III:29:520, my emphasis). The fact that Maimonides

must remind his philosophical reader that he, unlike the multitude, need not guard against the dangers of Sabianism only reinforces the point that he clearly does see a present danger especially for the philosopher from its seductive fables.

(3) After describing ancient Sabian cultic practices based on the evidence of the extant books, he adds:

> Some of the latter are generally known *at present in the world.* I mean the building of temples, the setting up in them of images made of cast metal and stone, the building of alters and the offering-up upon them of either animal sacrifices or various kinds of food, the institution of festivals, the gathering for prayer and for various kinds of worship in those temples in which they locate highly venerated places that are called by them the temple [*heikhal*] of the intellectual forms. (III: 29:521)

The phrase "temple of the intellectual forms," as Munk already noted, seems to refer to a Neoplatonic and, as the rest of the passage indicates, pagan place of worship, one that closely resembles, to the best of our historical knowledge, the Harranian "Sabian" meeting place, which served both as a philosophical academy and pagan house of popular religion.[32] For Maimonides there exists a single unbroken chain from the ancient Sabian temples, idols, and sacrifices, via festivals and prayer, to this contemporary Neoplatonic institution that combines philosophy with pagan popular worship, magic, and theurgy. Whether or not he had in mind the specific temple in Harran, the close connection drawn between these different activities in our text shows that Maimonides made no sharp differentiation among them. While he presumably believed that this contemporary form of Sabianism was a direct descendant of the ancient pagan religion, the name "Sabianism" now functions to refer more broadly to current—though probably more magical and theurgic—kinds of Neoplatonism. This shift is crucial to understanding why Maimonides sees so much of a threat in Sabianism.

(4) In I:63, Maimonides begins his account of the Tetragrammaton with "an introductory remark" in which he explains the meaning of Moses' statement that the Israelites will ask him "What is His name? What shall I say unto them?" (Exod. 3:13). After offering one interpretation, Maimonides says:

> You know that in those times the teachings of the Sabians were generally accepted and that all except a few men were idolaters. I mean by this that they believed in spirits, that they believed that those spirits can be made to descend among men, and *that they made talismans.* (I:63:153, my emphasis)

The underlined statement suggests that, according to Maimonides, the real reason why Moses thinks the Israelites will ask for the name of God is that they desire it for magical or theurgic purposes: to make talismans. However, Maimonides' concern does not seem to be restricted to ancient Israel. Here the association of talismans with Sabianism places in context various criticisms that Maimonides has raised in the two previous chapters against magical and superstitious uses of divine names in his own day:

> Do not . . . let occur to your mind the vain imaginings of the writers of charms (*qame'ot*) or what names you may hear from them or may find in their stupid books, names that they have invented, which are not indicative of any notion whatsoever, but which they call the names and of which they think that they necessitate *holiness* and *purity* and work miracles. (I:61:149)

In the same vein, Maimonides also says that

> when wicked and ignorant people found these texts [about the divine names], they had great scope for lying statements in that they would put together any letters they liked and would say: this is a name that has efficacy and the power to operate if it is written down or uttered in a particular way. Thereupon these lies invented by the first wicked and ignorant man were written down, and these writings transmitted to good, pious, and foolish men who lack the scales by means of which they could know the true from the false. These people accordingly made a secret of these writings, and the latter were found in the belongings left behind them, so that they were thought to be correct. (I:62:152)

Here Maimonides recounts the history of superstition, conceived in Sabianism, born of deceit, and sustained through pious innocence and naive goodness.[33] Although Maimonides concludes by saying that "the lack of validity" of these "vain imaginings . . . is manifest to every beginner in speculation" (ibid.), apparently he also believed that "the opinion concerning [these divine names and their meaning] that is generally accepted by the vulgar" made it absolutely necessary for him to go into the issue at such length. The present danger must have been real.[34]

(5) In the course of showing how the Mosaic laws of purity and impurity are in fact much less burdensome and unpleasant than corresponding Sabian practices, Maimonides refers to the "generally known . . . usages *observed up to our times* by the Sabians in the lands of the East, I refer to the remnants of the Magians" (III:47:595; my emphasis) who Pines identifies (ad loc.) as Zoroastrians. In the same passage, he also describes "another generally known usage of the Sabians that *continues to our time* [which] is to regard as unclean everything that is separated

from the body, that is, hair or nails or blood" (ibid.; my emphasis). Here Maimonides is possibly suggesting, as we shall see more explicitly in the next example, that what had once been a particular Sabian ritual has now become a more widespread element in popular religion and superstition.

(6) After describing the *molekh* rite, the pagan practice of passing one's child through fire, a practice that preyed on parents' special apprehensions about their children, who they were told would be endangered if this act was not performed; after describing this—we would think, now completely eradicated—practice, Maimonides says:

> Know that traces of this action subsist up to now as a consequence of its having been generally accepted in the world. You will see that midwives take small children in their swaddling clothes, throw a fumigant having a disagreeable odor upon the fire, and move the children over this fume above the fire. This is indubitably a sort of *passage through the fire*, which it is illicit to perform. Consider how perfidious was he who originated this opinion and how he perpetuated it through this imagining, so that its trace was not effaced though the Law has opposed it for thousands of years. (III:37:546)

Here, as in the previous example, Sabianism is presented as a myth in the Wittgensteinian sense, the sense in which a dead metaphor, mistakenly interpreted as literally true, continues to exercise an almost magical power over the way in which we think of some subject matter, like thinking of knowledge as an edifice with a foundation built from bottom up.[35] For Wittgenstein, these linguistic myths are the sources of deep cognitive errors, and it is the task of philosophy to demythicize or expose them as nothing more than dead metaphors, thereby curing us of our addiction to their ways of thinking. For Maimonides, the myth of Sabianism is more than a cognitive error, although its falsity is essential to his critique. Sabianism, built on its astrological beliefs in the power of the stars over humans, is false and prohibited by the Law *because* it is false.[36] But, as with linguistic myths, these falsehoods are not only failings of the intellect; they have become the stuff of people's imaginations and fantasies. Therefore, it is not enough for the philosopher simply to point out the fallacies and false premises from which the conclusions of Sabianism follow. The task of the philosopher is to free those caught in the grip of the Sabian myth. A crucial step in this process is exposing the Sabian origins of present-day "popular religion." In this last example, we would not even recognize the superstitious practice as a religious ritual, let alone as a form of magic or idolatry, if we were not able to recover its Sabian origins. Only then do we see how an originally idolatrous act was taken and perpetuated out of context, in its vulgar external meaning. Only then, with this knowledge in hand, can we disabuse ourselves of its magical hold.[37]

Maimonides sees a present danger in Sabianism because he believes that its grip still firmly holds captive the imaginations of his contemporaries—especially through the myths that continue to live on in astrology and the superstitious practices of popular religion. His use of Sabianism as the context in which to situate the legislation of the Mosaic Law should be understood, then, as both more specific and more general than idolatry *simpliciter*. It is more specific than general idolatry because it is focused on the worship of *stars*. It is more general because it essentially includes, besides idolatry, astrology, theurgy, and magic, both as these are incorporated in popular religion and as they are defended and elaborated by Neoplatonically inclined philosophers and thinkers. This Sabian triad of star worship, astrology, and magic must also be distinguished from the kind of idolatry Maimonides is concerned to deny and eliminate in the first part of the *Guide*: the cognitive, representational error in believing that God is corporeal, composite, and comparable. Readers of the *Guide* have typically focused on this first kind of idolatry as the main object of Maimonides' critique.[38] But when he says in Part III that the first intention of the Law—that is, the commandments—is to "efface," "reject," and "put an end to" idolatry (III:29:521, 30:523, 32:527, 32:529), Maimonides cannot have in mind, at least primarily, this first kind of intellectual error. For how could, say, sacrifice eliminate that kind of mistaken belief? It is instead the contemporary form of Sabianism manifest in popular religious belief in astrology, magic, and other superstitious practices against which commandments like sacrifice and the other *huqqim* are directed. This second kind of contemporary idolatry, this radically mistaken way of life, is Maimonides' target in Part III.[39]

The way in which the Mosaic commandments, and in particular sacrifices, "put an end" to astrology and magic is not only negative: by opposing, undermining, and weaning the people away from their practice. There is also a positive program: particular sacrifices cultivate an alternative type of personality, the kind of person who does not depend on astrology, magic, or superstition to decide how to act, who is instead responsible for his own actions and takes responsibility for them. To show this, let me now introduce a distinction to which I alluded earlier. Maimonides' initial historical explanation of the sacrificial cult in the *Guide* (III:26–32) does not distinguish among the various kinds of sacrifices. In later chapters, however, he sharply distinguishes the burnt offering (*'olah*) from the sin offering (*hat'at*). In the course of explaining why sin offerings are burned outside the camp, in contrast to burnt offerings, which are burned on the altar and produce a sweet smell, he says that the latter

> were performed with a view to putting an end to *idolatrous* opin-
> ions . . . As for the burning of these sin-offerings, its purpose was to
> signify that the trace of the sin in question was wiped out and had dis-
> appeared just as the body that had been burnt had disappeared, and
> that no trace remained of that action just as no trace remained of the
> *sin-offering.* (III:46:591)

Here Maimonides contrasts the reasons for the two kinds of sacrifices.
The purpose of the burnt offerings is now what was originally proposed
as the reason for all sacrifice: to negate Sabianism, star worship, astrology, and magic. The purpose of the sin offering is now said to be to
express symbolically to its offerer the complete elimination of his sinful
action: that he has utterly ceased to sin and changed his way of acting.[40]
Maimonides elaborates this reason in the next passage (discussed earlier
in Section II), in which he explains the reason for sending forth the
scapegoat: "All of these actions are parables serving to bring forth a
form in the soul so that a passion toward repentance should result"
(ibid.).[41] Now, the distinguishing feature of repentance for a sin, and the
symbolic content of the sin offering, is "one's being divested of it"
(III:36:540); that is, the person entirely ceases to perform the sin. "Complete" (or perhaps, "completed") repentance [*teshuvah gemurah*], Maimonides explains in the *Mishneh Torah*, obtains when the individual
finds himself in the identical circumstances in which he had sinned with
the ability to sin, but he separates [*peirash*] himself and does not sin
"*because* of his repentance."[42] Thus the purpose of the symbolism of the
sin offering is to bring about a "passion for repentance." However, its
significance in our context is still deeper.

Maimonides argues that humans, given their ignorance and passions, "cannot but sin and err" (III:36:540). Because of one's material
condition, one is *necessitated* to commit some sin at some time. But if
people believe that this necessity is due to external compulsion beyond
their control—that "this fracture could never be remedied, . . . that no
strategem remains" (ibid.) for them to act autonomously according to
their own will (even if it is necessitated)—they will fatalistically resign
themselves to their sinful state, take no responsibility for their actions,
"persist in [their] error and sometimes even disobey even more" (ibid.).
So, if people do not believe in the possibility of changing their actions—
as exemplified by repentance—they will adopt a fatalistic attitude of res-
ignation, absolving themselves of all responsibility for their own actions.
This is the same attitudinal consequence Maimonides elsewhere
attributes to belief in astrology and the power of the stars. The significance of belief in, or being passionate about, repentance is meant to
serve, then, as the very opposite of the Sabian astrological attitude: that

the individual *not* believe, if he sins, that he *must* forevermore sin, that he was and will be necessitated to sin, that he cannot change his ways, that his actions are not "up to him."[43] "If he believes in repentance, he can correct himself and return to a better and more perfect state than the one he was in before he sinned" (ibid.). Thus, the attitude presupposed by repentance is the opposite of that induced by astrology, magic, and the superstitious beliefs of Sabianism. And the point of the sin offerings, whose aim is to bring about a passion for repentance, is to inculcate and cultivate this alternative state of mind.

The two main classes of obligatory sacrifices thereby complement each other's role in overthrowing Sabianism. The *'olah*, or burnt offering, suppresses the wrong view: Sabianism in the broad sense of belief in astrology, magic, and superstition. The *hat'at*, the sin offering, impresses on the agent the proper positive attitude: that human agents are responsible for their actions and, because it is always within their power to act freely, or as they want to, that they have the responsibility to act as they should. Together the two kinds of sacrifices put an end to the whole way of life that Maimonides labels "Sabianism."[44]

To return, finally, to our broader argument: Let us suppose now that Maimonides believes that Sabianism survives to his own day and that the Law is still engaged in putting an end to it. There are two arguments why the reasons for the *huqqim* should nonetheless be concealed. First, if the underlying pathology of Sabianism—astrology and magic—has not yet been cured, the *huqqim* have yet to achieve their goal, a goal that requires that knowledge of their function be concealed from the multitude in order not to be self-defeating—no less now than at the time of the Mosaic legislation. Second, the fact that Sabianism "has not yet been effaced" testifies to its powerful grip on the human imagination. But it is also impossible to ignore the implication that the divine law has not been perfectly successful—which, in turn, might be used to argue that the divine law is less than divine. I mention this, not because this is what Maimonides himself believes is the right conclusion to draw, but because the multitude, those still in the hold of Sabianism, might all too easily make this potential inference. So the very same fact—that Sabianism is still alive, the consideration that counters the antinomian argument that the *huqqim* are at present obsolete—may also, on this alternative argument, furnish the ammunition for a different indictment of the Law. This, again, is a reason to conceal the explanation of the *huqqim* from the multitude while they simultaneously work to transform them. In either case, it is the *problematic* nature of the *huqqim* in light of their Sabian mythic background that distinguishes them.

IV

Thusfar I have suggested two explanations for why Scripture, the rabbis, and Maimonides conceal or obscure the reasons for the *huqqim* in
their respective works. Both of these are related to the external reasons
for the *huqqim*: their role as a means toward communal welfare, including the intellectual well-being of the community. There is, however, one
additional, more speculative, possible explanation for their concealment, which is due to a problem posed by their internal reason: their
purpose insofar as they teach or convey "wisdom that is useful for
beliefs concerned with the truth as it is" (I:Intro.:12). Maimonides gestures toward this internal reason when he mentions the "temple of intellectual forms," which we linked to the Neoplatonic orientation of Sabianism and its root doctrine, astrology. That is, this last problem posed
by the reason for the *huqqim* refers to "Sabianism" used as a label primarily for the more magical, hermetic school of Neoplatonism of Maimonides' own day whose doctrines were used in the service of astrology.[45] The internal reason of the *huqqim* is to deny these Neoplatonic
views and their astrological consequences. The problem posed by this
reason for Maimonides results from the fact that his own metaphysics
also rests on Neoplatonic theses.[46] Hence, he needs some criterion to distinguish his own "true" brand of Neoplatonism that serves (in part) as
the foundation of the Law from the false conception of Neoplatonism
that he believes is used to underpin astrology. However, given his skepticism about the possibility of human knowledge of metaphysics, Maimonides has no intellectual criterion to distinguish the one from the
other.[47] Under these circumstances, it may be better not to reveal reasons
that raise more questions than one can answer. Hence, their concealment.

To spell this out in more detail, let me first explain the grounds for
Maimonides' skepticism about the possibility of human knowledge of
metaphysics and, in particular, knowledge of purely immaterial forms
and their actions. Recall that knowledge in the strict Aristotelian sense
(other than direct apprehension of the forms) requires demonstration by
the intellect—where what is, and can be, demonstrated must be sharply
distinguished from what is simply *imagined* to be demonstrated. For the
imagination is a source of falsehood or, if you will, myth as opposed to
science, the object of the intellect. Now, one obstacle to metaphysical
knowledge lies in the fact that we do not possess a criterion by which
we can differentiate between the intellect and imagination or "between
that which is imagined and that which is cognized by the intellect"
(III:15:460–61). We lack such a criterion because knowledge, or intellectual cognition, requires a representation of the object of cognition.

However, the capacity whereby the intellect "forms" representations (even in internal speech, or thought) is mediated by the imagination which, because it is a bodily faculty, can conceive only of things that are themselves bodies or bodily.[48] Hence, the intellect cannot represent to itself an object of knowledge (like a separate intellect or the deity) that is purely immaterial, or nonbodily, without *making* it into—that is, without representing it to itself *as if* it were—a body of some kind, however abstract, for example, a substratum (or essence) possessing attributes or something that acts only mechanically or by way of bodily contact. Purported representations of purely immaterial forms therefore necessarily *mis*represent them. But if they misrepresent their object, they are false and, if they are false, they cannot be an object of knowledge.[49]

Now, Maimonides' case against Sabian astrology rests on the possibility of distinguishing its false claims—namely, that the stars "cause" not-purely-material or mechanical phenomena, for example, human actions, knowledge, and character traits—from true (and demonstrable) claims about both the genuine causal effects of the spheres and heavens on material and mechanical sublunar phenomena and the "causal" powers of the separate intellects, as elaborated in Aristotelian physics and metaphysics. I put *cause* (in the last clause) in quotation marks because, as Maimonides emphasizes, "causation" strictly speaking refers only to a relation that holds between bodies (II:12:277–80). For the nonbodily actions of the separate intellects and deity on the upper and lower worlds (or on each other), Maimonides instead uses the Arabic term *fayd*, which was used to translate the Neoplatonist notion (in English translation) of emanation, efflux, or (in Pines's translation) overflow.[50] Originally, Maimonides tells us, this term *fayd/overflow* was applied to the nonbodily actions of the separate intellects and of the Creator. "Sometimes," he goes on, it was also "applied in Hebrew to God."[51] Unfortunately, however, this was not the end of the history of the word. From the incorporeal separate intellects, or angels, the term was then illegitimately transferred to "the forces of the spheres," because of which it was also said that the sphere itself and the stars overflow—even though all their actions proceed from bodies (ibid.). "From there," Maimonides concludes, "astrology [or literally, as Pines adds in a note, "the judgments of the stars"] comes in" (II:12:280). Thus, the same term *fayd/overflow* came to be used indifferently, though illegitimately, for the actions of the separate intellects, deity, spheres, and stars.[52]

We can see a similar ambiguity in the use of the term *fayd/overflow* in accounts of prophetic revelation in the *Guide*. As is well known, Maimonides' own position is that "the true reality and quiddity of prophecy consists in its being an overflow overflowing from God . . . through the intermediation of the Active Intellect, toward the rational faculty in the first place and thereafter toward the imaginative faculty" (II:36:369). Yet he also reports how the Sabians use the same word *fayd/overflow* to describe the actions of the stars in their own descriptons of prophecy. The Sabians "set up statues . . . and *thought* that the forces of the planets *overflowed* toward these statues and . . . gave prophetic revelation to people . . . Similarly, they *said* of the trees assigned to the various planets that . . . the spirit of that planet *overflowed* toward that tree, [and] gave prophetic revelation to people" (III:29:517; my emphasis). Here, as in II:12, it is precisely because the Sabians adopt the same language as the philosophers for their astrological notions that Maimonides needs some criterion to distinguish the proper emanatory power that issues from God and the separate intellects in true prophecy from the merely purported emanatory power of the stars in the Sabians' spurious brand of prophecy. Likewise, in order to justifiably distinguish true prophecy—"that Law [that] is called by us divine Law"—from false prophecy—"the other political regimens, such as the nomoi of the Greeks and the ravings of the Sabians and of others" (II:40:381)—Maimonides must have a criterion to distinguish proper, intellectually demonstrable emanation from emanation that is merely imagined. But as he states in III:15, he has no such criterion.

Maimonides' use of *fayd/overflow* to describe Sabian prophecy should not be dismissed as little more than a report of the Sabians' own claims. Nor should the popular extension of *fayd/overflow* to designate the material actions of the sphere and stars simply be discounted as imprudent usage (encouraged perhaps by the tacit admission, in medieval Aristotelian science, of action at a distance to account for the physical causation of the planets).[53] Maimonides himself argues that these improper uses of *fayd/overflow* are unavoidable: that it is impossible for us to distinguish true from spurious *fayd*/overflow because *we* are unable to represent the distinction between the two kinds of actions of the separate intellects and of the stars. Maimonides writes as follows about the term *fayd/overflow*:

> Nothing is more fitting as a simile to the action of one that is separate from matter than this expression . . . *For we are not capable of finding the true reality of a term that would correspond to the true reality of the notion.* For the mental representation of the action of one who is separate from matter is very difficult, in a way similar to the difficulty of the mental representation of the existence of one who is separate from matter. For just as the imagination cannot represent to itself an existent other than a body or a force in a body, the imagination cannot represent to itself an action taking place otherwise than through the immediate contact of an agent or at a certain distance and from one particular direction . . . All this follows imagination which is also in

true reality the *evil impulse.* For every deficiency of reason or character is due to the action of the imagination or consequent upon its
action. (II:12:279–80; my emphasis)[54]

In other words, our powers of representation are dependent on the
imagination, a bodily faculty that can only represent bodies. Hence, we
cannot correctly represent that which is completely nonbodily or immaterial, namely, the immaterial "actions" of immaterial entities, like the
separate intellects, as distinct from the material actions of the stars. And
if our powers of representation cannot sharply distinguish the intellectually apprehensible overflow of the separate intellects and deity from
the so-called but really only imagined overflow of the stars and spheres,
then Maimonides also has no clear way of distinguishing astrology, the
object of the imagination, from philosophical metaphysics, the object of
the intellect.[55] Nor does he have a criterion to distinguish divine
prophecy and its product, the Mosaic Law, from the products of false
prophecy like Greek nomoi or the "ravings of the Sabians."[56]

Maimonides recognizes not only the impossibility of a correct representation of the purely nonmaterial and that a shift to emanatory
notions for bodily causal interactions is unavoidable. He also recognizes
the dangerous consequences that will follow. Referring to the causal
effects of the spheres on sublunar material phenomena, Maimonides
freely describes this relation using emanatory language: "Know that
there is a consensus of all the philosophers to the effect that the governance of this lower world is perfected by means of the forces *overflowing* to it from the sphere . . . and that the spheres apprehend and know
that which they govern" (II:5:260; my emphasis). However, in the very
sentence that follows this Maimonides moves to counter the obvious
objectionable consequences that might be drawn, especially because his
spheres are animate and possess intellects. Interpreting the last clause of
Deut. 4:19 as "expounding" the same idea, he states that this "means
that He made the spheres intermediaries for the governance of the created beings and *not for a view to their being worshipped*" (ibid., pp.
260–61). That is: *despite* the fact that the spheres are said by Scripture
itself to govern and rule, which in turn requires that they have knowledge of what they govern, they should nonetheless not be worshipped—
contra Sabianism and astrology. But the question remains whether Maimonides in fact has an argument to back up the difference he wishes to
maintain.

Finally, the problematic implications that follow from the impossibility of human knowledge of metaphysics—the absence of a criterion to
distinguish the true *fayd*/overflow of the separate intellects, which
underlies the metaphysics of the Law, from the spurious *fayd*/overflow
of the stars, which underlies astrology—may explain two curious aspects

of the *Guide*. First, it is striking how little Maimonides explicitly says in the way of philosophical critique of astrology in the *Guide*—indeed there is only the one sentence quoted earlier—despite his well-known opposition familiar from his more popular writings. However, once we recognize the problematic implications for Maimonides' own metaphysics and the Law that follow from the lack of a criterion to distinguish the two kinds of *fayd*/overflow, we can understand, perhaps, why he does not take on astrology openly and at length.[57]

Second, there is Maimonides' excessive fascination with the Sabian fables in III:29 and III:37. The same author who tells us that "the diction of this Treatise has not been chosen at haphazard, but with great exactness and exceeding precision" (I:Introduction:15), the same author who emphasizes the care with which he chooses every word, the same author goes on, page after page, in two of the longest chapters in the *Guide*, recounting these ridiculous, literally incredible Sabian myths. And despite the general prohibition against reading compositions on idolatry for fear that one might "incline after them,"[58] Maimonides also proudly tells us

> I have read in all matters concerning all of idolatry, so that it seems to me there does not remain in the world a composition on this subject, having been translated into Arabic from other languages, but that I have read it and have understood its subject matter and have plumbed the depth of its thought. [59]

Why the preoccupation with this literature? And why does Maimonides repeatedly draw our attention to his own preoccupation with it?

I want to suggest that Maimonides' point in dwelling at such length on these stories is to "refute" Sabianism—by which I take him to mean here not only the historical Sabians but also contemporary Neoplatonist astrology, magic, and popular religion—by holding up the example of its own literature for ridicule. That this is Maimonides' true intention becomes clear from his comment on the Sabian fables: "It is a wonder that people who think that the world is eternal should at the same time believe in these things that are impossible in nature for those who have knowledge of the speculation on nature" (III:29:516). In other words, the Sabians who believe both in the eternity of the world and in astrology and magic do not have the faintest understanding of the difference between the necessary and the impossible. This criticism is ad hominem, not a philosophical refutation of the sort Maimonides ascribes to the patriarch Abraham, the biblical philosopher who attacked the Harranian Sabians by reason. Instead it is an attack on Sabianism by ridicule, like the way Maimonides describes how his namesake, the biblical Moses, "commanded killing these people, wiping out their traces, and tearing out their roots" (III:29:517).[60] However, Maimonides has no alternative. He lacks a demonstration by the intellect that would *justify* a philosophical refutation of this kind of Sabianism. The potential consequences were it to become generally known that he lacks a criterion to distinguish Sabianism from his own philosophical metaphysics are highly volatile. Undesirable as it is, he must have thought, nothing less than this violent tactic is necessary to put an end to this form of idolatry and its astrological myths.

V

Maimonides' skeptical worries prompted by astrology, or "Sabianism," did not occupy his readers—including his own increasingly Averroistically influenced followers—in the post-Maimonidean thirteenth-century world of Christian Spain and Provence. As we mentioned earlier, many of his contemporaries and successors also did not share his negative opinion of astrology. However, his reconceptualization of the *huqqim*—from arbitrary divine commandments lacking reasons into problematic commandments whose reasons are not publicly revealed—nonetheless transformed the way these commandments were interpreted and explained by the next generation of scholars engaged in *ta'amei ha-mitzvot*. In the remaining sections of this chapter, I will trace the impact of Maimonides on the foremost among these *nach*-Maimonideans, Nahmanides, whose attitude toward astrology was the exact opposite of that of his predecessor. What I shall argue now is that Nahmanides adopts the structure of Maimonides' idea of a *hoq* to express a diametrically opposed content.

Like Maimonides, Nahmanides explicitly rejects the idea—that he finds in the Ashkenazic tradition of RaSHI—that the *huqqim* are arbitrary "royal decrees that have no reason" (*gezerot melekh she'ein ta'am ledavar*). Instead the *huqqim* are called "divine decrees" because they are "decrees that the king legislates in his kingdom without revealing their benefit to the people and from which the people do not benefit"; rather the people "think ill of the [king] in their hearts and accept [the *huqqim*] out of royal fear."[61] Here, following Maimonides, Nahmanides doubly qualifies the traditional rabbinic characterization of the *huqqim*. First, instead of seeing them as lacking reasons or as irrational laws, he makes them into laws whose reasons are not *known* or *revealed*. Second, those who do not know their reasons are specifically the "people" (*'am*) or "multitude" (*hamon*), implying that their reasons *are* known to the "counsellors of the king," figures like Moses and Solomon. Where Maimonides and Nahmanides differ concerns their respective explanations for the concealment of the reasons for the *huqqim*.

Maimonides' worries about the potential antinomian consequences that might be drawn from his explanation of the *huqqim* in terms of their extrascriptural Sabian context of legislation do not concern Nahmanides. The source of his worry about antinomianism is indeed the very opposite. Commenting on Lev. 26, 15, he explains that precisely because the reasons for the *huqqim* are not revealed to the multitude, they tend to hold them in contempt, saying "Why would God want me not to wear this garment woven of wool and linen?" or "Why should it benefit us if we burn the [red] heifer and sprinkle its ashes on us?" Here it is ignorance rather than knowledge of their reasons that is said to make the multitude, or people in general, despise or want to reject the *huqqim*.[62]

As for the use of extrascriptural historical information to explain the Mosaic commandments, it is true that Nahmanides does not appeal to historical explanations nearly as often as Maimonides. But he also never objects in principle to their use and he himself employs historical explanations, either in his own or Maimonides' name, either when he lacks a better account or when he wishes to supplement a more general reason to explain a detail. For example, Nahmanides appeals to Maimonides' explanation in terms of Sabian practices to explain the prohibition of leaven and honey and the requirement of salt in the sacrificial cult (C Lev. 2, 11); he uses the fact that ancient priests wore cultic magical garments (based on *Guide* III:37) to explain the prohibition of *sha'atnez* (C Lev. 19, 19); and he tells a similar story for the prohibition of *'orlah*, the forbidden fruit of a tree in its first three years (C Lev. 19, 23). In all these examples, the Maimonidean explanation is that the biblical commandment counters the idolatrous practice by prescribing its opposite; none employ Maimonides' more sophisticated idea of accommodation to idolatrous practice as a way of gradually weaning the people away from paganism. I'll return to Nahmanides' view of this second model of Maimonidean historical explanation in a moment.

Where Nahmanides sharply objects to Maimonides' appeal to historical reasons for commandments is where the scriptural text itself gives a reason Maimonides ignores in favor of the extrascriptural explanation. For Nahmanides, history has a place in explanation and interpretation, but it must always be subordinate to the words of the Torah. To appeal to an extrascriptural historical explanation when the Torah itself explicitly gives a nonhistorical reason for a commandment is to set up an independent and, we might add, naturalistic source of knowledge—the evidence of history—apart from and superior to the Torah. Not only does this impugn the very status of the Torah.[63] According to Nahmanides, the Torah is also encyclopedic—"*Torat ha-shem temimah*": it contains or encompasses *all* knowledge and wisdom.[64]

Therefore, if there were such an external source of historical knowledge, the Torah would not be "complete," containing all knowledge. Either the historical reason must be incorrect, and not the content of knowledge, or it ought to be given in, or discoverable from, the text of the Torah.

Perhaps the most striking example of this type is Nahmanides' discussion of the prohibition not to eat of the blood of slaughtered animals and of the commandment to cover the blood of wild beasts or birds with earth (Lev. 17; Deut. 12). According to Maimonides (III:46), the reasons for these and related laws are based on the historical fact that the Sabians held blood to be impure but also the food of devils, or the jinn. The Sabians consequently believed that they could fraternize with the jinn and learn the future from them by eating blood or near pools of blood. Therefore, the Torah declared, first, that blood is pure rather than impure; second, that it must be poured or sprinkled on the altar as part of sacrifical and purification rites; and, third, that the blood of all wild beasts and birds must be covered rather than left in open pools in the fields. Now, in both his commentaries on Lev. 17, 11 and Deut. 12, 22, Nahmanides explicitly recounts Maimonides' explanation.[65] But in his commentary on Leviticus, Nahmanides adds: "And these are fitting words (*devarim meyushavim*), but the verses do not so teach; for they always state that the reason for the prohibition is [the verse] 'for the life of all flesh is its blood'" (C Lev. 17, 14). He then goes on to give two alternative explications of the latter verse. The first claims that the prohibition on blood, which was assumed to be the locus of life in its bearer, is a trace of the original Adamic prohibition against eating any other animate creature.[66] The second (which follows the "ways of the Greeks," i.e., philosophers) argues that one is what one eats: since the locus of the life, or better identity, of a creature is in its blood, if one were permitted to eat the blood of animals, she would run the risk of becoming or taking on characteristics of the consumed thing. Now, despite his criticism of Maimonides, it should be noted that the contents of both of these latter reasons go considerably beyond what the "verse teaches," at least literally. However, they still have significantly more of a basis in Scripture than the Maimonidean explanation. The reason Nahmanides rejects Maimonides' historical reason is not, then, because of its historical content per se but because, unlike his own two reasons, it has *no* basis in the scriptural text. One might say that Nahmanides' two reasons are or are closer to *peshat*, although his conception of *peshat* must now be taken to be considerably richer and more variagated than the idea of the "literal meanings of words," subsuming philosophy and medicine as well.[67] On this view, Nahmanides rejects Maimonides' historical reason because it is not *peshat* where there is an an available explanation based on the *peshat*.

In his commentary on Deut. 12, 22, Nahmanides further qualifies his rejection of Maimonides' historical reason. He repeats his claim that the historical explanation cannot be the "main reason (*'iqar ta'am*) for the prohibition on [consuming] blood because Scripture explains its reason, namely, that "the blood is the life." But he now adds that the historical explanation *is* the reason the Torah *repeatedly* warns the Israelites not to consume blood and why it *emphasizes*: "But make sure [*rak hazak*] that you do not partake of the blood" (Deut. 12, 23). Here, again, there is no in principle objection to the use of historical information as explanans. Nahmanides only dissents from Maimonides on the specific focus of the explanandum. Indeed, in yet a third commentary, on Lev. 19, 26, a verse in which the prohibition on the consumption of blood is linked directly to prohibitions on divination, sooth-saying, and other magical and idolatrous practices, Nahmanides not only cites the Sabian practice as *the* reason for the prohibition; without even attributing it to Maimonides, he says that "according to the *peshat*, [eating blood] was one of the kinds of magic or divination because that is what we can infer about its explanation from its context [*ki hu davar lameid mi-'inyano*]" (Lev. 19, 26). Here Nahmanides' conception of *peshat* has been enriched to include the very same historical information that was excluded as the reason for the prohibition in the earlier context (Lev. 17). The only difference between the two verses is that in the latter an explicit scriptural reason is also given, displacing the historical reason.[68]

Nahmanides does not, then, object to Maimonides' general use of history for ta'amei ha-mitzvot so long as it remains subordinate to the scriptural text itself. Indeed, going even further than Maimonides, he does not conceal reasons that exploit the historical context in which the Torah was originally legislated. Yet, borrowing from Maimonides, Nahmanides also claims that the *huqqim* are *problematic*—and problematic rather than mysterious—that is, laws whose reasons are simply beyond or too deep for human comprehension. Furthermore, he shares the Maimonidean view that there is a deep connection between these commandments and astrology or the stars, the root doctrines of the Sabians. Now, for Maimonides what ties all these together—the problematicity of the *huqqim*, astrology, history, and the Sabians—is the idea that the Torah legislates the *huqqim* to deny astrology because it is radically false, and it adopts particular forms for commandments because they are modelled closely after the Sabian practices they aim to undermine— all of this despite the danger of making the Law highly contingent on historical circumstances. For Nahmanides, for whom astrology is *true*, what connects these various elements and what renders the *huqqim* problematic?

In his main discussion of the *huqqim* in his *Commentary on the Torah*, on the law of the scapegoat (Lev. 16, 8), Nahmanides quotes (with slight variation) the classic tannaitic passage on the *huqqim*, also cited by Maimonides (repeated here):

> "And these are my statutes (*huqqotai*)": These are things that I have prescribed for you (*huqqim shehaqqaqti likha*), about which you have not permission to think (*leharher*), which Satan denounces (*mekattereq*) and the Gentiles refute (*hagoyim meshivin aleihem*). And they are as follows: wearing wool and linen [garments] (*sha'atnez*), [the burning of] the red heifer, and sending forth the scapegoat. (BT *Yoma* 67b)

He then comments:

> And the rabbis [who authored this statement] did not attribute to the idolators a criticism of us concerning sacrifices because they are offered on the altar of God; they criticize us [only] for the scapegoat because they think that we are performing an action like their actions."[69]

Nahmanides does not name the author who held the view that he denies was the rabbis', namely, the view that *all* sacrifices are *huqqim*. But there is only one person he could have in mind: Maimonides, taking into account both his general explanation of sacrifices in the *Guide* and his *pesak halakhah* in the *Mishneh Torah* (repeated here), which affirms exactly what Nahmanides rejects: "All the sacrifices are in the category of *huqqim*" (MT *"Me'ilah"* viii, 8). Nahmanides denies that *all* sacrifices are *huqqim* for the reason that they are not commandments of the kind that the "Gentiles refute (*hagoyim meshivin aleihem*)." The reason they cannot be so refuted, he says, is because sacrifices are "offered on the altar of God." Hence, they will not be mistaken for idolatry. Only the scapegoat which is not offered on the altar in the Temple *looks like* idolatrous worship, "an act like their actions," and therefore counts as a *hoq*. Here we have a first stab at Nahmanides' general characterization of a *hoq*: a commandment that *looks like* a prohibited act, a commandment that makes the Law vulnerable to the criticism that it commands what it itself prohibits—in particular, that it is no different from idolatry.

There is also a hermeneutic difference between Nahmanides' idea of a *hoq* and Maimonides'. We noted earlier, in section III, that the enumeration of four or five commandments that follows the rabbinic characterization of the *huqqim* can be interpreted in two ways: either as a definitive list of the extension of the concept of a *hoq* or as representative examples of much broader classes of commandments, all of which would be *huqqim*. Maimonides, we argued, takes the second tack, boldly making the mode of explanation of the *huqqim* exemplary of the

Law as a whole, or at least of large blocs of commandments. Thus, the scapegoat is representative of all sacrifices (or at least burnt offerings), the red heifer of the laws of purity, sha'atnez of all prohibitions on crossbreeding. In contrast, Nahmanides' interpretation of the tannaitic passage is a conservative reaction to Maimonides' liberal reading. In this respect it is also typical of his general exegetical method, which is more sensitive than Maimonides' to the details of the Torah and less willing to sacrifice, or explain away, the messy complications that resist an elegant, philosophically systematic theory.[70] Here, for example, he focuses on the fact that the rabbis single out the scapegoat, which is prima facie hardly representative of sacrifice in general. The question he asks himself is, What *distinguishes* the scapegoat from other sacrifices to render it a *hoq*?

We can see a similar approach in his commentary on Lev. 19, 19, where he criticizes RaSHI for categorizing all prohibitions on interbreeding (including planting diverse seeds together and grafting trees) as *huqqim*: "The rabbis mentioned that its reason is hidden and that the Evil Inclination and the Nations of the World would refute it only with respect to *sha'atnez*, not with respect to the interbreeding of animals." The same criticism could have been levelled against Maimonides who generalizes from the single example of *sha'atnez* to most agricultural laws in the Torah, which he claims were instituted to counter Sabian agricultural practices connected to star worship. According to Nahmanides, *sha'atnez* is not representative of the agricultural laws in general; hence, we should focus on the reason the rabbis selected it alone.

As we shall see, the four or five examples in the list of *huqqim* in the original tannaitic passage will turn out, even according to Nahmanides, not to be absolutely exclusive and unique. In addition to the scapegoat, Nahmanides gives a similar reason for the red heifer, the (sacrificial) bird of the leper, the calf whose neck is broken (*'eglah 'arufah*), and three or four other sacrificial-like rites that are performed outside the camp or Temple precincts. Nonetheless, on Nahmanides' account, the *huqqim* remain a small class of commandments and, hence, an exception to the rule rather than, as they are for Maimonides, representative of the commandments in general.

Underlying Maimonides' and Nahmanides' different interpretive approaches are, however, very different substantive interpretations of the *huqqim*. To put these into focus, I shall now turn to Nahmanides' critique of Maimonides' reason for sacrifice and his own positive explanation of these commandments. Against this background, it will become clear what, on his account, makes commandments like the scapegoat problematic.

VI

In his commentary on Lev. 1, 9, on the burnt offering ['*olah*], Nahmanides presents one of his most vigorous and vituperative critiques of Maimonides focused on his explanation of sacrifice:

> Now in this verse there is the reason for the sacrifices: that they are "an offering made by fire, of a sweet savour to the Lord" (Lev. 1, 9). And the Rabbi [Maimonides] said in the *Guide of the Perplexed* [III:46:581–82] that the reason for the sacrifices is that the Egyptians and Chaldeans [*Khasdim*], in whose lands Israel were strangers and sojourners, always worshipped cattle and sheep, for the Egyptians worship the sheep and the Chaldeans worship the demons (*sheidim*) which appear to them in the shape of goats. And the people of India to this day will never slaughter cattle. For this reason [Scripture] commanded that they slaughter these three species to the Revered Name so that it be made known that the thing that [the Egyptians and Chaldeans] thought was the greatest transgression is what should be offered to the Creator, and through it sins will be atoned. In this way evil beliefs that are the sickness of the soul are cured because sickness and illness are cured only by their opposites. These are [Maimonides'] words, and he elaborated on them at length. Now, they are nonsense; they cure a great hurt and major difficulty superficially. They make the table of God despised, for its purpose is not only to remove [evil beliefs] from the hearts of the wicked and the fools of the world [i.e., the Egyptians and Chaldeans]. And Scripture states that [sacrifices] are "provision, an offering made by fire, of a sweet savour to the Lord." And, furthermore, the sickness of the Egyptians, according to their nonsense, will not be cured by this; rather the disease will be increased. For the intention of the aforementioned evil ones was to worship the constellation Aries [lamb] and the constellation Taurus [bull] which they think have power over them. Therefore they will not eat [sheep and bulls] out of honor to their power and their strength [*yesod*]. But if they sacrifice them to the Revered Name, that is a way of honoring and respecting them, and they themselves so act; as it is said: "And they shall no more offer their sacrifices to the satyrs [*si'irim*; lit: goats]" (Lev. 17, 7), and those who made the [Golden] Calf sacrificed to it. And the Rabbi [Maimonides] mentions that they used to sacrifice to the moon on the days of the new moon and to the sun in its ascent in the constellations known to them in their books. But the sickness would be better cured if we were to eat of them to our satisfaction, which is forbidden to them and despised in their eyes and something they would never do. Now, when Noah went out of the ark with his three sons, there were no Chaldeans or Egyptians in the world, and yet he offered a sacrifice and it found favor in the eyes of the Lord. And [Scripture] says concerning that: "And God smelled the sweet savour" (Gen. 8, 21) and, as a result, "He said in his heart: I

will not again curse the ground any more for man's sake" (Gen. 8, 21). "And Abel also brought of the firstlings of his flock and the fat parts thereof. And the Lord had respect for Abel and his offering" (Gen. 4, 4–5)—and there was not yet a trace of idolatry in the world. And Balaam said: "I have prepared the seven altars, and I have offered upon every altar a bullock and a ram" (Num. 23, 4). And his intention then was not to deny [his] evil beliefs and he was not commanded concerning that; but he did so in order to approach God so that the [divine] speech would reach him. And the [scriptural] language concerning sacrifices is: "My offering, the provision of my sacrifices made by fire, for a sweet savour to me" (Num. 28, 2). And Heaven forbid that there should be no benefit and no desired end [from sacrifice] but only the denial of idolatry from the opinions of fools.

Nahmanides' critique of Maimonides rests on three main claims. First, he repeats three times that Scripture itself gives the reason for sacrifice, implying that Maimonides' main mistake was to ignore Scripture's own internal explanation of its commandment. Yet he does not criticize Maimonides for using extrascriptural historical information per se. Second, he attacks the descriptive adequacy of Maimonides' explanation: it fails to apply to many of the narratives involving sacrifice found in the Torah. Third, he challenges its explanatory power, the degree to which sacrifice could effectively succeed as a cure for the disease of Sabianism.[71] But what is most striking about Nahmanides' critique—as Maimonides' medieval apologists, most notably, the RiTBaH, R. Yom Tov b. Abraham Al-Ishbili, already noted in his *Sefer HaZikaron*—is that it radically misrepresents Maimonides' general explanation of sacrifice, or so it appears.[72] Maimonides never claims that the reason for sacrifice is to change the beliefs of the Sabians (to whom Nahmanides, following Al-Harizi's translation of the *Guide*, refers as Chaldeans) or of the Egyptians. The aim of sacrifice is to reform the Israelites, to wean *them* away from the star worship to which they were accustomed, albeit because of their Sabian environment, and to bring them to belief in the one deity. As a reading of the *Guide*, either Nahmanides' interpretation shows extreme carelessness—which is unlikely given his many other insightful and subtle readings—or more is going on than meets the eye.

I will return immediately to the second alternative. But I would also like to suggest that Nahmanides' reading, while surely misleading, may not be as far off-target as some of Maimonides' medieval defenders like Al-Ishbili assume. It is true that the *immediate* function of sacrifice is to free the Israelites, not Gentiles, from the bonds of star worship and idolatry. However, Maimonides also indicates that the *ultimate* end of the *huqqim* is to reeducate not only Israel but also the Gentiles. To those who deny that the commandments have reasons, he replies with the verse: "Which shall hear all these statutes [*huqqim*] and say: Surely this great community is a wise and understanding people" (Deut. 6, 24), on which he comments: "Thus it states explicitly that even all the statutes [*huqqim*] will show to all the nations that they have been given with wisdom and understanding" (III:31:524). Now, the *huqqim*, we have argued, are commandments whose purpose is to reject and deny idolatry. Therefore, if the nations of the world acknowledge the *wisdom* of the *huqqim*, not only do they acknowledge that even those commandments that are typically believed to have no reason in fact do have a reason; they must also acknowledge the wisdom, or correctness, of the reason, namely, the falsity of idolatry. The ultimate end of the *huqqim* will be, then, to bring the "nations of the world," the archetypical idolators, to acknowledge the falsity of idolatry. This text, perhaps, is what led Nahmanides to read Maimonides' argument as he does.[73]

Nahmanides' misreading of Maimonides is not the only puzzling aspect of his discussion of sacrifice. After criticizing Maimonides, he goes on to endorse two reasons of his own. The first is what I have called its (parabolic) external reason—the reason whereby the commandment contributes to the practical and theoretical welfare of the community—and the second, its internal reason—whereby performance of the commandment serves to satisfy, complete, or perfect the deity or divine nature. I shall return to the internal reason; about its external reason, he writes:

> It is more fitting to accept the reason given for [sacrifices] that because the deeds of people are fulfilled through thought, speech, and action, God commanded that when one sins and brings a sacrifice; he should lay his hands on it corresponding to [*keneged*] the [sinful] action; confess with his mouth corresponding to the [sinful] speech; burn in fire the intestine and kidneys, which are the instruments of thought and desire, and the lower parts of the thighs, corresponding to the hands and legs of people that do their work; and sprinkle blood on the altar corresponding to the blood in their soul. Thus the person will think when he performs all of these that he has sinned against his God with his body and soul and that it is fitting for him to pour his own blood and consume in fire his own body were it not for the lovingkindness (*hesed*) of the Creator who took a substitute (*temurah*) [from him]. And this sacrifice will atone [for him]: its blood in place of his blood, soul for soul, the major limbs of the sacrifice in place of his major limbs, and the portions [given as gifts to the priests] to provide for the teachers of the Law in order that they will pray on his behalf. And [similarly] the daily offering is in order that the community will be saved from constantly sinning. These words are pleasing and attractive like sayings of Aggadah.

It is generally assumed that Nahmanides' source for this explanation is Abraham ibn Ezra who writes that the reason for "the burnt-offering and [other kinds of] sacrifice is that by giving each part [or: by each part's giving] at its time, the part which has a part [or: share] in the world to come is saved. Therefore the exegesis of *le-khaper* [to atone] is 'to pay ransom' [*kofer*]."[74] Both authors try to explain why certain parts, limbs, or organs of the animal are sacrificed by drawing some kind of connection with the corresponding part, limb, or organ of the owner of the sacrifice. Furthermore, although Nahmanides does not explicitly interpret *le-khaper* in terms of *kofer*, or ransom, it closely resembles his idea that a sacrifice is a *temurah*, exchange or substitute, for its owner. However, there is also one significant difference between the two. Ibn Ezra appeals to a theurgic effect of the parts of the sacrificed animal on higher astral forces, and the efficacy of the sacrifice is also said to depend on its timing. Neither of these astrological motifs enter into Nahmanides' account; instead he locates the power of sacrifice in its psychological effect on its owner's thought and attitudes, in the emotions of self-sacrifice and self-judgment that it evokes through the owner's reflection on the symbolism of its elements.

Although it is undeniable that Nahmanides draws on ibn Ezra, I want to suggest that there may be an additional, complementary source for Nahmanides' explanation: Maimonides' reason for sin offerings in the *Guide* III:46:589, the passage we discussed earlier and with which Nahmanides would have been well acquainted, since it belongs to the same chapter as the passage he openly criticizes.[75] Spelling out how the sacrifice is meant to bring its offerer to a "passion for repentance," Maimonides says:

> [T]he end of all these actions [i.e., the various sin sacrifices] is to establish firmly in the soul of every disobedient individual the constant need for remembering and making mention of his sin . . . and that he, his descendants, and the descendants of his descendants, must seek foregiveness for the sin by an act of obedience belonging to the same species as the act of disobedience. I mean by this that if the act of disobedience was in connection with property, he must extend his property in the act of obedience. If the act of disobedience consists in corporeal pleasures, he must weary and afflict his body by means of fasting and awakening at night . . . This was done . . . in the case of Aaron: for when he went astray in the action of the [golden] calf, it was prescribed that he and those of his descendants who would replace him, should sacrifice a bullock and a calf. When the act of disobedience concerned a kid of goats, the act of obedience also concerned a kid of goats. When these notions are consolidated in the soul, this leads without any doubt necessarily to one's taking a grave view of the act of disobedience and to an avoidance of it, so that the individual in

question will not, by stumbling into it, be in need of a long and unpleasant quest for foregiveness, which sometimes may not be achieved. Accordingly he will avoid and flee from the act of disobedience from the outset. (III:46:589)

Where Maimonides differs here from ibn Ezra is in the significance he assigns to the correspondence between the parts or features of the sacrificed animal, on the one side, and of the sin committed or of the person who brings the sacrifice, on the other. For ibn Ezra, as we said, the significance lies in the astral effects on the person of the corresponding sacrificial parts. For Maimonides it lies in its psychological impact. By coming to appreciate the severity of the sin he committed through the symbolic significance of certain features and aspects of the sacrifice, the person's attitude toward his act of disobedience changes. This psychological function of the sacrifice through a change of attitude is also largely preventive: as an effect of the sacrifice, the individual will "avoid and flee from the act of disobedience from the outset." This preventive theme is not explicit in Nahmanides' explanation but it must surely be on the mind of the individual as he sees the blood of the sacrificial animal poured on the altar and its body consumed in fire as a "substitute" for himself.

In sum, Nahmanides' stance toward Maimonides in these two passages is full of ambiguity. In the one case, Nahmanides seems to want to distance himself as far as possible from Maimonides, although it remains unclear whether he deliberately misrepresents or simply misunderstands the *Guide*. In the other case, Nahmanides' own explanation is surprisingly close to Maimonides', possibly even indebted to it. Nor is this complex discussion of sacrifices an isolated case of Nahmanides' obscure relation to Maimonides.[76] What I would like to suggest on a speculative note, to explain Nahmanides' ambivalent, tense relation to Maimonides, is that it reflects his own ambivalent, tense position in the Maimonidean Controversy.[77] The explanation of sacrifice Nahmanides attacks is a caricature of Maimonides' position, a possibly popular version of which Nahmanides could afford to be highly critical while assuming that his careful reader would know that this was not Maimonides' true position. At the same time, while Nahmanides knowingly adopts some of Maimonides' positions, he does not advertise it. Put a bit differently, Nahmanides may have wished to distance himself openly from some of the most radical of Maimonides' conclusions (or what they were commonly believed to be) while, or perhaps *because*, he also knew the degree to which his own explanations were in fact indebted to him. In language Nahmanides uses in his introduction to the *Commentary on the Torah* to describe his relation to another commentator, his relation to Maimonides is one of "open rebuke and concealed love." In either case, and most important for us, there is more common ground between the two figures than first meets the eye. It is against this shared background that their difference over the *huqqim* should be judged.

VII

What is problematic for Nahmanides about the scapegoat, we said in section V, is that it *looks like* idolatry. But in order to spell this out, we need to explain what, according to Nahmanides, is wrong with the worship of idols.

We know what Maimonides thinks is wrong with idolatry. Even if the idolator does not believe that the idols themselves, the artificial icons, have power, he believes that they are images of gods or celestial beings who are worthy of worship because they have power over humans. In fact, however, Maimonides argues, these purported beings are powerless or unreal. Therefore, their worship is based on a false and empty presupposition. What is fundamentally wrong with idolatry, then, is that it is founded on a cognitive error of the highest magnitude (I:36:82–83).

For Nahmanides, in contrast, what is wrong with idolatry is not that it is based on a false presupposition about its objects of worship. Just the opposite: idolatry is forbidden (to Israel) *precisely because its objects are real entities and powers.* In his *Commentary* on Exod. 20, 3, Nahmanides describes an elaborate metaphysical hierarchy, consisting of three classes of celestial beings each of which has dominion over certain peoples and places on earth, ranked in an order of power that also corresponds to the chronological order in which their respective kinds of idolatry historically emerged. The first, highest, and earliest objects of idolatry were the immaterial separate intellects, or angels. Some of these were originally believed to have power over specific nations and were therefore worshipped even while their respective nation recognized that there is a deity superior to them. Israel, however, was absolutely forbidden to worship any of these angels because it is the specially treasured people (*segulah*) of God who alone has power over them. Were the people of Israel to worship these "other gods" ['*elohim 'aherim*], it would be tantamount to a rejection of the one God for the others.

The second class of objects of idolatry were the visible heavenly bodies: the sun, moon, stars, and constellations who were also known to have power over specific nations. Unlike the idolatry associated with the first class, this second kind was also theurgic: by worshipping their respective star or constellation, its worshippers believed they could strengthen it and help it "victor" over its rivals, thereby improving their own fortune. These idolators were also the first to make physical shapes and idols whose timing was astrally significant. Through this elementary form of astrology, this brand of theurgic idolatry came to be associated with magic and to include the worship of certain humans whose power seemed closely linked to constellations.

The third species of idolatrous objects were the demons [*sheidim*], a class of spirits [*ruhot*] who, Nahmanides claims, are so-called because they dwell in destroyed or desolate [*shadudim*] places (C Lev. 17, 7). These devils are material but invisible, compounded of fire and air, an ontologically intermediate kind of being with some angelic and some human properties. Thus they eat and drink, especially blood; decompose and die; fly and inhabit the sky; and know the near future (news of which they overhear from higher celestial beings). Like the higher powers, they are also assigned to specific peoples but with dominion only over ruined, wild places where they are empowered only to harm enemies and those who fall victim to them. Nahmanides treats these devils with some contempt, as nouveau deities who lack the power to benefit their worshippers, who were not worshipped by the ancients, and who were "discovered" only by late Egyptian magicians. Yet he thinks they are no less real than the others. Indeed the most important point about all three classes of objects of idolatrous worship is that they are all real beings with real power—which is precisely why they are forbidden to Israel who is commanded to worship only the one God.

Nahmanides offers a similar explanation of the prohibitions against magic and divination. On the one hand, he sharply dismisses Maimonides' view that divination in particular "has absolutely no truth to it, for who will tell the raven or the crane what will be" (C Deut. 18, 9)? Making himself out to be even more of an empiricist than the Aristotelian—no doubt, it is Maimonides whom he has in mind—Nahmanides asks: "How can he deny claims well-known to the eyes of all viewers?"[78] On the other hand, he argues that there is a close ontological dependence between magic and the worship of stars and constellations, the second stage of idolatry during which he claims magic first emerged. According to Nahmanides,

> when God created the world *ex nihilo* He appointed the higher powers to govern the lower ones below, and He placed the earth and everything on it (Neh. 9, 6) in the power of stars and constellations . . . , as is demonstrated in the science of astrology [*hakhmat ha-'itztagninus*]. Furthermore, He placed governors over the stars and constellations: the angels and lords [*sarim*] which are their souls, and their [fixed] motion from the time they first came into being is for eternal duration according to the divine decree which He set out for them. But one of His great wondrous acts was that He put in the capacity of the higher

governors the ways of images [darkei temunot] and capacities to change the behavior of lower things. Thus, if the aspect [mabat] of the stars on the side facing the earth is good or bad for a land or nation or individual, the higher beings can change that very aspect . . . And it was made this way in order that God Himself could "change the times and the seasons" (Dan. 2, 21) . . . to do with them as He wills . . . without changing the nature [tiv'o] of the world and in order that the stars and constellations could continue their movements in their [present] order. (C Deut. 18, 9)

In line with his metaphysical hierarchy, here Nahmanides describes how a higher being governs and controls every creature and being on earth.[79] Furthermore, the lower celestial powers, the stars and constellations, are themselves subject to and governed by higher celestial beings, the angels or separate intellects. All of this is according to a fixed, lawful nature [tev'a] which was created by God to exist in perpetuity. But it is not inviolable or inevitable. Indeed precisely for it to be possible for God Himself to intervene in creation without "changing the nature of the world" and without disrupting the orderly motions of the heavenly bodies, He also instituted ways in which higher beings in the hierarchy could "change the behaviors" of lower things. And this possibility opened up the further opportunity for human magic and the employment by humans of techniques of astral change or theurgy. "The ways of images [of planets] [darkei temunot]" to which Nahmanides refers in the passage quoted was a species of astral magic known in the Middle Ages as horadat ruchaniyut ha-kokhavim, the lowering of the spiritual powers of the stars.[80] He describes, for example, how a person who draws a picture of a certain thing when the moon, stars, and constellation are in certain astral positions, inscribes on it the name of the hour and the angel appointed over that hour, and offers incense to it, will be able to change its aspect [mabat] for better or worse. This use of magic, Nahmanides emphasizes, involves only "the [ordinary] behavior of the moon through the power of its governor"; that is, it does not violate the laws of nature, it only manipulates them. It is based on the "science of astrology" (my emphasis) and indeed, as Nahmanides elsewhere states, all the ancient "sciences [hokhmot] were spiritual [ruhaniyot] [whose subject matter] was the subjects of demons, magicians, and the kinds of incenses offered to the heavenly host."[81] The only difference between the motion and aspect of the moon when it is magically changed through the spiritual sciences of astrology and demonology and its "natural" motion is that the latter is its "simple behavior" [hanhagah peshutah] and its "motion is the will [hefetz] of the Creator . . . while [its magically determined movement] is the opposite." But this difference is sufficient for astral magic to be prohibited. That is, the secret [*sod*] of [the kinds of] magic [*hakeshafim*] and of its power, concerning which [the Rabbis] said that they contradict the celestial host [*pamalyya shel ma'alah*] . . . is that [they] are the opposite of the simple powers [*hakohot hapeshutim*] and they contradict the [celestial] host in some or another way. For this reason, it is fitting for the Torah to prohibit them in order that the world should be left to its regularities and its simple nature that is the will of its Creator.

What is wrong with astral magic and theurgy is not, as Maimonides claimed, that they are unproductive, nonsensical, or vain, based on false beliefs about the powers of the stars and the possibility of changing nature. Instead, magic is productive and effective, derived from true doctrines about the nature of the celestial world and its metaphysical hierarchy of angels, stars, constellations, and even demons. The reason it is prohibited is that, in "contradicting" and subverting the original nature of the world, the magician challenges the deity who created it. Magic is wrong because it is an act of rebellion against the authority of God. By changing the divine, or natural, order of creation, the magician implicates that the world was not divinely created.[82]

VIII

With Nahmanides' conceptions of idolatry and magic in hand, let us now return to the *huqqim*, beginning with the *sa'ir la-'azazel*, the goat sent out to the *'azazel* as part of the cultic rite of the Day of Atonement. What makes this commandment problematic, we said earlier, is that it *looks like* a form of idolatry. We are now in position to make this idea more precise. To begin with, the ritual of the scapegoat, according to Nahmanides, originated in idolatry:

> They used to worship other gods [*'elohim 'aherim*], namely the angels, offering sacrifices to them . . . Now, the Torah absolutely prohibits accepting their divinity [*kabalat 'elohutam*] and any worship of them. However, the Lord commanded that on the Day of Atonement we should send a goat into the desert, to the minister who rules in places of destruction, which is appropriate for him because he is its master and through an emanation [*'azilut*] of his power destruction and ruin follow. For he is the cause of the stars of the sword, blood, wars, feuds, wounds, blows, divisions, and destruction. The principle is that [he] is the soul of the planet Mars [*Ma'adim*]; his portion among the nations is Esau [Rome] for that is the nation whose inheritance is the sword and wars; and among the animals, the he-goats and goats; and also in his portion are the demons [*sheidim*] who are called *mazikin* [destroyers] in the language of the Rabbis and *si'irim* [goats] in the language of Scripture, for both he and his people are called Sa'ir. (C Lev. 16, 8)

Like Maimonides, Nahmanides explains the rite of the scapegoat by situating it in the context of an idolatrous practice prevalent among the ancient Israelites. However, for Nahmanides unlike Maimonides, this earlier practice was not based on a pagan myth—that is, a false belief about gods or other celestial beings.[83] The "other gods" whom they worshipped are, according to Nahmanides, real beings with real powers over lower beings, peoples, and places. Indeed, as we mentioned in the previous section, he identifies some of these particular higher beings with the separate intellects (C Exod. 20, 3), and the specific angel/intellect to whom the scapegoat is addressed—whom Nahmanides also identifies with Sama'el, the midrashic adversary and prosecutor of Israel[84]— is the being who governs Mars, rules Esau (i.e., in medieval typology, the Romans or Christians), and has power over goats, places of destruction, demons, violent forces, and destructive actions. What was wrong with the ancient idolatrous rite from which the ritual of the scapegoat is descended was not its underlying beliefs about the nature and reality of its objects. What was wrong was the fact that these objects were acknowledged or accepted as deities worthy of the prerogative of worship.

There is a second critical difference between Maimonides' and Nahmanides' accounts. Maimonides explains that the *huqqim* were legislated to put an end to idolatrous practices and their underlying system of false astral beliefs. For Nahmanides, the rite of the scapegoat is a mechanism built into the Law to deal constructively with the genuine issues—especially potential harms—that follow from the reality of the astral beings that were illegitimately worshipped by the ancient idolators but whose existence cannot be ignored even by worshippers of the one God. In fact, because these celestial beings have a reality of their own, not only can the Torah not ignore them, it must deal with them on their own terms. This is the full force of the Gentiles' objection that the commandment of the *sa'ir la-'azazel* looks like idolatry. Because the scapegoat is not offered on the altar of God like other sacrifices but instead is sent outside the Temple to the particular domain—a desolate wilderness—where the minister of destruction reigns, the idolators specifically "think that we are performing an action like their actions." Indeed, given its open acknowledgment of the reality and power of this astral being, the most pressing question for Nahmanides' account is: Why is the rite of the scapegoat merely claimed to *look like* idolatry? Why is it *not* in fact idolatry?

Nahmanides' remarkable answer to this question is that there is no observable, behavioral difference between the rite of the scapegoat and idolatry. The difference between them is entirely a function of the *intention*, or *attitude*, of the individual performing the rite.

> The intention of the scapegoat is not, Heaven forbid, that it should be a sacrifice from us to [the minister of the desert]. Rather our intention should be to fulfil the will of our Creator who so commanded us. This resembles someone who made a feast for a master, who was commanded by the master to give a portion to a certain servant. The one who makes the feast himself [intends to] give nothing to that servant and does nothing out of honor for him. He gives everything rather to the master, and the master gives a reward to his servant. And [the one making the feast] keeps [the master's] commandment and out of honor to the master does everything he commanded him. However, the master, out of his good will for the host of the feast, wanted all of his servants to benefit from him so that they would praise and not speak ill of him. (Ibid.)[85]

In other words, the only element in the rite of the scapegoat that saves it from being idolatry is the absence of an intention to *worship*—or sacrifice to—the being to whom the scapegoat is addressed, coupled with the presence of a complementary intention to comply with the command of the one deity who is worthy of true worship. This difference, Nahmanides goes on to argue, is expressed in the fine details of the rite of the *sa'ir la-'azazel*, for example, the fact that both goats are initially set before God in the Temple and only afterward is one chosen, by lottery, as a gift from God to his minister, and sent to be killed in the desert. Nonetheless, for outsiders, and especially from the point of view of idolators, it is near impossible to distinguish the two: the rite of the scapegoat looks just like idol worship. This is why, according to Nahmanides, the classic midrashic description of the *huqqim* (BT *Yoma* 67b) characterizes them as commandments that Satan—or Sama'el—denounces (*mekatterek*) and the Gentiles refute (*hagoyim meshivin aleihem*): The people of Israel are denounced and refuted, not for opposing idolatry, but for engaging in it no different from their adversaries, whom they denounce and refute.[86]

The role Nahmanides assigns to intention in order to legitimate the scapegoat despite its idolatrous appearance is not unique to this case. He gives a similar role to proper intention for sacrifice in general where, on his view, an analogous problem exists.[87] The source of the difficulty is that Nahmanides recognizes not only all the astral beings—separate intellects, stars, constellations, and demons—that mediate between God and the world; he also posits a hierarchy or complex of divine attributes, beings, powers or—as they came to be called in medieval kabbalah—emanations [*sephirot*] *within* the deity. The details of Nahmanides' kabbalistic conception of God need not concern us. However, among these divine attributes he singles out the divine principles of justice and mercy [*midat ha-din ve-midat ha-rahamim*]. Now, the central idea of his internal reason for sacrifice is that the sacrificial animal is itself sustenance not for God but for the "fire" or "fires" ['isheh, 'ishim], which either symbolize or constitute the deity-internal principle of justice [midat ha-din] (C Lev. 1, 9). That is, the object to whom the sacrificial animal is immediately directed is not the Deity Himself but one of His attributes or principles. However, in order for the sacrifice to be "accepted" and "pleasing," it is crucial that the owner intend to offer it solely and only to the one deity signified by the Tetragrammaton. Where the agent instead intends to make the sacrifice to one divine attribute or principle like the principle of justice in isolation from the totality of attributes— even though that one attribute may in fact be the direct recipient of the sacrificial food—the act, as in the case of the golden calf, becomes an instance of idolatry, a denial of the unity of God (C Exod. 32, 1). So, both in the case of the sa'ir la-'azazel where the direct object who is addressed is external to God and in the case of sacrifice where the direct object is internal to God, an *intention* to worship only God as signified by the Tetragrammaton is necessary to render the ritual acceptable. What distinguishes the scapegoat from sacrifice in general is not the kind of intention with which the agent must perform the act, but the fact that the constraints that were imposed on sacrificial worship of God to distinguish it from idolatry are overriden with the scapegoat.

Nahmanides' explanation of the sa'ir la-'azazel is a bold attempt, then, to tie together three not easily resolvable theses:

(i)   That there actually exists the astral being, the "minister of the desert," to whom the scapegoat is sent, who possesses real, and potentially harmful, power which the Israelite community knows it must address.

(ii) That sending forth the scapegoat cannot be construed as a *sacrifice to* the astral minister of the desert on pain of counting as idolatrous worship; that it must be instead sent with the sole intention to obey a command of the deity—so that by sending the scapegoat *to* the astral minister, the community worships, not the minister, but God.

(iii) That sending forth the scapegoat nonetheless *looks* just like idolatry, the feature that accounts for its problematic character that marks it off (from sacrifices in general) as a *hoq*.

The philosophical problem that faces Nahmanides is to stake out the boundaries of an appropriate conception of worship that meets the constraints of these three claims. On the one hand, it is clear that this conception of worship cannot consist simply in the performance of certain ritual gestures; if it did, the ritual of the scapegoat, which is behaviorally and observationally indistinguishable from idolatry, would ipso facto constitute worship of its astral object. A specific attitude or intention is necessary to make the bodily action an act of worship. On the other hand, the relevant attitude or intention also cannot consist simply in the complex state of recognizing the power of the object, say, to harm oneself, that one must address the being, and that one must do what one can to appease it. As Nahmanides hints, quoting the *Chapters of Rabbi Eliezer*, this complex attitude would lead one to bribe the being, not worship it.

What is necessary for worship of something is to "accept its divinity." However, it is not entirely clear what such "acceptance" requires. Is it necessary that the agent truly accept something as a divinity to worship it or is it sufficient if she simply *represents* herself *as if* she accepts the thing as a divinity? The ambiguity I have in mind is already hinted at by Nahmanides in the parable (*mashal*) (quoted earlier) through which he illustrates the status of the scapegoat. The host of the feast does not himself intend to benefit or honor the master's servant; he treats him well only out of deference, or honor, to the master whom he does want to benefit and honor. The master, however, wants his servant to be treated well so that he will praise the host. But, of course, in order for the servant to want to praise the host, he must *believe* that the host himself wants to treat him well. If the servant were to learn that he is being well treated only because his master has so commanded the host, there would obviously be little cause for him to praise the host. Hence, the master's strategem must remain unknown to the servant; the host must *represent* himself *as if* he himself wants to treat the servant well.

Now, how does this parable bear on the *sa'ir la-'azazel*? On Nahmanides' account, the scapegoat is said not to be sent as a gesture of worship to the astral minister of the desert; the community, or its priestly representative, sends it as a "bribe," or means of appeasement, at the command of God. However, the parable suggests that the minister does not regard the scapegoat merely as a crude bribe, simply as a way of paying him off. Just as the servant must believe that the host's own desire is to treat him well, so, one might argue by analogy, the minister of Mars must think that he is accepted as a divinity in order for the scapegoat to effectively appease him. Now, for the minister to *think* that he is accepted as a divinity, it is not necessary that the appeasing agent actually accept him as one. But it is necessary for the agent minimally to *represent* himself *as if* he accepts the minister as a deity. However, this in turn will be problematic if representing himself as if he accepts something as a divinity already constitutes worship of it. For even if the agent has one intention to send forth the scapegoat only, or really, because God so commanded, the fact that the ritual gesture is performed with an additional intention to represent himself as if he worships the minister may already suffice to render the act an instance of idolatry.

Whether worship of something as a deity requires, then, that the agent truly accept it or whether it is enough that the agent so represents himself will affect, then, whether the scapegoat ritual is or is not idolatry. This unresolved ambiguity concerning the required attitude or intention for performance of the scapegoat ritual may be yet a further reason why the reason for this *hoq* cannot be openly revealed. At this point we might also recall Nahmanides' explanation that the *huqqim* are called divine decrees [*gezerot*], not because they have no reason, but because they are "decrees that the king legislates in his kingdom without revealing their benefit to the people and from which the people do not benefit"; rather the people "think ill of the [king] in their hearts and accept [the *huqqim*] out of royal fear." This description fits well with our understanding of the reason for the *sa'ir la-'azazel*. Because of its problematic relation to idolatry—the fact that the minister to whom the *sa'ir* is sent does have power and must be appeased but, at the same time, cannot be worshipped—the king does not reveal the benefit that will accrue to the people from performing the rite. If he did reveal its utility, the slide to idolatrous worship would be all too smooth. Not knowing the reason for the commandment, the people therefore "think ill of the [king] in their hearts"—possibly even because it looks like forbidden idolatry. Yet, like the host of the feast, they accept the commandment "out of royal fear."

IX

The *sa'ir la-'azazel* is the most perspicuous example of Nahmanides' Maimonidean conception of a *hoq*: a commandment whose reason is problematic rather than simply unknown or without a reason. However, he applies the same model of explanation to a series of additional commandments: the purification rite of the individual stricken with the plague of *tzara'at* (C Lev. 14, 4), the purification rite for a house stricken with the plague of *tzara'at* (C Lev. 14, 53), the rite of the red heifer [*parah 'adumah*] (C Num. 19, 2), the rite of breaking the neck of a young heifer ['*eglah 'arufah*] (C Deut. 21, 4), the burning of the bullock for the consecration of the High Priest (C Exod. 29, 14), and the paschal sacrifice celebrated in Egypt (C Lev. 14, 4).[88] Each of these commandments is problematic. Sacrifices are strictly prohibited except within the Temple precincts on pain of being mistaken to be acts of idolatry. All of these rites either appear to be sacrifices or belong to more complex ceremonies with sacrificial overtones. Yet they are performed, not only outside the Temple, but in the very kinds of places—untilled open fields, desolate areas—that are associated specifically with idolatrous cults and especially with the worship of astral beings associated with destruction. Hence, one would expect all such rites to be absolutely forbidden by the Torah. Nahmanides' explanation for why they are nonetheless commanded is not spelled out in detail, but the reason hinted at in his commentaries is the same as his explanation of the *sa'ir la-'azazel*. These rites are not, despite their appearance, actually sacrifices or acts of worship; instead they are acts performed at the command of the deity to appease potentially hostile powers.

The reasons for these commandments, like that of the scapegoat, presuppose the truth of the metaphysical and astrological beliefs of the idolatrous practices they resemble. They differ from idolatry only in their respective attitudes toward their objects, only with respect to the intentions with which they are performed. Hence, there is the same kind of ambiguity surrounding their performance as there is with the scapegoat: do they express just the acknowledgment of a dangerous power who must be dealt with and appeased or are they really worship of the idolatrous object? One can see cause in their case, as in the case of the scapegoat, not to reveal their underlying reason to the community-at-large who are unable to clearly distinguish between idolatrous worship and necessary acknowledgment of an evil power. For all these reasons, Nahmanides considers all these commandments, like the scapegoat, *huqqim*.

The problematic feature of the *huqqim* we have thusfar explained by analogy to the *sa'ir la-'azazel* is a matter of idolatry. Their model of explanation, however, suggests a common structure for all problematic commandments, the idea that is the core of the notion of a *hoq* that Nahmanides adopts from Maimonides. Let me make the structure of this notion of a *hoq*—the problematic commandment—more explicit.

We typically explain an individual commandment by classifying it with other commandments with similar characteristics for which we give a common reason. However, there can obviously be different kinds of characteristics on which to base our classifications. In particular, a classification can be based on superficial, observable characteristics, the kind available to the ordinary member of the community, or on deeper, more theoretical features, the kind accessible only to those with privileged knowledge. Let us call the former an *ordinary* classification, the latter an *expert* classification. In many cases, two classifications of a single thing, one ordinary, the other expert, will turn out to be coextensive. But with the *huqqim* they do not.

Suppose an individual commandment c is ordinarily categorized as belonging to a class of commandments C (perhaps like the classes among which Maimonides divides all of the commandments in *Guide* III:35). This *ordinary* classification is based on superficial, observable characteristics of *c*—for example, whether it looks like a sacrifice, or involves cross-breeding of species, or concerns sexual behavior. The class *C* is given a general reason *R*, a common explanation for why each of its member commandments was legislated. However, given the general reason *R* for *C*—and despite the superficial resemblance between *c* and the other members of *C*—it may happen that *R* excludes *c* from *C*. That is, whereas *R* explains why the other commandments in *C* are prescribed, *R* implies that *c* in particular ought to be prohibited or not be prescribed (or perhaps not-*c* ought to be prescribed). Or if *R* explains why the other actions in *C* are prohibited, it also implies that *c* ought to be permitted or prescribed (or perhaps not-*c* ought to be prohibited). In this case, we will say that *c* is *problematic* relative to the reason *R* for the class of commandments *C*. We might even make this more explicit. Nahmanides, following Maimonides, insists that the reasons for the *huqqim* are problematic for, or not understood by, specifically the community-at-large or multitude. Hence, let's say that *c* is problematic to the multitude *M* relative to *R* for *C*. In order to explain why *c* is none the less commanded (or prohibited), it is necessary, then, to reclassify it in some other class of commandments *C'* for which the explanation is a different reason *R'*, usually an expert (or more expert) classification based on deeper characteristics of *c*.

Now, given this account of what it is for a commandment to be problematic, we can say what it is for a commandment to be a *hoq*. A commandment *c* is a *hoq* just in case, for some multitude *M* and some reason *R* for the ordinary class *C* in which *M* would expect *c* to be classified, *c* is problematic relative to *R* for *C*; that is, *R* entails that *c* should not belong to *C*. If *C* is a class of prescriptions, *c* should not be prescribed; if *C* is a class of prohibitions, *c* should not be prohibited.[89] For example, if *c* is the commandment of the *sa'ir la-'azazel*, it prima facie belongs to the class of commandments concerning sacrifice (*C*). However, given the explanation (*R*) for sacrifice that restricts them to the Temple precinct with the intention to worship the deity signified by the Tetragrammaton, it follows that the *sa'ir la-'azazel* should be prohibited (or the multitude *M* would expect it to be prohibited). Therefore, Nahmanides denies that the *sa'ir la-'azazel* really is to be categorized as a sacrifice; instead he re-classifies it among acts of appeasement to astral powers commanded by the deity, that is, in an alternative class *C'* with its own explanation *R'*.[90]

What I wish to show in the remaining pages of this chapter is how Nahmanides applies this formal notion of a *hoq*, not only to the class of commandments (enumerated earlier) to which the scapegoat belongs, but to at least two other commandments in the classic rabbinic enumeration of *huqqim*: *sha'atnez* (the prohibition against wearing garments woven of wool and linen together) and *shi'eir 'arayot* (prohibitions against sexual relations with specific relatives). Their explanations on this model are not, in my opinion, quite as compelling as the explanations of the scapegoat and its analogues, but they persuasively show the degree to which the Maimonidean notion of a *hoq* as a problematic commandment influenced Nahmanides and the extent to which Nahmanides developed and applied this idea in terms of its structural characterization. I will begin with *sha'atnez*.

Just as he begins his account of the *sa'ir la-'azazel* by criticizing Maimonides' thesis that all sacrifices are *huqqim*, Nahmanides begins his account of *sha'atnez* by criticizing the view that all commandments prohibiting cross-breeding (*kil'ayim*) are *huqqim*. "The Rabbis said that their reason is hidden and that the Evil Inclination and the Gentiles refute them only concerning *sha'atnez* and not concerning the cross-breeding of animals" (C Lev. 19, 19). The figure to whom he explicitly attributes the view he attacks is RaSHI, but it could equally as well have been Maimonides. For just as he takes the *sa'ir la-'azazel* to be representative of the whole class of sacrifices he counts as *huqqim*, so Maimonides takes the example of *sha'atnez* in the midrashic enumeration of *huqqim* (in BT *Yoma* 67b) to be representative of all commandments bearing on cross-breeding and perhaps even of all commandments concerned with cultic practices associated with agriculture. In any case, Maimonides' influence on Nahmanides' own explanation of the *hoq* of *sha'atnez* as a problematic commandment is unmistakable.

Nahmanides singles out two reasons for all prohibitions concerned with cross-breeding. This is significant but not because these commandments, *kil'ayim*, have reasons while *sha'atnez* does not. Indeed Nahmanides proposes two additional reasons for *sha'atnez*. The point of the contrast between *kil'ayim* and *sha'atnez* is that it is relative to the *reasons* for the general reference class of *kil'ayim* that *sha'atnez* stands out as an anomaly, a problematic commandment.

The two reasons Nahmanides offers for the prohibitions against cross-breeding may at first sight appear to be mutually incompatible. The first reason is that God created each species with the power to preserve itself as a distinct species for as long as He wills the existence of the world.[91] Therefore, "the one who cross-breeds two species [or grafts one species onto another] changes and denies the account of the beginning. It is as if he thinks that the Holy One did not bring to completion in the world all that is necessary, so he wants to assist in the creation of the world by adding creatures to it" (Ibid.). The second reason is surprisingly Maimonidean in spirit: cross-breeding is prohibited because cross-bred species cannot reproduce themselves. Hence, acts of cross-breeding and grafting are "contemptible and vain" (Ibid.). In other words, cross-breeding is forbidden because it is based on false beliefs and is therefore unproductive. But these two reasons are, of course, prima facie inconsistent. If cross-breeding is not productive and issues forth in no new species, then the cross-breeder, whatever he thinks, performs no action that in fact changes the order of the world by adding new species. A real change in the original nature created by God can only be effected by a permanent change, that is, a change in the number of species, contrary to the second reason.

It should be remembered that all attempts to change nature and its natural kinds are, on Nahmanides' account, cases of magic. More precisely, actions like cross-breeding have the same aim as astral magic and other forms of prohibited theurgy: to subvert and deconstruct the natural, or divine, order fixed in creation. Thus, in the course of his explanation of magic in his commentary on Deut. 18, 9, the passage we discussed in Section VII, Nahmanides adds that kil'ayim, cross-breeding, is prohibited for the same reason as magic:

> There will come to be from the graftings plants that will perform strange functions [pi'ulot nakhriyot] that will give birth to changes from the customary way of the world [miminhago shel 'olam], either for good or bad, apart from the fact that they themselves are a change in creation. (Deut. 18, 9)

If we recall Nahmanides' distinction between the "simple behaviors" and magically induced behaviors of celestial beings, we might also resolve the contradiction between his two reasons. The second reason claims that following the *simple* behavior of species, cross-breeding will never be productive, generating new self-preserving species. However, that "simple" fact is not incompatible with the state of affairs presupposed by the first reason according to which the individual is able by *magical* means to effect a genuine but "nonsimple" change in the natural world—for example, a new species. Furthermore, what is wrong with actions that attempt to induce such a change in the created "simple" world is not, as Maimonides argues, that they are vain and ineffectual, based on false presuppositions about the celestial powers. To the contrary, Nahmanides once again cites the midrashic statement that each terrestrial species has a celestial ruler that governs it (*Genesis Rabbah* 10:7), to which Scripture refers as the huqqot ha-shamaiyim [celestial statutes]. What is wrong with actions like cross-breeding is that they implicate that the doctrine of the divine creation of the world is false—that is, cross-breeding, like magic, is prohibited because it is an effective but rebellious act against the deity, an attempt to "mix up [mi'areiv] and deny the account of the beginning [*ma'aseh bereishit*]" (C Lev. 19, 19). In short, whereas Maimonides holds that the *huqqim* are commandments that come to deny the *huqqot ha-goyim*, Nahmanides holds that the *huqqim* are commandments that come to uphold the *huqqot ha-shamaiyim*.

Therefore, the most general reason for the ordinary class of commandments to which the prohibition against *sha'atnez* prima facie belongs—the general class of prohibitions against cross-breeding—is that, like magic, they attempt to subvert the natural order and thereby rebel against God, a reason that presupposes that such theurgic acts are effective. But if this is the reason for the class as a whole, it is problematic, as Nahmanides himself recognizes, why *sha'atnez* should be prohibited. Wearing a garment woven of thread from a plant species (linen) and of thread from the hair of an animal species (wool) is not, despite its superficial similarity to mixing diverse kinds, a kind of magic. There is no presupposition underlying *sha'atnez* that wearing such garments will have an effect on, or cause a change in, the natural created order. Such an action creates no new species. Indeed *sha'atnez* should be no more prohibited than cooking a meat and vegetable soup![92] Therefore, relative to its prima facie ordinary classification among prohibitions against cross-breeding, and the reasons for those laws, the prohibition against *sha'atnez* is problematic—hence, a *hoq*.

But to say that *sha'atnez* is problematic relative to the reason for one class of commandments is not to say that it has no reason, indeed no nonproblematic reason relative to another class of commandments. Nahmanides goes on to give two such reasons for *sha'atnez*. The first is to "take precautionary measures against [*leharhik*] mixing species; therefore [Scripture] forbade [mixing] the [different species] from which it is usual to make a garment" (C Lev. 19, 19). The second reason—which possibly reflects Nahmanides' own dissatisfaction with his first reason—is that of Maimonides in the *Guide* (III:37:544): that there was a garment made of *sha'atnez* that was well known to the priests who practiced magic during ancient times that had special powers. Therefore the Torah forebade that garment (and others made like it) because "the Torah comes to eradicate their actions and to destroy their memory" (Ibid.). Both of these reasons may strike us as little more than subtle variations on the problem-creating reason rejected by Nahmanides. However, his use of the Maimonidean explanation is also full of irony. For Maimonides, the garment is forbidden because it is based on false beliefs about magic, which is absolutely vain and silly. For Nahmanides, the garment is prohibited precisely because it is magically effective and its underlying metaphysical beliefs are true. However, both of these reasons strictly speaking avoid the problematic features of the ordinary classification and explanation of *sha'atnez*.

X

Our last example of a *hoq* is Nahmanides' explanation of the prohibitions against sexual relations with relatives who are near of kin ['*ervat shi'eir basar*] and, specifically, the relatives enumerated in Lev. 18, 6–18.[93] After saying that the reason for these specific prohibited relations is not stated explicitly in Scripture, Nahmanides first presents the reason given by Maimonides and Abraham ibn Ezra: that the general purpose of all these prohibitions is to minimize sexual intercourse tout cour and to accustom people to satisfy themselves with the least sex. The specific relatives that are singled out in the Torah are simply those with whom the man or woman is most frequently in contact in the household.[94] In other words, although Maimonides and Abraham ibn Ezra do not explicitly draw this conclusion, the moral to which their explanation points is that the particulars that are mentioned in the Torah are exemplary rather than exclusive. The reason for the ordinary class of commandments to which the *'ervat shi'eir basar* should belong is to restrict, constrain, and minimize sexual desires and activities *with anyone*.

As we have seen with other *huqqim*, Nahmanides opposes this liberal hermeneutic move. His objections to Maimonides' and ibn Ezra's "weak reasons" also serve to show how problematic are the prohibitions of *'ervat shi'eir basar* when they are explained relative to the reason for the ordinary class of commandments concerning sexual abstinence. Why, Nahmanides objects, "should relations with these particular relatives—just because they are frequently around each other—incur divine punishment by premature death [*karet*] while individuals are permitted to marry hundreds and even thousands of wives? And what will it hurt if someone marries his daughter to his son—as is permitted to Noahides? Or if he marries two sisters, as did Jacob the Patriarch?" (C Lev. 18, 6). In other words, if the reason is to teach sexual restraint or abstinence, why is it that these particular sexual relations and not others are singled out for excessively harsh punishment? Indeed, given the general reason, one might argue to the contrary that these relations ought to be permitted or even encouraged. "There is no more proper marriage for a person than to marry his daughter to his son who is older than her, that they should inherit his property and multiply and be fruitful in his house" (Ibid.). Hence, relative to the reason for this ordinary class (sexual restraint), these particular prohibitions are problematic—hence, *huqqim*.

But this is not the end of Nahmanides' story. While, or perhaps *because*, these prohibitions are problematic relative to their ordinary explanation, Nahmanides goes on to give an expert explanation, in fact two alternative reasons. The first is a kabbalistic explanation concerning the secret of the transmigration of souls [*sod ha-'ibur*].[95] The second, like Nahmanides' second reason for *sha'atnez*, is at first glance Maimonidean in spirit. Taking an extremely negative view of sex, he argues that sexual intercourse is permitted only insofar as it is conducive to procreation; sex that is not productive is nothing but the expression of lust [*zimah mahshevet ta'avah*]. That is, the Torah forbids such actions because they are vain, unproductive, and based on mistaken presuppositions, desires, and values. However, as with *sha'atnez*, there may be more here than meets the eye. Nahmanides' distinction between the "simple behavior" of beings as established in divine creation and their "nonsimple" magically induced behavior may lie behind his second reason. Sexual relations among relatives of near kin, the *shi'eir basar*, is unproductive according to their "simple" divinely created natures. However, the prohibition may be aimed, not at this, but at attempts through magic to subvert and change the natural "simple" order that underlies the differences among the *shi'eir basar* that prevent them from being productive. The correct class of commandments among which the prohibitions of *'ervat shi'eir basar* should be classified and explained would be, then, those designed to combat magic and the rebellious subversion of divine creation.

XI

We have followed two parallel lines of development in the explanation of the *huqqim* from Maimonides to Nahmanides. The first focuses on their opposing attitudes toward astrology and magic, and their metaphysical presuppositions, as they enter into their respective explanations of the *huqqim*. The second concentrates on the reconceptualization of the idea of a *hoq* as a problematic commandment. Although Maimonides may not have been the first Jewish thinker to refer to idolatry, or astrology and magic, in his account of *ta'amei ha-mitzvot*, what I have tried to show is how the Maimonidean revolution, one of whose central aims was to naturalize rabbinic Judaism, shaped the subsequent discussion and, in particular, Nahmanides' reaction. For Maimonides the "naturalization" of the Law meant, first, that the commandments are always subject to rational explanation and, second, that the primary end of the commandments is to eradicate falsehood and myth, the greatest of which is idolatry or, more specifically, Sabianism, a heading under which he includes astrology, magic, popular religion, and superstition, contemporary as well as ancient. Nahmanides did not share Maimonides' ideal of naturalization but, in any case, he also sharply disagreed over the specific truth-value of astrology and astral magic. It is no small irony that Maimonides' characterization of the *huqqim* as problematic commandments funished Nahmanides with the very apparatus he needed in his explanatory repertoire in order to acknowledge and address astrology and magic as true but forbidden doctrines within the constraints of the Law.

Nahmanides, I have also tried to show, articulates the idea of a *hoq* as a problematic commandment in terms of an abstract structural notion that applies to different areas of the Law. With this analysis he advances considerably beyond Maimonides' original idea, which was closely tied to a substantive criterion, namely, the rejection of Sabianism. At least since the seventeenth century we have associated this kind of formalization, abstraction, and systematization with the characteristics of an emerging science. It is a second irony that this abstract refinement of the idea of a problematic commandment was developed by Nahmanides in the service of a defense of astrology and astral magic in reaction to Maimonides' naturalistic critique. Maimonides' explanation of the *huqqim* attempted to bring about the fall of myth in Judaism. Instead it led, through its formative influence on Nahmanides just one generation later, to the resuscitation of the same myths.

NOTES

CHAPTER 1. *TA'AMEI HA-MITZVOT* AND THE PHILOSOPHICAL FOUNDATIONS OF JUDAISM

1. I ignore Philo because his important, and massive, writing on *ta'amei ha-mitzvot* had no recognizable influence on medieval Jewish philosophy.

2. See, e.g., Idel (1990).

3. This antinomian argument should be distinguished from a more general objection, based on the consideration that most reasons for commandments are merely sufficient, not necessary, conditions. That is, the proposed reason explains a commandment by identifying an end for which it is a sufficient means. But if the commandment is not also necessary for that end, there is always the danger that an agent will reject the particular means (furnished by the commandment) and try to achieve the end through some other means of his own design. On this argument, see Maimonides' discussion of King Solomon at the end of *SHM*, Negative Commandment 365.

4. Maimonides' answer to this question turns, I would argue, on a parallel he wishes to draw between the eternity a parte poste of the world and of the Law. All change in either domain, he says, can be due only to inherent excesses or deficiencies that require correction. But neither the world nor the Law, he claims, are inherently deficient or excessive. I hope to develop this argument elsewhere. On the eternity of the world a parte poste, see now Feldman (1986) and Weiss (1992–1993).

5. This problem should, in turn, be distinguished from yet another issue: that attention to bodily actions like the commandments may not only be foreign and irrelevant to higher forms of worship like contemplation, but a disruption or obstacle for the perfected philosopher to complete concentration on the latter. I develop this idea at length in Stern (ms. a). But the problem rears its head in chapter 5 below.

6. See Harvey (1988).

7. See the various writings of Leo Strauss, e.g., his (1952) and (1963). Since Strauss the terms have been widely but uncritically used in the literature.

8. However, neither the parabolic external nor internal meaning should be identified with the *linguistic* meaning of the text, the lexical meanings of the words, or the *peshat* (in the sense of the Andalusian tradition of biblical exegesis: the meaning of the words in their (linguistic, historical, literary) context). I discuss these issues further in the coming chapters.

9. On terminological grounds, one might therefore classify the *Mishneh Torah* as an exoteric text and the *Guide* as an esoteric one. However, closer

analysis shows, I shall argue below, that this characterization is also incorrect.

10. For a few examples of Maimonides' broad and varied use of the term *parable (mathal, mashal)*, compare I:60:143; II:11:275; I:59:140ff.; III:51:628; II:17:296.

11. On the latter, see Stern (ms. a).

12. See Stern (1989), (forthcoming b), (ms. b, c).

CHAPTER 2. PROBLEMATIC COMMANDMENTS I

1. For a general overview of the subject, see Heinemann (1954) vol. 1; on the Rabbinic literature, Urbach (1971), 321–47; and on Maimonides: Ben-Sasson (1960), Hartman (1976), 139–86; Hyman (1979–80); Twersky (1980a), 356–514; and Nehorai (1983).

2. Cf. Exod. 15:25; Lev. 18:26, 26:46; Num. 9:3; Deut. 4:1, 4:5, 4:8, 4:14, 4:45, 5:1, 5:28, 6:1, 6:20, 7:11, 8:11, 11:32, 12:1, 26:17; note that the term *mitzvot* is also sometimes scripturally contrasted with *huqqim* and *mishpatim*.

3. For these two views of the *mishpatim*, see Saadiah Gaon (1970–71/ 1948) and Ibn Daud (1852/1982), respectively. Saadiah does not explicitly call his rationally known laws *mishpatim* (though he indicates that his distinction is scripturally based) but he is so interpreted by Maimonides in *EC* 6. Except in passing, I shall not discuss the *mishpatim* further.

4. As we shall see, Maimonides will attempt to "naturalize" (though not eliminate) the reference to God in his answers to this question. One might equally well state the question without mentioning a deity: Why were particular Mosaic commandments, or the Mosaic Law as a whole, legislated to Israel at the time of the Mosaic (so-called) revelation?

5. It is not, however, as clear that the Ash'arites, in light of their description in I:71, are the proponents of the first opinion of III:26. Cf. Hyman (1979–80) who suggests that these are (Jewish?) Mu'tazilites. Note also that in III:28 Maimonides restricts the first opinion of III:26 to "commandments from whose external meaning it does not appear that they are useful": i.e., the *huqqim* or a putative Mu'tazilite analogue. Contrast with this the reference in III:31 to "a *group of human beings* who consider it a grievous thing that causes should be given for any law" [my emphasis], a description that fits only Ash'arites who possibly are described by the odd and necessarily vague phrase "a group of human beings" precisely because they are not Jews.

6. Note Maimonides' prooftext in I:54—Gen. 1:31—also quoted as the penultimate verse of III:25.

7. See Pines (1979).

8. Though the two also significantly differ: e.g., the Law is a function of the imagination unlike Nature.

9. Cf. Rosenberg (1981), especially 130–33.

10. Pines (1960), 197; cf. Pines (1963), cxii–cxiii; Altmann (1974); and Stern (1997).

11. Though Aristotle himself would, of course, disagree with this analogy.

12. See *SHM* Negative 365 and *MT "Meʻilah,"* viii, 8 for two additional types of antinomianism; and cf. Twersky (1980a), 407–408, the first, to my knowledge, to emphasize the central role of antinomianism in Maimonides' thought.

13. Two general remarks on rabbinic sources for the notion of a *hoq*: *Sifra* (*'Aharei*) 13:10 (cf. also BT *Yoma* 67b), cited in Maimonides' three major discussions of *taʻamei ha-mitzvot*: *EC* 6; *MT "Meʻilah"* viii, 8; and *Guide* III:26. (I) In *EC*, Maimonides identifies the Rabbinic *huqqim* with Saadiah's "traditional laws" (*torot shimʻiyyot*) (though he does not mention Saadiah by name), which he further describes as "[laws which] if not for the Torah would not be bad at all"; i.e, their validity solely depends on the divine will manifest in the Torah, for no reason independent of their being commanded, a view he vigorously disputes in the *Guide*. (Note also that in *EC* the transgression of illicit sexual unions [*gilu'i ʻarayot*] is classified, for reasons unclear to me, among the *huqqim* rather than among the *mishpatim,* as in the original text.) Already in the *Mishneh Torah*, however, Maimonides abandons this view and holds, as in the *Guide*, that *huqqim* "are commandments whose reason is not *known*" (my emphasis), unlike ordinances [*mishpatim*] "whose reason is obvious" (*MT "Meʻilah"* viii, 8; cf. also *MT "Temurah"* iv, 13). On these *halakhot*, cf. Twersky (1980a), 407–14 and (1980b). Twersky (1980a), 458–59 also claims that the crux of Maimonides' objection to Saadiah's characterization of his first class of laws as *rational* is "that not *some* but *all* laws are rational . . . he objects to [the] limited application [of the term *rational* [*sikhliyot*] and the resultant implication that other laws are nonrational. *All* laws are rational . . ." This reading slides invalidly from Maimonides' opinion that all laws are rational in the sense of *having a reason* to the (Kalam-Saadianic) view (which Maimonides rejects) that they are rational in the sense of *being the object of the faculty of Reason (Intellect)*. On the significant al-Farabian influence on this subject, see Macy (1982). (II) The Rabbinic description of the *huqqim* raises two general questions of interpretation: (1) the identities of its typological figures—the Evil Impulse (in *MT "Meʻilah"*), Satan (in the *Guide*), and the Nations of the World and (2) the status of the examples of *huqqim* cited in each: are these meant as exhaustive and exclusive lists for which the term *hoq* is simply an abbreviation or as examples of general conditions of *"hoq*-hood" under which we should subsume other commandments? I pursue these questions below.

14. On this passage, see chap. 3.

15. See also Maimonides' impassioned polemical remarks with which he concludes the same passage of III:26:509. His strong language can be understood only on the assumption that he is concerned, not with the empty results of vain inquiry, but with the reasons that such inquiry will uncover and the potential dangers of certain knowledge in the wrong hands; the point of his intense language is to dissuade certain groups from inquiry.

16. On the ends of the Law, see Galston (1978), Harvey (1980).

17. For the possible source of this example, see Aristotle (1984), *Nicomachean Ethics* 5, 7.

18. See Aristotle (1984), *Metaphysics* 5.26 1023b 12–37; *Topics* 1.2.101b 17–24; Porphyry (1975), 41 (I thank Dr. C. Manekin for bringing these sources to my attention); and *SHM*, Principles 11–12.

19. Similarly, contrast (i) III:30 with (ii) III:32. In III:30 Maimonides explains the particular details of the Deuteronomic covenant in terms of particular Sabian idolatrous agricultural beliefs and the general institution of covenantal curses and blessings as a first intention; in III:32 it is the institution of curses and blessings, "commandments and prohibitions, rewards and punishments" (528–29) which is the particular explained by a second intention and general belief in the Law, however that end is accomplished, is the sole generality.

20. A "literal" paraphrase of this passage might be this: "Necessarily some particulars 'lack' causes because whichever one was commanded, we could (would?) always ask, Why was it rather than another commanded? It is necessary only that *some* species or *some* number be commanded. Like 'the possible,' what is necessitated is only, given any two possibilities P and not-P, that one will be realized at some time. But there is no necessity that P in particular be realized or not-P." On this reading, the argument depends, not on the "reversability of the question," but on the alleged "resemblance" of particulars to the "nature of the possible." But that the possible has this nature is itself simply *asserted*. Nor is it demonstrated that there *exist* such undetermined possibilities and, similarly, that there exist uncaused particulars. So, while faithful to the language of the passage, this reading does not yield a sound argument; yet interpretations (including that below) that provide better arguments are not as faithful to the text.

21. Al-Ghazali's view is quoted, and criticized, in Averroes (1954), 18–19, 21. The Shem Tob-al-Ghazali interpretation has recently been urged by Hyman (1979–80), 339–43. Cf. also Rescher (1959/60) and Ullmann-Margalit and Morgenbesser (1977).

22. As Ullmann-Margalit and Morgenbesser (1977), 768, argue, in the general case of Buridan's Ass the agent might have *equally weighty* reasons for selecting A to the exclusion of B *and* B to the exclusion of A, thereby undercutting inferences to the conclusions both that the agent's reasons will always *determine* his selections (the Aristotelian position) and that wherever a selection is not so determined, it will be arbitrary, random, or without reason. (Note that my use of *choose* does not follow that of Margalit-Morgenbesser.)

23. See Pines (1963), cxxvi–cxxxi; cf. Guttmann (1979) and Rosenberg (1978a) and (1978b), especially 121ff.

24. Cf. II:19:302, 308, 310; III:32:524; II:25:329; Pines (1963), cxxx–cxxxi; and compare Averroes (1954), 249, n.2 with III:31:523–24.

25. For a diametrically opposed interpretation of this passage, see Funkenstein (1977), 87–90; and Twersky (1980a), 398. Our differences of interpretation recall Maimonides' comment that the only difference between the Law and the philosophers is that "they regard the world as eternal and we regard it as produced in time" (III:256:506). For a different sort of evidence for the ontological reading, see also Twersky (1980a), 398ff.

26. E.g., III:37:540, 544, 546, 547, 548; III:41:561; III:45:577, 578; III:46:581, 582, 585, 586; III:48:599.

27. Cf. Ibn Tibbon's entry for *huqqah* in his terminological glossary to *MN*. It should also be noted that Maimonides deems a practice to be magic only with respect to its historical context of prohibition; see III:37:543–44. There-

fore, despite the fact that we may *now* know—something that Maimonides *in fact* did know (III:37:544)!—that what was in ancient times believed to be medically required is in fact false or ineffectual, the practice is nonetheless *not* considered a form of magic.

28. This halakhah is a superb example of a passage in the *Mishneh Torah* with both external and internal interpretations. On its external reading, the laws of impurity are *huqqim* in the sense of "decrees" either with no reason or with a reason that transcends human understanding. For its internal interpretation, see III:33:47; and chap. 3 below.

29. See Maimonides' revealing comment that "as for the offering of wine, I am up to now perplexed with regard to it: *How could He have commanded* to offer it, since the idolators offered it? No reason for this has occurred to me" (III:46:591; my emphasis).

30. I am indebted here to Noam Zohar.

31. See Maimonides' exegesis of Jer. 7:22–23 (III:32:530). On the account presented in the text, the "first" and "second" intentions of commandments are their *primary* and *secondary* intentions. But Maimonides also gives "another way of interpreting" the Jeremiah verse according to which the first and second intentions refer *chronologically* to the intentions of the first legislation at Marah (Exod. 15, 22–27) and the second legislation at Sinai; see III:32:530–31. In the course of giving this interpretation, note that Maimonides also changes the meaning of the word *hoq*: first, in Exod. 15, 25–26 "the statute referred to is the Sabbath" (cf. BT *Sanhedrin* 56b; also III:24:498f.); later, as part of the Sinaitic revelation, it refers to the statutes exemplified by the sacrifices.

32. Maimonides' explanation that the *huqqim* result from realizing a first intention of the Law within the bounds of natural necessity also raises a second problem concerning divine omnipotence—an objection he explicitly addresses in III:32:527–29. On this, see also II:25:505.

33. See Harvey (1980).

34. See Moses of Narbonne's (1852/1961) comment on III:32 (attributed, significantly, to "other students of the *Guide*") "that so long as man exists on earth idolatry will also exist." For further discussion along this line, see below chap. 6.

35. See Moses of Narbonne (1852/1961) on III:34; Abarbanel (1579), "Introduction" to Lev.; Thomas Aquinas (1941) Ia, IIae 101–103; Benin (1982) and references therein to William of Auvergne and John of la Rochelle; Macy (1982); Scholem (1961), 29; Agus (1959), 202; Hartman (1976), 176ff.; Harvey (1980), 203ff.; Rosenberg (1981), 141–43; Berman (1959), 104–107; and Epstein (1959).

36. The one conclusion I believe Maimonides did not intend his philosophical audience to draw was that the *huqqim*, e.g., the sacrifices, are no longer binding. This *is* a corollary of his historical explanation—and therefore must be countered—but I know of no good argument that he intended this as the true "esoteric" conclusion to be drawn from his account. For the alternative view, see, however, Berman (1959), who claims that the "clear implication [of III:32:526 (quoted below)] is that had Moses come at the time of Maimonides, during conditions that did not exist during his own life, he would not have leg-

islated reformed statutes of sacrifice, because there would have been no need for them" (106). This claim is not implied by the text and, in any case, the question is not whether a different legislation would require sacrifice but whether the Mosaic legislation of sacrifice—even if it were motivated by historical considerations—should remain valid or binding. One might grant that a contemporary Law would not include sacrifice, yet hold that, if sacrifice in fact was commanded, then it retains its obligatoriness. Furthermore, the obligatoriness of the *huqqim* would seem to follow from (1) the parallel Maimonides draws between the commandments and nature and (2) his view that the natural world is eternal *a parte post*. Therefore, for *philosophical* (not theological) reasons—the presumed source of his "esoteric" interpretations—he ought to endorse the eternal validity of the *huqqim*.

37. On this passage, and especially concerning the subject of personal equity and justice, see Rosenthal (1968); Rosenberg (1982); Kirschenbaum (1984); Shein (1984); Levinger (1984). The problem of equity is *formally* similar to the problem raised by the *huqqim*, though their solutions may differ. I believe Maimonides addresses both questions in III:34.

38. On the perfection of the Law and, in particular, on the historical relativity of such judgments, see II:39:380, II:40:382, and III:39:554. Not only its *explanation* but also *evaluation* of its "wisdom" requires knowledge of its historical context of legislation. Nonetheless there remains considerable tension between Maimonides' historicism and the claim that the Law is eternally binding.

39. This distinction between the unchangeable and changeable within the Law parallels, for Maimonides, the traditional distinction between the Written and Oral Laws. Compare his comment that "at present my purpose is to give reasons for the [biblical] texts and not for the pronouncements of the legal science" (III:41:558, 567); cf. Levinger (1968).

40. Inasmuch as the philosopher also belongs to the community, whatever grounds obligate the community to continue to obey the Law, also obligate him; see II:40:381ff.; III:27:511. Yet, Maimonides' view is not free of all tension; see III:51:621.

41. Maimonides never makes this implication explicit, but the analogy would suggest that prayer, reciting the Torah, and similar commandments all have a status like the *huqqim*. Terminology aside, the important point is that the notion of a *hoq* serves Maimonides as a general model for understanding an extremely wide range of commandments.

42. See Rosenberg (1981), 141ff.

43. See the anthropocentric/theocentric distinction in Ben-Sasson (1960), 274–81.

44. On III:27, see Galston (1978), 28, who does not even include III:51–52 among the three sections of the *Guide* she says "form the core of Maimonides' teaching about the purpose of the Law," thus attesting to the remarkable success with which Maimonides concealed their relation to his account of *ta'amei ha-mitzvot* in III:26–49. See also the classification of III:51–52 in Strauss (1963) p. xiii, which completely severs their connection to III:26–49. On my view, the account of *ta'amei ha-mitzvot* extends from III:25 to III:52 inclusive; III:50,

despite its common themes with III:49, is inserted between the two accounts primarily to conceal the apparent contradiction between them.

45. Note Maimonides' deliberately open-ended phrase "the performance of the other commandments," with which he concludes his carefully chosen examples.

46. To perform the commandments as training of this type is *not* to say that they were willed arbitrarily by God, nor does it entail any view of their legislation as opposed to their performance. But through such informed performance of the *huqqim* as training the ordinary member of the community is, perhaps, given a glimpse of the highest state of divine worship; compare III:51:624–28 with the end of *MT "Me'ilah"* viii, 8.

CHAPTER 3. PROBLEMATIC COMMANDMENTS II

1. See Shem Tob's commentary in *MN* and Moses of Narbonne (1852/1961) both on *Guide* III:48; Twersky (1980a), 448, n.224, 471, n.285; and Levinger (1967).

2. With the one important qualification that we may be ignorant of the reason; on its significance, see below.

3. See also *Guide* III:26:508f., where Maimonides rejects the law of animal slaughter as an example of a particular with no reason even according to his own "revised" interpretation of the *Bereshith Rabbah* passage. The reason actually given there—that it is "intended to bring about the easiest death in an easy manner"—is the same reason given in III:48.

4. See *MT "Me'ilah"* viii, 8; *MT "Temurah"* iv, 13, and Twersky (1980a), 407ff., 416f.; and Twersky (1980b).

5. See the *halakhot* cited in the previous note.

6. Although Maimonides attacks Saadiah (though not by name) in *EC* 6, his criticism is entirely directed against Saadiah's Kalamic characterization of the *mishpatim* (ordinances) as rational laws, i.e., laws which are the object of Reason or the faculty of the intellect. According to Maimonides, these laws, which mainly concern the moral or, more generally, the good and the bad, are conventional (*mefursamim*) and, thus, the object of the imagination. However, Maimonides agrees with Saadiah on the division of the commandments into two classes and on his conception of the *huqqim*.

7. See *MT "Me'ilah"* viii, 8; *MT "Mikva'ot "* xi, 12; and discussion in chap. 2.

8. On Nahmanides' criticism of Maimonides on this issue, see below chap. 4. See also Weiss (1989) who argues that Maimonides holds that, while divine providence does not extend to individual nonhuman animals, divine mercy does, on the assumption that "providence and mercy are not the same thing and do not necessarily imply one another" (p. 357). I myself would agree, but it is not at all clear that Maimonides distinguishes between them in the case of the deity; see, e.g., his uses of the terms *mercy* (Heb. *rahum*), *providence* (Ar. *'inaya*) and *governance* (Ar. *tadbir*) in *Guide* I:54 and III:54. Furthermore, throughout her discussion, Weiss misidentifies Maimonides' references to "the

Law" with references to the deity. Thus she writes that "Maimonides, in discussing the Law's exhortation to be merciful to animals, compares animals to human beings in respect of their common ability to experience pain . . . [e.g.,] 'If the Law takes into consideration these pains of the soul in the case of beasts and birds, what will be the case with regard to the individuals of the human species as a whole?' [III:48:600]. Here "the Law" clearly cannot be interpreted as referring to the deity. Maimonides' point is rather that if the Law requires *us* humans to take into consideration the pains of beasts and birds, surely it expects *us* to act with comparable mercy toward our fellow humans. This passage is irrelevant to the question whether or not God Himself is merciful toward birds and beasts.

9. On the Talmudic use, see Urbach (1971), 330, 335f.; "*Gezerat Ha-Katuv.*" Among medieval Talmudists who give the phrase the meaning of arbitrary or lacking reason are RiTBA in his *Novellae* on BT *Baba Metzi'a'* 11a "*VeH'a*" and RaSHI in his *Commentary on the Torah*, Gen. 26:5, Lev. 18:4, and Lev. 19:19. Note that for RaSHI this sense of *gezerat ha-katuv* is linked to his concept of a *hoq*; on the general connection between these two, see below.

10. It should also be noted that Maimonides does not label all those *halakhot* that he in fact states have no reason as *gezerot ha-katuv*. See, e.g., MT "*Mekhirah*" vi, 8; xxii, 9; and MT "*Zehi'iah u-Matanah*" vi, 15. Thus the term and its purported explicans are not even coextensive.

11. See Assaf (1975), vol. 4, 76.

12. See Twersky (1980a), 471, n. 285.

13. See, e.g., BT '*Avodah Zarah* 18a; and compare Maimonides' other uses of the phrase with essentially the same meaning in MT "*Sheluhin ve-Shutafin*" vi, 5 (where *divrei ta'am* are contrasted with *derekh ve-ha-din ha-'emet*); MT "*She'eilah ve-Pikadon*" vii, 12; MT "*Malveh ve-Loveh*" xxi, 1; MT "*To'en ve-Nit'an*" viii, 10; and MT "'*Ishut*" iv, 19.

14. As a general feature of scriptural commandments, see *Guide* III:34.

15. See, however, the Lehem Mishneh and RaDBaZ, ad loc., who question how Maimonides can give a reason for a *gezerat ha-katuv*, and their attempt to reconcile the *halakhah* with the Talmud. Note also that in the *Guide* III:33 and III:41 Maimonides does not hesitate to give reasons for the law of the stubborn and rebellious son—indeed two independent reasons whose relation to one another requires reconsideration. On Maimonides' view of the role of the customary and the usual in the explanation of scriptural commandments, see *Guide* III:34.

16. See also MT "*Temurah*" iv, 13 where Maimonides also offers a psychological explanation immediately after writing that "all statutes [*huqqei*] of the Law are decrees [*gezerot*]."

17. See also Maimonides' shift to the phrase "*gezerat ha-melekh* [decree of the king]" at the end of the passage; and compare Nahmanides' use of this phrase in his *Commentary on the Torah*, e.g., Lev. 19:19. Cf. also RaDBaZ, ad loc. who explicitly states that a *gezerat ha-katuv* is a law whose reason we do not know.

18. See BT *Sanhedrin* 27a and RaSHI, ad loc. Although this is not emphasized in our *halakhah*, a major function of calling a given law a "*hiddush*"—

which is one reason the Talmud calls our case of 'eidim zommimim a hiddush—
is to prohibit drawing legal analogies to other laws or cases.

19. See, e.g., Tur on Hoshen Mishpat 37.

20. This section of the chapter has been entirely rewritten and differs sub-stantively from the corresponding section in the earlier Hebrew version of the paper.

21. For another example of Maimonides' use of the term remez, see MT "Shi'ar 'Avot Ha-Tum'ot" vi, 1: "The impurity of idolatry is an enactment of the scribes (divrei sofrim) but it has a remez in the Torah: 'Remove the foreign gods that are in your midst and purify yourselves and change your clothing,'" suggesting perhaps that the impurity of idols is a reality.

22. In the Guide it is the Sabbath that is explained by reference to creation, although it is not clear that the notion as it is so employed is incompatible with the doctrine of eternity. See III:43:570; II:31:359f.; and I:67:162.

23. See the commentary of Moses of Narbonne (1852/1961) on III:43. Narbonne adds that this is especially true when the practice in question also agrees with the intellect (sekhel), explicitly referring to Maimonides' earlier remarks in III:43 on the reason for the seven days of Passover and possibly to his homiletical explanation of the sounding of the shofar (which Narbonne con-trasts with the kabbalistic explanation of the "toranniyim" [lit.: scholars of the Law] according to whom the sounding of the shofar is for the benefit of God [tzorekh gavoha], serving to unify the divine attributes [sefiroth]). On the idea of tzorekh gavohah, see below chap. 4.

24. See chap. 2.

25. LA (Heb.) 311, (Eng.) 351.

26. Guide III:36:539; MT "Ta'aniyot" i, 1–2. From Maimonides' discus-sion, it is clear that the same kind of explanation applies both to sounding of trumpets and the shofar.

27. On the Arabic usage of the name Sabians to designate all pagans, but in particular to translate the term Hellenes as it was used by Christian authors to designate pagans (like Epicureans) prevalent in the Roman Empire during the first centuries C.E., see Pines (1963), cxxiv, and chap. 6 below.

28. See Maimonides' use of this prooftext both in III:17:464, to describe the Epicurean "unbelievers" in Israel, and in III:32:530, to describe the idolators to be abolished by the Law, idolatry Maimonides takes to be exemplified by Sabian star worship.

29. For elaboration, see chap. 6.

30. On the relation between the Mishneh Torah and Guide on this point, see also Levinger (1967), who claims that Maimonides elevates what was only a "remez" in the former—a text directed to the multitude from whom he wishes to conceal the reasons for commandments—to the status of a "reason" in the latter—a text directed to the elite to whom reasons can be revealed. But why Maimonides should want to deemphasize, let alone conceal, the type of reason given in this remez is not explained by Levinger, who also does not take into account Maimonides' comments there on "midrashic" reasons. For further dis-cussion of Maimonides' remarks here on midrashic interpretations, see Stern (forthcoming a) and (ms. a).

31. Compare the similar, if not even broader, use of *gezerot* in *MT* "*Temurah*" iv, 13.

32. This is not, of course, to deny that Maimonides' language here is highly ambiguous or that it is possible to read the *halakhah* in the first innocuous sense; indeed I believe that the ambiguity is deliberate.

33. See also *EC 6*, where Maimonides uses the Rabbinic phrase "*gazar 'alei*" [decreed (that it be forbidden) upon me] to describe specifically the *ḥuqqim*. (I am indebted to David Shatz for reminding me of this passage.)

34. These three purposes are not unconnected but a hierarchy; on their relation, see *MT* "*Tum'at 'Okhlim*" xvi, 12.

35. Compare his use here of *Sifra Lev.* 11, 44 with its use in III:33:533.

36. Cf. III:45:580 on the annointing oil.

37. I suggest that we also interpret the phrase "*da'ato shel 'adam*" in *MT* "*Me'ilah*," not as "human understanding," but as "the understanding of the multitude"; on this meaning of *'adam*, see *Guide* I:14.

38. In contrast, Maimonides says, to the commandments of *MT* "*De'ot*," which are "all explicitly stated to have as their purpose the acquisition of the noble *moral* qualities in question" (ad loc., my emphasis). For related terms within moral contexts, see also the concluding statement of *MT* "*Temurah*" iv, 13 and *Guide* III:49:605: "In this way bad moral habits are cured, when the *divine command* is the physician" [my emphasis].

39. See *Guide* III:34; Blau, Responsum #252, 460; Rosenthal (1968); Rosenberg (1982).

40. The same precautionary motif runs through the explanation of the nazarite law in the remaining passage of III:48. See Levinger (1967), who argues that there also exists a contradiction between this passage and the *Mishneh Torah*, which should be resolved along the same lines that he resolves the contradiction over *shiluah ha-ken*. I cannot pursue this topic here, but the question whether there is indeed a *contradiction* on this point should be distinguished, in my opinion, from the question of Maimonides' general attitude toward asceticism, which is certainly different in the two works.

41. On Maimonides' conception of the Oral Law, see Levinger (1968); Blidstein (1978); and Blidstein (1986).

42. See BT *Berakhot* 33b; BT *Megillah* 25a; JT *Berakhot* V; JT *Megillah* III.

43. On the general question of Maimonides' relation to his sources, see Levinger (1965). If he is correct about the general case, ours may be an exception.

CHAPTER 4. MAIMONIDES AND NAHMANIDES ON PARABLES AND COMMANDMENTS

1. See, e.g., Baer (1966), vol. 1, 245. For this image in the context of *ta'amei mitzvot*, see Matt (1986) 376, 379–82; Henoch (1978) vii–xxiv and 65–69.

2. See, in particular, Septimus (1983); Idel (1983), (1990); Berger (1983); Wolfson (1989); Halbertal (1990).

3. Wolfson (1989), 122.

4. One topic I shall not discuss here is the difference between Maimonides' and Nahmanides' concepts of a *mitzvah*, or biblical commandment. Suffice it to say that Maimonides draws a sharp distinction between scriptural *mitzvot* and all other obligations and prohibitions in the Law, both scriptural and rabbinic, and that he explicitly states in the *Guide* that he gives reasons only for biblical commandments according to the "external meaning" of the biblical text (III:41:567). Nahmanides, in contrast, has a much broader conception of the commandments, and he repeatedly includes rabbinic as well as biblical prescriptions and prohibitions among those acts for which he gives *ta'amei ha-mitzvot*. For further discussion of Maimonides' and Nahmanides' conceptions of *mitzvah*, see Golding (1987) and Halbertal (1990).

5. See Galston (1978).

6. For an alternative explanation of the *huqqim*, see now Frank (1993).

7. For further discussion of this question, see chap. 6.

8. See Heinemann (1954), 97–128, although a comprehensive study of post-Maimonidean philosophical *ta'amei ha-mitzvot* has yet to be written.

9. See Idel (1990), 42–50. I cannot discuss here the interesting question, pursued by Idel, of whether the Maimonidean "revolution" caused the first Kabbalists to create, or invent, new theosophical or theurgic reasons to counter the philosophical ones of the *Guide* or whether it merely forced them to crystalize, systematize, and make public an older esoteric tradition of reasons for the commandments that they already possessed. It is also important to keep in mind, as Idel shows, that Maimonides' philosophical, naturalized Aristotelian reconstruction of the classical bodies of esoteric truth, *ma'aseh merkabah* and *ma'aseh bereshith*, elicited an analogous reaction from the Kabbalists who viewed it as an innovation discrediting a tradition they inherited. The two topics must be evaluated conjointly.

10. *SHM*, 394, based on BT *Sanhedrin* 21b. Compare also Maimonides' statements in *MT* "*Me'ilah*" viii, 8; *Guide* III:26:507–508; and the discussion in Twersky (1980a) 391–401. On Maimonides' use of the figure of Solomon, see now Klein-Braslavy (1990) and (1996).

11. For an alternative, more Ash'arite interpretation of this passage, see Leibowitz (1980).

12. On this distinction, see chap. 2 and Shatz (1991). Here I depart from my earlier explanation in chap. 2, section V where I argued that Maimonides shifts in III:51 from an account of reasons of the legislator to an account of reasons for a performer. Of course, to say that the account of III:51–52 also concerns reasons of the legislator does not mean that such a reason, when known by the performer, cannot also serve as a (indeed *the* proper) motivating reason for him to perform the commandment.

13. It should be added that Maimonides also sometimes, amphibolously, calls the vulgar meaning of a verse its "external meaning"; see I:Intro.:11.

14. See, e.g., I:26:56f.; I:36:84.

15. Apart from these two "wise" reasons, some individual commandments may also have what we might analogously call a "vulgar" reason; e.g., in the case of the commandment to bury one's excrement, the sanitary value of the act; in the case of the Sabbath, physical rest; in the case of circumcision, improve-

ment of the physical organ. About the first two cases, Maimonides makes no explicit judgment; the third, as we shall see in chap. 5, he openly attacks.

16. On the first example, see Stern (ms. a); on the second, chap. 5 below. I intend to discuss the example of the Sabbath elsewhere.

17. See *Guide* II:40:383ff.

18. Two complicating qualifications do not, as far as I can tell, affect my general point. First, Maimonides' description of the class of commandments for which he intends his explanation in III:51—"the practices of the worship, such as reading the Torah, prayer, and the performance of the other *commandments*"—is left, apparently deliberately, open-ended. On the one hand, the specific examples he mentions all fall in the ninth class of commandments according to the categorization of the *Guide* or, as Maimonides himself adds (III:35:537), in the "Book of Adoration" in the *Mishneh Torah*. On the other hand, Maimonides seems to be specifically concerned with them insofar as they involve "action" or performance "with one's limbs—as if you were digging a hole in the ground or hewing wood in the forest" (an allusion, I believe to the commandment of Deut. 23:14), in other words, use of one's body (including the bodily organ of speech). This might suggest that the explanation ought to apply generally to all and only commandments that involve action or the body. Yet a third possibility, based on Maimonides' comparison of prayer to sacrifice in III:32:526, is that the explanation of III:51 should be extended to all similar acts of worship—concerning the Temple, sacrifice, purity and impurity, and the other acts introduced to counter idolatry. In short, it remains open how broad a class of commandments should be explained under the parabolic structure of III:26–49 and III:51–52. The second qualification I would mention concerns the content of the internal meanings of parables and internal reasons of commandments. If, as some scholars (myself included) have argued, Maimonides held a skeptical or critical view of the possibility of human knowledge of metaphysical truth or, more generally, of the possibility of human attainment of the status of an acquired intellect, then the requirement of dissasociation from "this world" as a precondition for this kind of state must also be suitably qualified.

19. On this reason, see C Lev. 19:19 on the prohibition of interbreeding. Nahmanides states this reason in C Deut. 22:6 only in passing, but it is clear that it is his intended argument.

20. Or so at least it has been supposed by most scholars. For a dissenting opinion that Nahmanides himself knew Arabic and read the *Guide* in the original, even though he may also have utilized translations like Al-Harizi's *SMN*, see now Jospe (1987). On this particular mistranslation, see 93, n.50.

21. Note that the rejected rabbinic opinion here is not the mishnaic dictum itself but one of the Amoraic explanations for the dictum in the Babylonian Talmud, that of R. Jose bar Zebida (BT *Berakhot* 33b). As we just saw, however, earlier in the text Maimonides himself appears to endorse this reason in MT *"Tefillah"* ix, 7. Hence, Maimonides would *appear* to contract himself in the *Guide* and *Mishneh Torah*. Note also that in PM *Megillah* IV, 7, Maimonides explicitly calls the commandment of *shiluah ha-ken a shim'it*, adopting the Saadyanic terminology for a purely volitional revealed law. On these apparently contradictory passages, see above chap. 3.

22. He at most alludes to it by saying that Maimonides recognized that the midrash poses a difficulty for his view [*hukshah 'alav*].

23. See especially his citation of BT *Sanhedrin* 21b, the same text about Solomon cited by Maimonides in *SHM*, which Nahmanides cites to show that every commandment has a reason.

24. Novak (1992), 2–4, 99–104, seems to hold that Nahmanides' aim in ascertaining *ta'amei ha-mitzvot* is to determine the content of the proper intentions (*kavvanot*) with which the commandments should be performed. Although there is surely a connection between *ta'amei ha-mitzvot* and proper *kavvanah*, Novak's account fails to distinguish between reasons of a legislator and reasons for a performer.

25. See also C Lev. 19:19.

26. Nahmanides distinguishes such benefits and goods from "rewards from the Legislator." Neither, it should also be noted, is a mystical effect or a kind of kabbalistic significance that attaches to performance of the commandments. At the very end of the commentary, Nahmanides does allude [*romez*] to a kabbalistic reason, a *sod*, but this only serves to underline its absence from the earlier part of his discussion. On kabbalistic theurgic reasons, see below.

27. Cf. Hyman (1979–80), 343.

28. On Nahmanides' conservativism, and the essential role he gave to tradition in his conception of Kabbalah, see Idel (1983) and (1990).

29. Compare Nahmanides' statement on knowledge of kabbalistic *ta'amei ha-mitzvot* in his "Sermon on the Words of Kohelet," in *K* 1, 190; see also Idel (1990), 45.

30. Compare Nahmanides remarks in *"Derashat Torat Ha-Shem Temimah,"* *K* 1, 163, 167.

31. Quoted in Wolfson (1988), 226. Cf. also Matt (1986), 379–82, 394f.; and Faierstein (1983). The terminology *"tzorekh gavoha"* and *"tzorekh hedyot"* is, of course, Talmudic in origin where the former refers to the "needs of the Temple" and the latter to "lay or profane needs or uses." According to Faierstein, Nahmanides was the first to employ the phrases in their kabbalistic sense.

32. *K* 1, 180. On this passage and Nahmanides' general theory of interpretation, see Wolfson (1989), 122ff.

33. Here I differ from Wolfson's (1989) interpretation of Nahmanides' terminology according to which *mashal* and *melitzah* synonymously refer to "the external sense of that which is uttered or expressed, whereas *hakhmah* and *hidah* are used to connote the internal sense and hence the *sod* of the matter" (p. 124). In a recent paper, Wolfson, revising his earlier view, now claims that *"mashal* here, as elsewhere in Nahmanides' ouevre, denotes the figurative or parabolic sense" [Wolfson (1993), 193, n. 29]. On my interpretation of the passage, *mashal* does not denote any sense or meaning at all—either external or figurative—but the kind, or genre, of the passage or text to be interpreted, namely, that it is a parable. *Melitzah*, *hakhmah*, and *hidah* refer to the different kinds of meanings that can be given the passage.

34. One wonders whether there is a deliberate play on the words *tzorfim*—the silversmiths who craft the "silver filigree-work" that figuratively represents Maimonides' external meaning—and *letzareif*—the purification accomplished

by the commandments according to Nahmanides' external explanation of Deut. 22:6.

35. Note his example, the *etrog* and other members of the four species. Here, too, one wonders whether the example was deliberately chosen in light of Maimonides' disapproving statements about the parabolic interpretation of this particular commandment in the introduction to the *Guide*, p. 11, and in III:43:572–73.

36. Nahmanides, notes, in *SHM*, 44–45.

37. For many striking examples of these two phenomena, see Wolfson (1989), 129–53. For an intriguing discussion of the legal implications (in their conception and enumeration of commandments) of these hermeneutical differences in Maimonides and Nahmanides, see Halbertal (1990), 473–76.

38. *SHM*, 45; see also Wolfson (1989), 128.

39. As a consequence, Nahmanides' notion of *peshat* is, of course, much richer than Maimonides'; see Septimus 1983, p. 18.

40. Nahmanides, notes, in *SHM*, 44.

41. One would think that this denial is based on opposition to corporeal descriptions of the deity. However, Nahmanides' general treatment of this issue is much more ambivalent and qualified than Maimonides' rigorous denial of all such ascriptions; e.g., C, 1, Gen. 46:1, pp. 246–49. For a brief discussion, see now Novak (1992), 41–42. The topic requires further evaluation.

42. C 2, p. 117.

43. This passage also raises a different question. Performing a commandment because it is the will of the deity is clearly a proper reason to do so, whereas performing it simply to be rewarded is improper. But where do the naturalistic external reasons of Deut. 22:6 stand in this ranking of agents' reasons for performing the commandments? On the one hand, because they aim at human goods or perfections, both practical and intellectual, they lack the theocentric condition Nahmanides seems to require for *'avodah me-'ahavah*, service out of love of God. On the other hand, they also do not fall under the low bill of *'avodah shelo' leshmah 'al menat leqabeil peras*, service not for the sake [of heaven] but [simply] in order to be rewarded, at least where such a reward is taken to be an improper motive. I do not know whether, or how, Nahmanides resolves this question concerning the normative status of the external reasons for the commandments as motives for their performers.

44. See C 2 on Lev. 18:25, 110–11; Deut. 11:18, 394; "Sermon on the Words of Kohelet," K 1, 200–1; and chap. 6 below.

CHAPTER 5. MAIMONIDES ON THE PARABLE OF CIRCUMCISION

1. Saadiah (1970–71/1948) III, X, 7/177.

2. See II:39:380 and III:49:605, especially Maimonides' use of Deut. 32:4 as prooftext both for the "consumate perfection" of nature and the "consumate justice" of the commandments.

3. See also Maimonides' citation of *Gen. Rabbah* LXXX.

4. *EC* chaps. I–IV and *MT* "*De'ot*," chaps. i–iii.

5. *EC* chap. IV.

6. On this chapter, see Stern (1997) and (ms. a).

7. See BT *Baba Batra* 16a; compare Rashi, Gen. 12:11.

8. Compare the role of accommodation in Maimonides' explanation of the institution of sacrifices in chap. 2.

9. See, however, *MT "Milah"* iii, 8, based on *M. Nedarim* 3. There, too, the kind of perfection to which Maimonides refers would appear to be moral rather than congenital or natural, although the figure of Abraham seems to be used to exemplify something closer to the mean. On the use of the term *tamim* [*perfect*] in the sense of the mean, see also II:39:378–81. Maimonides' conception of the mean appears, however, to shift from the *Mishneh Torah* to the *Guide;* for discussion, see the references cited in the next note.

10. For a similar interpretation of the ethics of the *Guide* and of the mean, see now Davidson (1987). Although it seems to me still open whether Maimonides intends this conception of the mean to hold for all characteristics of the soul, I am almost entirely in agreement with Davidson's description of Maimonides' position in the *Guide.* I would disagree, however, at least in part with his explanation for the shift in Maimonides' view from *EC* and *MT "De'ot"* to the *Guide.* As I argue at greater length in "Excrement and Exegesis" (ms. a), this shift reflects one of several ways, according to Maimonides, in which matter comes to be an obstruction both to apprehension of and concentration on God. I discuss this subject further in ms. a, b, c.

11. Cf. *MT "Bi'ot 'Asurot,"* xiii, 14.

12. Compare Maimonides' later statement, among his reasons for why circumcision is performed in childhood, that "a grown-up man would regard the thing, which he would *imagine* before it occurred, as terrible and hard" (III:49:610, my emphasis) and, therefore, may well not perform it.

13. Maimonides' source for this interpretation may be the biblical story (Gen. 34) of Shekhem the son of Hamor who, after raping Dinah, agrees along with his people to be circumcised in order to unite with the Israelites. Note, however, that this story may undercut the claim that circumcision is a good test of the would-be convert, since the text suggests that the motive of the Shekhemites is to marry the Israelite women and profit from the association. Furthermore, instead of preventing outsiders from deceiving the community, circumcision is primarily used by Jacob's sons to deceive the outsiders. It is also not clear from the passage in our text how Maimonides wishes us to contrast circumcision and "an incision in the leg or a burn in the arm." Are the latter meant to be idolatrous practices, like the mourning gashes of Lev. 21? Does Maimonides emphasize this difference to circumvent a possible parallel between the two?

14. Cf. *MT "Milah"* iii, 8 ("Whoever nullifes the covenant of our ancestor Abraham and retains his foreskin or stretches it, even if he possesses knowledge of the Torah and practices good deeds, has no portion in the World to Come"), based on *M. Avoth* III, 11. Maimonides' use of the rabbinic phrase "World to Come" in this *halakhah* may refer to membership in the community of Israel, following its use in the "Introduction to Heleq" in *PM* or it may refer to the immortality of soul. In the latter case, Maimonides' negative formulation of his *halakhah* may be significant since circumcision is at best a necessary but not suf-

ficient condition for the kind of perfection that could yield immortality, or "permanent preservation" (III:27:511).

15. This midrashically based depiction of the ancient Israelites in Egypt is in sharp contrast to other *midrashim* that emphasize the degree to which they had attempted to preserve their distinct identity throughout their Egyptian captivity, e.g., by preserving their distinct names and clothing.

16. MT *"Bi'ot 'Asurot,"* xiii, 1–3, based on BT *Kritot* 9a.

17. Ibid. xiiii,, 2.

18. To be sure, the two covenants are not entirely distinct. The Levites, from whom Moses is descended, are said not to have ceased practicing circumcision, continuing the Abrahamic covenant. Similarly, in MT *"'Avodah Zarah,"* i, 3, Maimonides states that throughout their sojourn in Egypt the Levites, unlike the rest of the Israelites, never engaged in idolatry. Thus the Mosaic covenant builds on the Abrahamic rather than simply replaces it. I return to the contrast between the two covenants later.

19. For Maimonides' opinion that Muslims believe in the unity of God (and deny idolatry or polytheism), see his letter to Obadiah the Convert, in Blau 2, Responsum #248, 725–28 and Shailat, 238–41. For his view that Christians do not truly believe in divine unity, see I:50:111: "the Christians [who] say: namely, that He is one but also three, and that the three are one" "resemble" the one "who says in his words that He is one, but believes Him in his thought to be many." Likewise, see *PM 'Avodah Zarah* I, 3, where Christians are explicitly described as idolators. On the contrast between Muslims and Christians, see also Blau, 1, #149, 284ff; and Shailat, 215ff. For further discussion, see Novak (1986), 233–50; Kaplan (1986); and Schlossberg (1990). To avoid a possible misunderstanding, I should add that my remarks in the text are not meant to suggest that Maimonides' comprehensive attitude toward Islam was uniformly positive. As Schlossberg shows, his attitude toward Islam as a historical reality, especially in light of its treatment of the Jews, was quite negative and surely much more critical than the idealized view depicted in the text.

20. For a similar distinction, see Kellner (1991), chap. 9, on the two communities "Jews" and "Israel."

21. MT *"Milah,"* iii, 9; based on BT *Nedarim* 31b.

22. I am indebted to Michael Fishbane for pointing out to me this pun on the words *hit'arvu*, intermingled, and *'aravim*, Arabs.

23. On this *halakhah*, see also BT *Sanhedrin* 59b. Note, as Maimonides emphasizes in his opening sentence, that circumcision was never commanded to the Noahides at large but only to Abraham and his descendants; hence, it might be classified specifically as an Abrahamic law to be distinguished both from the Noahide laws and the Mosaic commandments. For an opposing view, see, however, *PM Hullin* VI, 6 (based on BT *Makkot* 23b), where he writes, in illustration of the principle of a law "prescribed from Sinai," that "we do not circumcise because Abraham circumcised himself and the members of his household but because God commanded us, through Moses, to become circumcised as had Abraham." It would appear, then, that Maimonides changed his position sometime between this earlier work and the *Mishneh Torah*, although the matter requires further investigation. For discussion of the passage in question, see Lichtenstein (1975).

24. Compare Maimonides' ruling with RaSHI, BT *Sanhedrin* 59b, who interprets the obligation as devolving only on the six immediate sons of Keturah and not their descendants, an interpretation with considerable textual support. Note also that, according to standard midrashic interpretation, "Keturah" is simply another name for Hagar, the mother of Ishmael; in which case, the descendants of Keturah and of Ishmael are ultimately all descendants of the same pair of ancestors. Cf. also "Bnei Keturah" (1954).

25. Cf. *MT "Nedarim"* ix, 21–22. In the first of these two *halakhot,* Maimonides repeats the traditional rabbinic exclusion of the Ishmaelites from the commandment of circumcison, based on Gen. 21:12, repeating almost verbatim *MT "Melakhim"* x, 7. But in the second of the two *halakhot* in *"Nedarim,"* he adds (commenting on the law of the person who vows to forbid himself any benefit from the uncircumcised): "'The uncircumcised [*ha'arlah*]' only refers to idolators, as it is said: 'For all the nations are uncircumcised' (Jer. 9:25); and by this [i.e., by the phrase 'the circumcised'] are meant only those who are commanded to perform circumcision and not those who are not commanded to perform it." That is, "the circumcised" refers only to those who are de jure circumcised (whether or not they are in fact circumcised), namely, Israel; not to those who are de facto circumcised whether or not they were so commanded. On the face of it, this ruling in the second of the two *halakhot* would seem, then, simply to corroborate the traditional ruling in the first *halakhah,* which excludes Ishmaelites, thus contradicting the outcome of *"Melakhim"* x, 7–8. Whether or not the latter should be viewed as a gloss on *"Nedarim"* needs further investigation. Note also Maimonides' citation of Jer. 9:25 in *"Milah"* iii, 8, based on M. *Nedarim* 3: "Repulsive is the foreskin, for the nations are made repulsive by it, as it is stated in Scripture, 'For all the nations are uncircumcised' (Jer. 9:25)." Here also circumcision seems to function to differentiate Israel from *all* other nations.

26. Cf. Kellner (1991) and Novak (1986).

27. As Joel Kraemer has suggested to me (personal communication), there may also be a polemical dimension to Maimonides' explanation here and in *MT "Melakhim,"* x, 8: after having included the Moslems within the Abrahamic covenant of circumcision, Maimonides justifies the Jewish practice to circumcise the child on the eighth day after birth and criticizes the Muslim practice to defer circumcision to puberty. For a similar proposal, see also Kasher (1995)

28. See III:48:599; the context is the explanation of the prohibition of Lev. 22:28. Note that parental love, insofar as it is a function of the imagination, is not even specific to the human species.

29. Harvey (1980).

30. Cf. Kreisel (1989).

31. For a sample of these modes of symbolization, see Stern (1987).

32. This stands, of course, in complete contrast to Maimonides' enthusiasm for historical-anthropological explanations or even ethical explanations for obscure commandments. For a good example of Maimonides' disdain for symbolic interpretations of commandments or ritual acts and gestures, see his explanation of the festivals in III:43:570–74, where he does not offer a single symbolic interpretation and, on the contrary, appears to criticize midrashic explanations

for their symbolic interpretations. For further discussion of that passage, see Stern (ms. a).

33. Cf. also *MT* "*'Avodah Zarah*" i, 2; *Guide* II:39:379f.

34. *Guide* II:33:364. Of course, all such speculation and reasoning is an "overflow" of the deity or, more precisely, active intellect. However, this detracts in no way from the naturalistic character of the intellectual process to which Maimonides is referring in the case of Abraham.

35. On this theme, see also Maimonides' letter to Obadiah the Proselyte, in Blau, 2, Responsum #248, 725–28 and Shailat, 238–41, in which Abraham, rather than Moses, is portrayed as the father of *everyone* who rejects idolatry and professes belief in the unity of God, and especially of the proselyte to Judaism.

36. Cf. also the general reference to "representation of the unity of the Name" (I:50:151), *MT* "*'Avodah Zarah*" i, 3; and the letter to Obadiah the Proselyte (see note 35).

37. The same phrase was used by Maimonides' father, R. Maimon, and by his son, R. Abraham; it parallels the Arabic *basmalah*: "In the name of Allah, the merciful, the compassionate" (*bismi'llah al-rahman al-rahim*). For brief comments, though the references are incomplete, see Lieberman (1947), "Introduction," 5, n.7.

38. Here Maimonides follows Ibn Sina's doctrine that the deity and only the deity is necessarily existent in itself, as opposed to all other beings, which are possibily existent in themselves and necessitated to exist through a cause. On Maimonides' underlying theory of meaning here, see Stern (1989) and (forthcoming b).

39. *Tanhuma, Tzav,* 14; cf. also *Shemini,* 8.

40. See Wolfson (1987), who traces the development of this doctrine from the *Tanhuma* passage quoted in the text through the Hasidei Ashkenaz and Spanish kabbalah. He does not discuss Maimonides, but his illuminating study inspired this conjecture and, as I hope is clear, it would not be surprising to find Maimonides an heir to the same esoteric doctrine.

41. This section of the chapter has been extensively rewritten and differs substantively from the corresponding section in the earlier published version of the essay.

42. I discuss this topic at greater length in (ms.a).

43. As I argued in chap. 4, this is not Maimonides' only account of *ta'amei ha-mitzvot.* His first, internal, reason for circumcision fits the second, internal, explanation of the Law as a whole sketched in III:51–52.

44. See, e.g., Twersky (1980a), 283–84.

45. On Maimonides' identification of love of God with knowledge, see *MT* "*Teshuvah*" x, 6; *Guide* III:28:512–13; I:39:89; and III:51:621. For a similar analysis of the *Book of Love,* see now Kreisel (1996).

46. For the opposing view, see Strauss (1952), 94.

CHAPTER 6. PROBLEMATIC COMMANDMENTS III

1. Pines's translation "learned man" in the *Guide* follows Ibn Tibbon's "*'ish hakham*" in *MN.* However, as Joel Kraemer has noted (personal commu-

nication), the Arabic original is a rare expression that means something like "man of the sciences," i.e., a scientist. In the Graeco-Arabic translation literature, the same Arabic term is also used to translate the Greek term for mathematician. See also Langermann (1994), n.40, who cites an anonymous Yemeni commentary to the *Guide* (ms. Berlin Or. oct. 258 [Cat. Steinschneider 108], f. 106a), which reads: "They say that *al-'ulumiyyin* are those who have knowledge of the science[s] of motions, observations, and astral magic (*al-instinzalat*)." Langermann notes that this last Arabic phrase literally means "the bringing down" of the celestial forces. We shall return below, in our discussion of Nahmanides, to this action and its relation to astronomy and astrology. In any case, "learned man" should not be understood to mean that the individual in question is learned in the Law.

2. See Munk, 1, 38, n.1. There is no scholarly consensus over the source of Maimonides' analogy. Dr. Sarah Stroumsa (personal communication) has suggested that Maimonides is alluding to the story of Ishtar and the fallen angels. Dr. T. Langermann (personal communication) has suggested as a possible source Abraham bar Hiyya (1860), e.g., 5, where he mentions certain wise but evil individuals who are simultaneously rewarded and punished by being confined eternally to the celestial realm. This last suggestion would complement my view below that Maimonides uses "Sabians" as a label for then contemporary astrologers, like bar Hiyya, and theurgically or magically oriented forms of Neoplatonism.

3. Cf. Harvey (1988), (1993).

4. The other kind of idolatry is representational: belief in divine corporeality, attributes, and other features that suggest that the deity is not one but plural, composite, or comparable. This kind of idolatry is the subject of much of the first part of the *Guide*.

5. The one possible exception, who may have influenced Maimonides, is Abraham ibn Ezra (1976); see, e.g., his commentary on Lev. 16, 18; 17, 7; 19, 26. However, ibn Ezra's reasons of this kind are hardly explicit and at most limited to individual commandments. See now Regev (1990); Twersky (1993). I return to ibn Ezra below.

6. See Urbach (1971), 330–33; and now, for a comprehensive review of the texts, Havlin (1995), who argues on comparative textual evidence that for the rabbis the *huqqim* were distinguished because of their apparent connection to idolatrous practices, but that this explanation was eclipsed by the *geonim*. I am sympathetic to this conclusion, although Havlin's arguments read, I believe, too much Maimonides back into the rabbis.

7. For variants, see *Peskita DeRav Kahana* (1962) ; *Sifra Aharei Mot*, 372–73.

8. For historical background on Sabianism, see Chwolsohn (1856); Pines (1963), cxxiii–iv; Burnett (1986), 87f.; Munk 3, 217–43; Hjårpe (1972); and now Tardieu (1986). (I am indebted to Sarah Stroumsa and Gad Freudenthal for bringing Tardieu's essay to my attention.) On the *Nabatean Agriculture*, see Sezgin (1971), 318–29.

9. Here I follow Tardieu, 12–13, 17–18, 25, 27–29.

10. *MT* "*'Avodah Zarah*" xi, 15, *MT* "*Teshuva*" v–vi; *EC* chaps. V–VIII; *LA*. Especially noteworthy is Maimonides' explanation that the Temple was

destroyed and the "kingdom lost" because the Jews occupied themselves with star gazing instead of the art of war (*LA*, 465). See also Lerner (1968). For another popular statement of Maimonides' view, see his "Letter of Responsa to Obadiah the Convert, Second Question" (Heb.), in Shailat 1, 236–38; Blau 2, 714–18. On Maimonides' view of astrology, see now Langermann (1991), 123–58; Freudenthal (1993), 77–90; Barkai (1987), 7–35 and, on Maimonides, 12–15; and Kreisel (1994), 25–31.

11. See Bahya ibn Paquda (1928/1973), 276–301; Saadiah (1973), 194–95. On Abraham ibn Ezra, see now Langermann (1993), 28–85; Jospe (1994). On all of these figures, see also Kafih (1988). (I am indebted to Gad Freudenthal for bringing this essay to my attention.) For an interesting discussion of the status of astrology in ninth- and tenth-century Islam, see Kraemer (1986), 150–62 and notes. On Nahmanides' attitude toward astrology, see below.

12. See Freudenthal (1993), 77–83.

13. For the latter, see, e.g., Baer (1966), 1, 245; and in the context of *ta'amei ha-mitzvot*, Henoch (1978), vii–xxiv and 65–69; and Matt (1986), 376. For a much more balanced, subtle interpretation in the former vein, see now Septimus (1983), 11, n.1; Novak (1992); Langermann (1992), 223–45; and chap. 4 above.

14. On Ha-Levi's influence on Nahmanides, especially his view of science, astrology, and magic, see Langermann (1992) and now Ruderman's (1995) brief but interesting discussion, 35–40.

15. Idel (1990), 50.

16. *Guide* III:26–32; Nahmanides, C Deut. 22:6.

17. To avoid a possible misunderstanding, note (1) that a reason, as I use the term, is not necessarily an object of the faculty of reason, or intellect, what Saadiah calls a *mitzvah sikhlit*. For discussion, see chap. 2, n.12. (2) As in chap. 2, the *ta'amei ha-mitzvot* with which I am concerned, are reasons, or explanations, why the commandments were legislated, not reasons for agents to perform them. Although many of the former will also serve as the latter, not all will—as we shall see below.

18. I:Intro.:9, 11. In fact the situation is somewhat more complicated: sometimes the vulgar meaning coincides with the external or internal parabolic meaning; at other times (say, where it describes God corporeally or expresses Sabian myths), it expresses harmful falsehoods that the author does not believe and he believes should not be believed by any reasonable person—although it may have been necessary, or unavoidable, to use such language in its original context of utterance (see, e.g., *Guide* 1:26:56f.; 1:36:84); and at yet other times, the "vulgar" meaning may be innocuous: neither wisdom nor harmful falsehood. At bottom, Maimonides is not concerned with ascertaining the meanings of words, or *peshat*. He is concerned with what we ought to believe, and "belief is not the notion that is uttered but the notion that is represented in the soul" (*Guide* 1:50:111).

19. These are in addition to the "vulgar" reason for the commandment: e.g., for the commandment to bury one's excrement, its sanitary value; for the Sabbath, physical rest; for circumcision, improvement of the physical organ.

About the first two cases, Maimonides makes no explicit judgment; the third, he openly attacks.

20. On the scapegoat, see also III:47:597. On the use of parables in the Law, see also Maimonides' comment that some of the opinions communicated by the Law "are set forth in parables" (III:27:510)—perhaps parabolic commandments? In the course of giving reasons for the commandments, Maimonides also sometimes refers to their external meaning [*zahir*]; see III:46:590; III:41:567. I would argue that he is referring to the parabolic exernal meaning of the commandments.

21. See II:40:383ff; Kreisel (1989).

22. C Exodus 29:46

23. I do not mean here "mysterious" (or "enigmatic") in the Hellenistic sense of *enigmata* or mystery religions, but rather in the sense of things whose explanation lies completely beyond human capacities. On the notions of problem and mystery, see Morgenbesser and Levi (1964).

24. See also *LA* and *Guide* III:49:612.

25. For Maimonides' earliest description of the Sabians, see *PM 'Avodah Zarah* VII, 7.

26. Cf. Langermann (1991), 146–51.

27. An especially important case of the latter sort is Maimonides' explanation of the agriculturally related curses and blessings, or rewards and punishments, in III:30:522–23. Maimonides seems to hold that the very fact that the Israelites were told that there *are* rewards and punishments (in this world) for the Law is itself a strategem to counter Sabianism. I cannot explore it here, but this is crucial for understanding Maimonides' notion of providence, which should not, then, be defined in terms of divine reward and punishment.

28. This kind of antinomianism was my primary explanation for concealment of the *huqqim* in chap. 2; I now think that it is not the whole story. So, even while Sabianism may still be alive according to Maimonides (as I shall next argue), there remains the *general* problem of "obsolete commandments": the grounds for the obligatoriness of commandments when the explanation for their legislation is no longer a reason for agents to perform those commandments. This *general* problem is, of course, not solved simply by showing that certain commandments in fact may not be obsolete. I cannot pursue this question here, but I hope to do so on another occasion.

29. See, however, Maimonides' comment in III:49:612 where he denies first-hand acquaintance with the Sabians whose "opinions have disappeared two thousand years ago or even before that." Also III:50:615: "The doctrines of the Sabians are remote from us today."

30. The meaning of this reference is not clear.

31. See (3) below; also Moses of Narbonne (1852/1961) ad loc. who emphasizes the widespread use of talismans.

32. See Munk's comment in Munk 3, 242, n. 1; Tardieu (1986), 17–19. According to Chwolsohn, cited by Tardieu, 17, sacrifice was a regular part of the Sabian rite on their festivals. On Maimonides' use of the Hebrew term *heikhal*, see Tardieu's comment on Chwolson's understanding of the Arabic

word *magma'* for the Sabian meeting house: "*magma'* serait donc synonyme de *haikal*, 'temple'" (17).

33. This history should be compared with Maimonides' history of idolatry at the beginning of MT "'*Avodah Zarah*."

34. Cf. Burnett (1986).

35. Cf. Halbertal and Margalit (1992), 77, and Margalit (1990).

36. On Maimonides' criticisms and scientific objections to astrology, see Langermann (1991). The objections concern specific empirical errors (found mainly in the *PM 'Avodah Zarah* IV,7), misuse of the notion of *fayd*, or overflow (see II:12), and methodological considerations: that the astrologers base their claims on inductive observation and experience rather than on a theory with first principles. As Langermann mentions, this methodological question was discussed widely in the contemporary literature and debates on astrology, although Maimonides himself addresses it directly only in a medical context. This is significant because Maimonides may have learned of the issue from the classical debate between medical dogmatists and empiricists, as recounted by Galen (1944), who is also a main source of medieval knowledge of the skeptical tradition as it was preserved in the medical tradition. Hence, this may have been a route by which Maimonides also became acquainted with the kind of skeptical argument I discuss below. On this history, see Stern (ms.b). Besides scientific objections, Maimonides also criticizes astrology on practical grounds (that it leads to neglect in acquiring essential practical skills and because it leads to fatalism). On the latter, see Stern (1997).

37. This may also explain why Maimonides is so concerned with the particulars of the *huqqim*, down to the number and animal gender of every sacrifice. Rituals, as scholars of religion often observe, are either performed exactly, down to the smallest detail, or not successfully performed at all. Therefore, in order to succeed in exposing the myth, or to transfer the practices from their idolatrous context to worship of the deity, it was essential for Maimonides to attend to *all* particulars.

38. See, for example, Halbertal and Margalit (1992), who give an excellent analysis of Maimonides' theory of attributes and linguistic representation as a cognitive form of idolatry, but entirely ignore the Sabian idolatry of Part III of the *Guide*.

39. I do not want to exaggerate the differences between the two kinds of idolatry, in Parts I and III. Both turn on the illegitimate role of the imagination that corrupts the intellect. Both turn on ways in which matter controls form. And both kinds of refutation involve, at the external level, negation and, at the internal level, a kind of skeptical dilemma. That is, affirmative attributive statements about God are to be reinterpreted (externally) as negations of privations, just as the commandments that, according to their vulgar meaning, express practices like that of Sabianism, are in fact to be explained (externally) as attempts to negate those practices. On the internal meaning of divine attributions, see Stern (1989), (forthcoming b), and (ms. b). On the internal meaning of the *huqqim*, see below.

40. On this notion of symbolic expression, see Stern (1987).

41. The meaning of the phrase "to bring forth a form [*tzurah*] in the soul" is not clear. Presumably the idea is that repentance involves some kind of actualization of the human soul, i.e., the material intellect. Whether the form is necessarily an intelligible is less evident.

42. MT *"Teshuvah"* ii, 1.

43. See Stern (1997).

44. On human autonomy in Maimonides, see Hartman (1976) and (1985); Gellman (1990); and Shatz (1990).

45. On the Platonic and Neoplatonic traditions in Islamic philosophy, see Peters (1979), including his pessimistic comments concerning research prospects into the origins of nonscholastic Islamic Platonism and Neoplatonism, such as Sabianism (14).

46. On Neoplatonic influences on Maimonides, see now the series of studies by Ivry (1985a), (1985b), and (1991).

47. The locus classicus for contemporary discusssions of Maimonides' skepticism is Pines (1979), but see also his (1981), (1986), and (1987). Pines's papers have generated a huge body of literature; for references, see Stern (ms.b) The argument for skepticism I give in this section, based on Maimonides' philosophy of language, is a counterpart to arguments I give in the papers cited in note 39. For a second set of skeptical arguments with respect to astronomy, see Stern (ms.c). For a rather different kind of appeal to Maimonides' skepticism in connection with his view of astrology, see Freudenthal (1993).

48. *Guide* I:73:209ff. Cf. Altmann (1987), 75 . For a different account of Maimonides' theory of the intellect and extended criticism of Pines, see now Davidson (1992–93).

49. For further discussion of this argument, see Stern (1989) and (forthcoming b). For a valuable discussion by the Yemini Maimonidean Hoter b. Shlomo of the distinction between the intellect and imagination and their role in cognition, see now the texts and notes in Langermann (1994). These texts may throw significant light on Maimonides' own understanding of the distinction.

50. As Ivry (1985b) argues, Maimonides also attempts to play down the causal, ontic role of the separate intellects. Clearly this is of a piece with his desire to distance himself from attributing any causal power to the stars.

51. *Guide* II:12:79f. It is not clear from the text whether the contrast Maimonides intends to draw is between the Creator (= the Active Intellect?) and God or between what is *"always* designated" (my emphasis) using a certain term and what is designated in that way in Hebrew (alone?).

52. In the same passage Maimonides describes how the separate intellects, sphere, and stars were also assimilated in the opposite direction, i.e., how all their actions were subsumed under a kind of material causation. A well-known difficulty within medieval science, already noted by Aristotle, was how to explain the purported material actions of the spheres and stars on the sublunar elements given that they were not mechanical, i.e., body on body, but some kind of action at a distance. To save the theory, it was therefore postulated that all these apparent actions at a distance (like the magnet; cf. II:12:277) were really material in virtue of taking place via contact through a medium. Similarly, Mai-

monides describes how "some among the multitude," having realized that the deity is not a body and not in space, could still not "imagine" any action taking place except by contact and in virtue of standing in some spacial relation; therefore, "they imagined that He gives commands to the angels and that they accomplish the actions . . . through immediate contact and the drawing near of one body to another . . . they also imagined that the angels were bodies" and that He issues commands only "through the instrumentality of letters and sounds—and that in consequence that thing is affected" (II:12:280). In other words, they attempt to explain the actions of the deity and separate intellects as mechanical actions, no different from those of the spheres and star, by positing contact through a medium. (Throughout this note I am indebted to personal correspondence with Gad Freudenthal.)

53. Here I am also indebted to Gad Freudenthal (personal correspondence) who raised these alternatives in reply to my argument.

54. Maimonides' identification of the evil impulse (*yetzer hara'*) with the imagination in this passage should be coupled with his identification of Satan with the evil impulse in III:22:489. This may throw some light on his understanding of the tannaitic statement of BT *Yoma* 67b on the *huqqim* in which it is said that Satan criticizes Israel for these commandments. The criticism stems from the imagination, on a number of levels.

55. Maimonides may have a similar problem, stemming from his lack of a criterion to distinguish the intellect from the imagination, justifying the distinction he surely wanted to draw between determinism (which he may have upheld) and fatalism (which he explicitly rejects). Cf. Freudenthal (1993), 88f.

56. On this curious term *raving* (*hathiyan*), see now Gellman (1991) who concedes, however, that this occurrence of the term, as well as its occurrences in III:29, fall outside his account.

57. For additional problems Maimonides himself seems to recognize that render problematic his *justification* of a distinction between improper astrology and proper celestial physics and metaphysics, see Kreisel (1994). Although I generally agree with Kreisel's argument, his claim that Maimonides acknowledges in *Guide* II:37 that there is some knowledge that emanates to the imagination of magicians and diviners does not seem to me supported by the text.

58. MT "'*Avodah Zarah*" ii, 2.

59. LA 229

60. On this contrast between Moses and Abraham, see Kaplan (1985) and above chap. 5. See also Maimonides' apology for his own use of a "rhetorical mode of speech in order to support" the doctrine of creation in which he counters that he is acting no different from Aristotle who "used rhetorical speeches" in support of eternity. Citing BT *Baba Bathra* 116a, Maimonides then asks: "If he refers in support of his opinion to the ravings of the Sabians, how can we but refer in support of our opinion to the words of Moses and Abraham . . . ?" (II:23:322)

61. C Lev. 19, 19; cf. C Lev 18, 6; 26, 15; C Deut 6, 16; 6, 20; 16, 12. This is not Nahmanides' only interpretation of the word *hoq*. See C Exod. 15, 25 where he interprets *hoq* as *minhag*, i.e., what is customary or habitual; also C Gen. 26, 5; C Deut. 11, 32; C Deut. 16, 12; C Lev. 25, 23. In a number of these

cases, Nahmanides seems to mean by a *hoq* any commandment whose reason is not explicitly written in the Torah.

62. Cf. *MT* "*Me'ilah*" viii, 8 for a similar concern by Maimonides.

63. For similar remarks concerning Nahmanides' attitude toward science in general, see Langermann (1992).

64. "Introduction to Genesis," C 1, 2–7; "*Derashat Torat HaShem Temimah*" in *K* 1:141–75, 142–45; Langermann (1992), 232.

65. Following Al-Harizi's Hebrew translation *SMN*, Nahmanides refers the idolatrous practice to "Chaldeans" (*Khasdim*) rather than Sabians. Cf. *SMN* III:46:286ff.

66. Here Nahmanides follows Saadiah and HaLevi rather than Maimonides.

67. Cf. Septimus (1983).

68. In addition, Nahmanides sometimes objects to Maimonides' historical explanation on purely descriptive grounds: its generality fails to do justice to the details and complexities of the commandment as stated in the Torah. See, e.g., Nahmanides' criticisms of Maimonides' explanation for the prohibition on the use of metal in building the Temple altar, in Exod. 20, 2; and below, on sacrifice.

69. The passage reoccurs almost verbatim in the "*Derashat Torat HaShem Temimah*," *K* 1, 165. This statement should, however, be contrasted with Nahmanides' comment on Deut. 11, 32 where he seems to include *all* sacrifices among *huqqim*.

70. Cf. Halbertal (1990).

71. For a similar criticism of the explanatory power of another of Maimonides' *ta'amei ha-mitzvot*, see C Deut. 21, 4, on *'eglah 'arufah*, the commandment to break the neck of a heifer when an unidentified murder victim is discovered outside a city. In *Guide* III:40:557, Maimonides explains the rite as a strategy to publicize the murder and thereby expose the murderer. Nahmanides objects, among other things, that if this were the reason, "it would be more fitting that it be performed on a good field that is fit to be sown which people will notice, for in the case of a rough ravine that has never been tilled people won't know why it is not worked." As we shall see, Nahmanides instead classifes the commandment among the *huqqim*.

72. Al-Ishbili (1956), 53–58. See also Abarbanel (1579/repr. frequently); Arama (1522/1849); and Moses of Narbonne (1852/1961), III:32 who attacks without mentioning Nahmanides.

73. This interpretation, of course, will not save Nahmanides' misreading if he means that the aim of the *huqqim* is to reeducate *only* the Chaldeans and Egyptians. In his defense, it might be added that the text he cites, Maimonides' statement that "it was in order to efface the traces of these incorrect opinions that we have been ordered by the Law to offer in sacrifices only these three species of quadrupeds" (III:46:581), does not unambiguously state *whose* incorrect opinions are to be effaced. But anyone who has read III:26–33 would know that it is the opinions of the Israelites and not Chaldeans or Egyptians. It is also curious that Nahmanides chooses this passage in III:46 to represent Maimonides' position rather than the more sustained discussions in III:29, 32, or 37.

For a similar problem about Nahmanides' choice of Maimonidean texts, see chap. 4.

74. Ibn Ezra *Com.*, Lev. 1, 1. I have used the translation of Langermann (1993), 35. That Nahmanides is referring to ibn Ezra is claimed, e.g., by Chavel, C 2, Lev. 1, 9 , n.11, p. 12. Likewise, in *"Derashat Torat HaShem Temimah,"* K 1, 163–66, Nahmanides explicitly recommends ibn Ezra's explanation, saying that it is a "fine reason that should be accepted."

75. Maimonides' explanation itself, of course, may have been influenced by ibn Ezra's. On ibn Ezra's influence on Maimonides, see now Twersky (1993) and Harvey (1987).

76. For a similar problem concerning whether all commandments have reasons in III:26–28 and in III:48, see chap. 3; also Berger (1983).

77. On Nahmanides' stand in the Maimonidean Controversy, see Septimus (1983); Berger (1983).

78. C Deut. 18, 9; cf. Nahmanides' argument for miracles in *"Derashat Torat HaShem Temimah,"* K, 1, 130; C Exod. 13, 16; and Berger (1983), 109–10.

79. See also his repeated invocation of *Genesis Rabbah* 10:7 in C Gen. 1, 11; 2,8; Lev. 19, 19.

80. On the history of astral magic, and this form in particular, see the important series of articles by Schwartz (1992a), (1992b), (1992c), to whom I am also indebted for discussion. Because he concentrates on the fourteenth century and later, on which Nahmanides does not seem to have had significant impact, Schwartz does not discuss him at length. It is worth noting, however, that Nahmanides' position seems to be unique among the various stances taken by Jewish thinkers toward astral magic. Schwartz describes four such positions: those who take astral magic to be (1) absolutely false and forbidden, (2) dubiously or possibly true (in part) and forbidden, (3) false but psychologically useful and nonetheless forbidden, and (4) true and permissable. Nahmanides' view is that astral magic is definitely true and *therefore* forbidden, i.e., forbidden *because* it is true.

81. *"Derashat Torat HaShem Temimah,"* K, 1, 147. This important passage contains a history of the decline of the spiritual sciences among the Jews reminiscent of and unquestionably directed against Maimonides' history (*Guide* I:71) of the decline of the philosophical sciences, physics and metaphysics, among the Jews. Like Maimonides, Nahmanides also blames the decline of the sciences on the Exile and on their esoteric, oral character, which limited their transmission and accessibility. However, Nahmanides adds that the true spiritual sciences were also suppressed under the dominating power of the "Greeks" and "the well-known man," namely, Aristotle, who "denied everything other than what can be perceived by the senses [*murgash*]" and who insisted that all science be based on "natures" [*tiv'aim*]. On this passage, see also Langermann (1992), 331–32; Vajda (1954), 113–16.

82. Cf. Halbertal and Margalit (1992), 190–97.

83. It should also be noted that, while Nahmanides acknowledges the important influence of Abraham ibn Ezra, they disagree on the reality of the object of idolatry. For ibn Ezra, the objects of the ancient idolatrous rite corre-

sponding to the *sa'ir la-'azazel* were *sheidim* [demons] who, he says, are also called *si'irim* [goats] because that is how they appear in visions or hallucinations to the mad. Hence, for ibn Ezra, unlike Nahmanides, *sheidim* are only imagined in visions and hallucinations, but do not really exist. For ibn Ezra this raises a further question: if demons do not exist, to whom, then, is the *sa'ir la-'azazel* sent? On this question in ibn Ezra's supercommentaries, see Langermann (1993), 39–42.

84. Cf. *Genesis Rabbah* 65:10; *Chapters of Rabbi Eliezer* 46.

85. Cf. C Num. 19, 2.

86. Cf. "*Derashat Torat HaShem Temimah*," K, 1, 165.

87. Cf. Halbertal and Margalit (1992), 190–97 on monolatry.

88. On the paschal sacrifice, see also C Exod. 5, 3 and C Lev. 4, 2, where Nahmanides also employs the fact that the communal bulluck sin-offering (Lev. 4, 13–21) is in part burnt outside the camp to explain why Scripture does not use the expressions "a fire offering to God" or "a sweet savior to the Lord." He does not, however, call it a *hoq*. On the significance of the fact that it is a bulluck or heifer that is offered, see C Exod. 24, 5.

89. On this view, the predicate "is a *hoq*," insofar as that means "is problematic," is not, then, (in modern terminology) a one-place predicate (or property) of commandments, but a four-place relation between a commandment c, a (reference) class of commandments C, a reason R for C, and a population M. To be sure, Nahmanides seems to take the "multitude" to be a somewhat stable group for different communities, but the point here is that to be a *hoq*, a commandment need not be problematic for everyone—though if it is problematic for the *multitude M*, it will be a *hoq* for *everyone* in the community including those for whom it is not problematic.

90. This is not to say that the true, expert categorization C' and its reason R' is always or ever revealed to the multitude M for whom the commandment c is problematic relative to the reason for its ordinary classification. For the reasons discussed in the text, it may be preferable that M accept c simply as a "divine decree" whose reason they do not know and are not told.

91. Note Nahmanides' disagreement with Maimonides who (explicitly) claims (*Guide* II:28–29) that, even if the world is created, it may be (and is) eternal *a parte post*. More consistently with Aristotelian philosophy, Nahmanides infers from the fact that the world is created by the will of God (and, hence, subject to composition) that it also only continues to exist so long as He so wills (because it is also subject to decomposition).

92. Although it could hardly count as a case of cross-breeding, it might be noted that Nahmanides does not seem to consider another classical rabbinic example of a *hoq*, the prohibition against cooking (and eating) milk and meat— in scriptural terms: cooking a kid in its mother's milk (Exod. 23, 19; 34, 26; Deut. 14, 21)—as a *hoq* at all. Unlike Maimonides who explains it in terms of its idolatrous Sabian context of legislation (III:48:599), Nahmanides argues that the reason for the scriptural prohibition against cooking a kid in its mother's milk (which is then generalized to all mixing of meat and milk) is to teach us humans not to be cruel (C Deut. 14, 21). For other explanations of this kind, see chap. 3.

93. The prohibitions of *'Ervat she'eir basar* or *'arayot* [prohibitions against various sexual activities] are not mentioned as *huqqim* in the enumeration of BT *Yoma* 67b, according to the version cited either in the *Guide* or in Nahmanides' *Commentary*. Maimonides does, however, include them in his enumeration of *huqqim* in *EC*, chap.VI in *PM*, 392.

94. *Guide* III:49:606; ibn Ezra, *Com.*, Lev. 18, 6.

95. On Nahmanides' introductory phrase here "We have no kabbalistic tradition on this," see Idel (1983).

BIBLIOGRAPHY

Abrabanel, Don Isaac (1579/repr. frequently) *Commentary on the Torah* (Heb.), Venice.

Abraham bar Hiyya (1860), *Hegyon ha-Nefesh*, ed. Isaac Freimann, Leipzig: Vollrath.

Abraham ibn Daud (1852/1982), *Sefer Ha-Emunah Ha-Ramah (Exalted Faith)*, Heb. trans. Solomon b. Labi, ed. Samson Weill, Frankfurt a.M.: Sifriah LeMahshevet Yisra'el.

Abraham ibn Ezra (1976), *Commentary on the Torah (Sefer HaYashar)*, ed. Asher Weiser, Jerusalem: Mossad HaRav Kook.

Agus, Jacob B. (1959), *The Evolution of Jewish Thought*, London and New York: Abelard-Schuman.

Al-Ishbili (RiTBa), R. Yom Tov b. R. Abraham (1956), *Sefer HaZikaron* (Heb.), ed. Kalman Kahana, Jerusalem: Mossad HaRav Kook.

Altmann, Alexander (1974), "The Religion of the Thinkers: Free Will and Pre-destination in Maimonides," *Religion in a Religious Age*, ed. S. D. Goitein, Cambridge, Mass.: Association for Jewish Studies, 25–53.

—— (1987), "Maimonides on the Intellect and the Scope of Metaphysics," in *Von der mittelalterlichen zur modernen Aufklärung*, Tubingen, Germany: J. C. B. Mohr, 60–129.

Arama, Isaac (1522/1849) *'Aqedat Yitzhaq* (Heb.), ed. H. Pollak, Pressburg: V. Kitseer.

Aristotle (1984), *The Complete Works of Aristotle* (Revised Oxford Translation), ed. Jonathan Barnes, Princeton, N.J.: Princeton University Press.

Assaf, David (1975), *Concordance of the Mishneh Torah of Maimonides* (Heb.), Haifa: Makhon Le-heker Kitve Ha-Rambam.

Averroes (Ibn Rushd) (1954), *Tahafut al-Tahafut*, Eng. trans. S. van den Bergh, London: E. J. W. Gibb Memorial.

Baer, Yitzhaq (1966), *A History of the Jews in Christian Spain*, 2 vols., Philadelphia: Jewish Publication Society.

Bahya ibn Paquda (1928), *Sefer Torat Hovot Ha-Levavot (The Book of Direction to the Duties of the Heart)*, Jerusalem; (1973) Eng. trans. M. Mansoor, London: Routledge & Kegan Paul.

Barkai, Ron (1987), "Theoretical and Practical Aspects of Jewish Astrology in the Middle Ages," in *Science, Magic, and Mythology in the Middle Ages* (Heb.), Jerusalem: Makhon Van Leer, 7–35.

Benin, Stephen D. (1982), "Maimonides and Scholasticism: Sacrifice as Historical Hermeneutic," *Proceedings of the Eight World Congress of Jewish Studies*, Jerusalem, Division C: 41–46.

Ben-Sasson, Yonah (1960), "A Study of the Doctrine of *Ta'ame ha-Mitzvot* in Maimonides' *Guide*" (Heb.), *Tarbiz* 29: 268–81.

Berger, David (1983), "Miracles and the Natural Order in Nachmanides," in *Rabbi Moses Nachmanides (Ramban): Explorations in His Religious and Literary Virtuosity*, ed. Isadore Twersky, Cambridge, Mass.: Harvard University Press, 107–28.

Berman, Lawrence. V. (1959), *Ibn Bajjah and Maimonides: A Chapter in the History of Political Philosophy*, Hebrew University Ph.D. thesis (Heb.).

Blidstein, Gerald (Ya'akov) (1978), "Maimonides on 'Oral Law,'" *The Jewish Law Annual* 1: 108–22.

―――― (1986), "*Mesoret ve-Samkhut Mosdit le-Ra'ayon Torah She-Be'al Peh be-Mishnat Ha-RaMBaM*," *Da'at* 16: 11–27.

"Bnei Keturah" (1954), (Heb.), *Encyclopedia Talmudit*, III:392–93, Jerusalem: Hotsa'at Encyclopedia Talmudit.

Burnett, C. S. (1986), "Arabic, Greek, and Latin Works on Astrological Magic Attributed to Aristotle," in *Pseudo-Aristotle in the Middle Ages*, ed. J. Kraye, W. F. Ryan, and C. B. Schmitt, London: Warburg Institute, 84–96.

Chwolsohn, D. (1856) *Die Ssabier und der Ssabismus*, 2 vols., St. Petersburg, Russia.

Davidson, Herbert (1992–93), "Maimonides on Metaphysical Knowledge," *Maimonidean Studies* 3: 49–103.

―――― (1987), "The Middle Way in Maimonides' Ethic," *Proceedings of the American Academy for Jewish Research* 54: 31–72.

Epstein, Isadore (1959), "Le-shitat ha-RaMBaM be-ta'amei ha-mitzvot" (Heb.), in *Yad Sha'ul, Memorial Volume for Rabbi Dr. Saul Weingurt*, Tel Aviv: 145–52.

Faierstein, Morris (1983), "God's Need for the Commandments in Medieval Kabbalah," *Conservative Judaism* 36: 45–59.

Feldman, Seymour (1986), "The End of the World in Medieval Jewish Philosophy," *AJS Review* 11: 53–77.

Frank, Daniel (1993), "Ad Hoq," *S'vara* 3, 1:91–94.

Freudenthal, Gad (1993), "Maimonides' Stance on Astrology in Context: Cosmology, Physics, Medicine, and Providence," in *Moses Maimonides: Physician, Scientist, and Philosopher*, eds. Fred Rosner and Samuel Kotteck, Northvale, N.J./London: Jason Aronson, 77–90.

Funkenstein, Amos (1977), "Maimonides: Political Theory and Realistic Messianism," *Miscellanea Mediaevalia* 11: 81–103.

―――― (1982), "Nachmanides' Symbolical Reading of History," in *Studies in Jewish Mysticism*, ed. Joseph Dan and Frank Talmage, Cambridge, Mass.: Association for Jewish Studies, 129–50.

Galen (1944), *Galen on Medical Experience*, trans. R. Walzer, London: Oxford University Press.

Galston, Miriam (1978), "The Purpose of the Law According to Maimonides," *Jewish Quarterly Review* 69: 27–51.

Gellman, Jerome (1990), "Radical Responsibity in Maimonides' Thought," in *The Thought of Moses Maimonides*, ed. Ira Robinson et al., Lewistown, N.Y.: Edwin Mellon Press, 249–65.

—— (1991), "Maimonides' Ravings," *Review of Metaphysics* 45, 2:309–28

"*Gezerat Ha-Katuv*" (1954) (Heb.), *Encyclopedia Talmudit*, V: 564, Jerusalem.

Golding, Martin (1987), "Maimonides: Theory of Juristic Reasoning," in *Maimonides as Codifier of Jewish Law*, ed. Nahum Rakover, Jerusalem: 51–59.

Guttmann, Julius (1979), "The Problem of Contingency in the Philosophy of Maimonides" (Heb.), in *Religion and Knowledge*, Jerusalem: Magnes Press, 119–35.

Halbertal, Moshe (1990), "Maimonides' *Book of Commandments*: The Architecture of the Halakhah and its Theory of Interpretation" (Heb.), *Tarbiz* 59, 3–4: 457–80.

Halbertal, Moshe, and Margalit, Avishai (1992), *Idolatry*, Cambridge, Mass.: Harvard University Press.

Hartman, David (1976) *Maimonides, Torah, and Philosophic Quest*, Philadelphia: Jewish Publication Society.

—— (1985), *A Living Covenant*, New York: Free Press.

Harvey, Warren Zev (1980), "Political Philosophy and Halakhah in Maimonides" (Heb.), *Iyyun* 29: 198–212.

—— (1987), "The First Commandment and the God of History: Judah Ha-Levi and R. Hasdai Crescas vs. R. Abraham ibn Ezra and Maimonides" (Heb.), *Tarbiz* 2, 57: 203–16.

—— (1988), "How to Begin to Study the *Guide of the Perplexed*, I, 1" (Heb.), *Da'at* 21: 5–23.

—— (1993), "Anti-fondamentalisme maimonidien," *Les retours aux écritures: fondamentalismes presents et passés*, ed. E. Patlagean and A. LeBoulluec, Louvain-Paris: 313–18.

Havlin, Shlomo Zalman (1995), "Hukkim and Mishpatim in the Bible, Talmudic literature, and Maimonides" (Heb.), *Annual of Bar-Ilan University: Studies in Judaica and Humanities* 1995, XXVI–XXVII, ed. Z. A. Steinfeld, Ramat Aviv: 135–66.

Heinemann, Isaac (1954), *Ta'amei ha-Mitzvot be-Sifrut Yisra'el* (Heb.), 3d ed., 2 vols., Jerusalem: Jewish Agency Press.

Henoch, C. (1978), *Nachmanides: Philosopher and Mystic*, Jerusalem: Torah Laam Publications.

Hjårpe, J. (1972), *Analyse critique des traditions arabes sur les sabéens harraniens*, Uppsala, Sweden.

Hyman, Arthur (1979–80), "A Note on Maimonides' Classification of Law," *Proceedings of the American Academy for Jewish Research* 46–47: 323–43.

Idel, Moshe (1983), "We Have No Kabbalistic Tradition on This," in *Rabbi Moses Nachmanides (Ramban): Explorations in His Religious and Literary Virtuosity*, ed. Isadore Twersky, Cambridge, Mass.: Harvard University Press, 51–74.

—— (1990) "Maimonides and Kabbalah," in *Studies in Maimonides*, ed. Isadore Twersky, Cambridge, Mass.: Harvard University Press, 31–81.

Ivry, Alfred (1985a), "Islamic and Greek Influences on Maimonides' Philosophy," in *Maimonides and Philosophy*, ed. Shlomo Pines and Yirmiyahu Yovel, Dordrecht: Martinus Nijhoff/Kluwer Publishers, 148–51.

—— (1985b) "Providence, Divine Omniscience, and Possibility: The Case of Maimonides," in *Divine Omniscience and Omnipotence in Medieval Philosophy*, ed. Tamar Rudavsky, Dordrecht: Martinus Nijhoff/Kluwer Publishers, 143–59.

—— (1991), "Neoplatonic Currents in Maimonides' Thought," in *Perspectives on Maimonides,* ed. Joel Kraemer, Oxford: Oxford University Press, 115–40.

Jospe, Raphael (1987), "Nachmanides and Arabic" (Heb.), *Tarbiz* 62, 1: 67–93.

—— (1994), "Abraham ibn Ezra on the Torah and Astrology " (Heb.), *Da'at* 32–33: 31–52.

Kafih, Joseph (1988), "The Order of the Stars and Constellations and Events" (Heb.), in *Essays*, ed. J. Tuvi, vol. 1, Jerusalem.

Kaplan, Lawrence (1985), "Maimonides on the Singularity of the Jewish People," *Da'at* 15: v–xxvii.

—— (1986), "Maimonides on Christianity and Islam," *L'Eylah* 22: 31–34.

Kasher, Hannah (1995), "Maimonides' View of Circumcision as a Factor Uniting the Jewish and Muslim Communities, in *Modern Perspectives on Muslim-Jewish Relations*, ed. R. Nettler, London: Harwood Academic Publishers, 103–108.

Kellner, Menachem (1991), *Maimonides on Judaism and the Jewish People*, Albany: State University of New York Press.

Kirschenbaum, Aaron (1984), "Equity in Jewish Law," *Da'at* 13: 43–54.

Klein-Braslavy, Sarah (1990), "King Solomon and Metaphysical Esotericism According to Maimonides," *Maimonidean Studies*, vol. 1. New York: 57–86.

—— (1996), *King Solomon and Philosophical Esotericism in the Thought of Maimonides*, Jerusalem: Magnes Press.

Kraemer, Joel (1986), *Humanism in the Renaissance of Islam*, Leiden: E. J. Brill.

Kreisel, Howard (1989), "Intellectual Perfection and the Role of the Law in the Philosophy of Maimonides," in *From Ancient Israel to Modern Judaism: Intellect in Quest of Understanding, Essays in Honor of Marvin Fox*, 3 vols., ed. Jacob Neusner et al., Atlanta: Scholars Press, vol. III: 25–46.

—— (1994), "Maimonides' Approach to Astrology" (Heb.), *Proceedings of the Eleventh World Congress of Jewish Studies*, Division C, Jerusalem: vol. II: 25–31.

—— (1996) "Love and Fear of God in the Writings of Maimonides" (Heb.), *Da'at* 37: 127–51.

Langermann, Y. Tzvi (1991), "Maimonides' Repudiation of Astrology," *Maimonidean Studies*, vol. 2: 123–58.

—— (1992), "Acceptance and Devaluation: Nahmanides' Attitude towards Science," *Journal of Jewish Thought and Philosophy* 1: 223–45.

—— (1993), "Some Astrological Themes in the Thought of Abraham ibn Ezra," in *Rabbi Abraham ibn Ezra: Studies in the Writings of a Twelfth-Century Jewish Polymath*, ed. Isadore Twersky and Jay M. Harris, Cambridge, Mass.: Harvard University Press, 28–85.

—— (1994), "The Debate between the Philosopher and the Mutakallim," *Proceedings of the American Academy for Jewish Research* LX: 189–240.

Leibowitz, Yeshayahu (1980), *The Faith of Maimonides* (Heb.), Tel Aviv: Israel Defense Ministry.

Lerner, Ralph (1968), "Maimonides' Letter on Astrology," *History of Religions* 8: 143–58.

Levinger, Jacob (1965), *Darkhei ha-Mahashavah ha-Hilkhatit shel ha-RaMBaM* (Heb.), Tel Aviv: Yavneh.

—— (1967), "Abstinence from Alcohol in the *Guide of the Perplexed*" (Heb.), *Bar Ilan University Annual: Decennial Volume 1955–65*, Jerusalem: 299–305.

—— (1968), "The Oral Law in Maimonides' Thought" (Heb.), *Tarbiz* 37: 282–93.

—— (1984), "Halakhah and Personal Perfection" (Heb.), *Da'at* 13: 61–66.

Lichtenstein, Aharon (1975), "Does Jewish Tradition Recognize an Ethic Independent of Halakhah?" in *Modern Jewish Ethics*, ed. Marvin Fox, Columbus, Ohio: Ohio State University Press, 62–88.

Lieberman, Saul (1947), *Hilkhoth Ha-Yerushalmi (The Laws of the Palestinian Talmud) of Rabbi Moses ben Maimon* (Heb.), New York/Jerusalem: Jewish Theological Seminary Press.

Macy, Jeffrey (1982), "The Theological-Political Teaching of *Shemonah Peraqim*: A Reappraisal of the Text and of Its Arabic Sources," *Proceedings of the Eighth World Congress of Jewish Studies*, Jerusalem, Division C: 31–40.

Margalit, Avishai (1990), "Animism Animated," *S'vara* I: 41–49.

Matt, Daniel (1986), "The Mystic and the Mizwot," in *Jewish Spirituality from the Bible throughout the Middle Ages,"* ed. Arthur Green, New York: Crossroad Press, 367–404.

Morgenbesser, Sidney, and Levi, Isaac (1964), "Belief and Disposition," *American Philosophical Quarterly* I, 3 :221–33.

Moses b. Joshua of Narbonne (1852/1961), *Commentary on the Guide of the Perplexed*, ed. J. Goldenthal, Vienna; repr. in *Three Ancient Commentators on the Guide of the Perplexed*.

Nehorai, Michael (1983), "Maimonides' System of the Commandments" (Heb.), *Da'at* 10: 29–42.

Novak, David (1986), "The Treatment of Islam and Muslims in the Legal Writings of Maimonides," in *Studies in Islamic and Judaic Traditions*, ed. W. Brinner and S. Ricks, Atlanta: Scholars Press, 233–50.

—— (1992), *The Theology of Nachmanides Systematically Presented*, Atlanta: Scholars Press.

Pesikta de-Rav Kahana (1962), ed. B. Mandelbaum, New York: Jewish Theological Seminary.

Peters, F. E. (1979), "The Origins of Islamic Platonism: The School Tradition," in *Islamic Philosophical Theology*, ed. Parviz Morewedge, Albany: State University of New York Press, 14–45.

Pines, Shlomo (1960), "Excursis: Notes on Maimonides' Views Concerning Human Will," *Scripta Hierosolymatina* 20: 195–98.

—— (1963), "Translator's Introduction: The Philosophic Sources of *The Guide of the Perplexed*," in Moses Maimonides, *The Guide of the Perplexed*, trans., S. Pines, Chicago: University of Chicago Press, lvii–cxxxiv.

—— (1979), "The Limitations of Human Knowledge According to Al-Farabi, ibn Bajja and Maimonides," in *Studies in Medieval Jewish History and Literature*, ed. Isadore Twersky, Cambridge, Mass.: Harvard University Press, 82–102.

—— (1981), "Les Limites de la Métaphysique selon Al-Farabi, ibn Bajja et Maimonide; Sources et Antitheses de ces Doctrines chez Alexandre d'Aphrodise et Chez Themistius," *Miscellanea Mediaevalia* 13: 211–25

—— (1986), "Dieu et L'être selon Maïmonide: Exégèse d'Exode 3,14 et doctrine connexe," in *Celui qui est: Interprétations juives et chrétiennes d'Exode 3, 14*, ed. A. De Libera et E. Zum Brunn, Paris: Les Editions du Cerf [Collection "Patrimoines"], 15–24.

—— (1987), "The Relation between Maimonides' Halakhic and non-Halakhic Works," in *Maimonides and Philosophy*, ed. S. Pines and Y. Yovel, Dordrecht: Martinus Nijhoff/Kluwer Publishers, 1–14.

Porphyry (1975), *Isagoge*, trans. E. W. Warren, Toronto: Pontifical Institute of Mediaeval Studies.

Regev, Shaul (1990), "Ta'amei Ha-Mitzvot in R. Avraham ibn-Ezra's Commentary: Secrets," in *Abraham ibn Ezra y su tiempo*, ed. Fernando Diaz Esteban, Madrid: Asociación Española de Orientalistas, 210–17.

Rescher, Nicholas (1959/60), "Choice without Preference: A Study of the History and Logic of the Problem of 'Buridan's Ass,'" *Kant Studien* 51:142–75.

Rosenberg, Shalom (1978a), "Possible and Assertoric in Medieval Logic" (Heb.), *Iyyun* 28: 56–72.

—— (1978b), "Necessary and Possible in Medieval Logic" (Heb.), *Iyyun* 28: 103–55.

—— (1981), "The Interpretation of the Torah in the *Guide*" (Heb.), *Jerusalem Studies in Jewish Thought*, 1/1:85–157.

—— (1982), "Again 'For the Most Part'" (Heb.), in *The Jewish Spiritual Leadership in Our Time*, ed. E. Belfer, Tel Aviv: Devir, 87–103.

Rosenthal, E. S. (1968), "For the Most Part" (Heb.), *Peraqim* I:183–224.

Ruderman, David (1995) *Jewish Thought and Scientific Discovery in Early Modern Europe*, New Haven, Conn.: Yale University Press.

Saadiah Gaon (1970–71/1948), *Sefer Emunot VeDe'ot (Book of Doctrines and Beliefs)* (Heb.), trans. J. Kafih, Jerusalem: Sura Press; Eng. trans. S. Rosenblatt, New Haven, Conn.: Yale University Press.

—— (1973) *Book of Theodocy* (Heb.), trans. and ed. J. Kafih, Jerusalem: HaMaqor Press; (1993); Eng. trans. as *Saadiah ben Joseph al Fayyumi's Book of Theodocy, a Tenth Century Arabic Commentary and Translation of the Book of Job*, trans. L. E. Goodman, New Haven, Conn.: Yale University Press.

Schlossberg, Eliezer (1990), "The Attitude of Maimonides towards Islam" (Heb.), *Pe'amim* 42: 38–60.

Scholem, Gershom (1961), *Major Trends in Jewish Mysticism*, New York: Schocken Press.

Schwartz, Dov (1992a), "The Dispute over Astral Magic in Fourteenth-Century Provence" (Heb.), *Zion* 58: 141–74.

—— (1992b), "Different Forms of Magic in Spanish Jewish Thought of the Fourteenth Century" (Heb.), *Proceedings of the American Academy for Jewish Research* 57: 17–47.

—— (1992c), "Astrology and Astral Magic in R. Solomon Al-Qonstantin's *Migaleh 'Amuqot*" (Heb.), *Jerusalem Studies in Jewish Folklore* 15: 37–82.

Septimus, Bernard (1983), "'Open Rebuke and Concealed Love': Nachmanides and the Andalusian Tradition," in *Rabbi Moses Nachmanides (Ramban): Explorations in His Religious and Literary Virtuosity*, ed. I. Twersky, Cambridge, Mass.: Harvard University Press, 11–34.

Sezgin, F. (1971), *Geschichte des arabischen Schrifttums*, 4 vols., Frankfurt a.M.: 318–29.

Shatz, David (1991), "Worship, Corporeality, and Human Perfection: A Reading of *Guide of the Perplexed*, III:51–54," in *The Thought of Moses Maimonides*, ed. I. Robinson et al., Lewistown, N.Y.: Edwin Mellon Press, 77–129.

Shein, Chaim (1984), "'The Majority Rules'—Illusionary Argument" (Heb.), *Da'at* 13: 55–60.

Stern, Josef (1987), "Modes of Reference in the Rituals of Judaism," *Religious Studies* 23: 109–28.

—— (1989), "Logical Syntax as a Key to a Secret of the Guide of the Perplexed" (Heb.), *Iyyun* 38: 137–66.

—— (1997), "Maimonides' Conceptions of Freedom and the Sense of Shame," in *Human Freedom and Moral Responsibility: General and Jewish Perspectives*, ed. Charles Manekin and Menachem Kellner, College Park, Maryland: University Press of Maryland.

—— (forthcoming a), "Philosophy or Exegesis: Some Critical Comments," *Studies in Jewish-Muslim Relations*.

—— (forthcoming b), "Maimonides on Language and the Science of Language," in *Maimonides and the Sciences (Boston Studies in the Philosophy of Science)*, ed. H. Levine and R. Cohen, Dordrecht: Martinus Nijhoff/Kluwer Publications.

—— (ms. a), "Excrement and Exegesis."

—— (ms. b), "Maimonides in the Skeptical Tradition."

—— (ms. c), "Maimonides on the Growth of Knowledge and the Limitations of the Intellect."

Strauss, Leo (1952), "The Literary Character of *The Guide of the Perplexed*," in *Persecution and the Art of Writing*, Westport, Conn.: Greenwood Press, 38–94.

—— (1963), "How to Begin to Study *The Guide of the Perplexed*," in Moses Maimonides, *The Guide of the Perplexed*, trans. S. Pines, Chicago: University of Chicago Press, xi–lvi.

Tardieu, Michel (1986), "Sabiens Coraniques et 'Sabiens' de Harran," *Journal Asiatique* CCLXXIV: 1–44.

Thomas Aquinas (1941), *Summa Theologiae*, 4 vols., Ottowa, Ont.

Twersky, Isadore (1980a), *Introduction to the Code of Maimonides.* New Haven, Conn.: Yale University Press.

—— (1980b), "Concerning Maimonides' Rationalization of the Commandments: An Explication of Hilkhot Me'ilah viii, 8" (Heb.), *Studies in the History of Jewish Society in the Middle Ages and in the Modern Period*, Jerusalem: Magnes Press.

—— (1993), "Did Ibn Ezra Influence Maimonides?" (Heb.), in *Rabbi Abraham ibn Ezra: Studies in the Writing of a Twelfth-Century Jewish Polymath*, ed. Isadore Twersky and Jay Harris, Cambridge, Mass.: Harvard University Press.

Ullmann-Margalit, Edna, and Morgenbesser, Sidney (1977), "Picking and Choosing," *Social Research* 44: 757–85.

Urbach, Ephraim E. (1971), *The Sages: Their Concepts and Beliefs* (Heb.), 2d ed., Jerusalem: Magnes Press.

Vajda, Georges (1954), *Judah ben Nissim ibn Malka, philosophe juif marocain*, Paris.

Weiss, Roslyn (1989), "Maimonides on *Shilluah Ha-Qen*," *Jewish Quarterly Review* 79, 4: 345–66.

—— (1992–93), "Maimonides on the End of the World," *Maimonidean Studies* III: 195–218.

Wolfson, Elliot (1987), "Circumcision and the Divine Name: A Study in the Transmission of Esoteric Doctrine," *Jewish Quarterly Review* 78: 77–112.

—— (1988), "Mystical Rationalization of the Commandments in *Sefer ha-Rimmon*." *Hebrew Union College Annual* 59: 217–51.

—— (1989), "By Way of Truth: Aspects of Nachmanides' Kabbalistic Hermeneutic." *AJS Review* 14, 2: 103–79.

—— (1993), "Beautiful Maiden without Eyes: *Peshat* and *Sod* in Zoharic Hermeneutics," in *The Midrashic Imagination: Essays in Rabbinic Thought and Interpretation*, ed. Michael Fishbane, Albany: State University of New York Press, 155–203.

INDEX

Abraham (the Patriarch), 90–91, 93,
   95–97, 100–1, 111, 118, 132
   Abrahamic covenant, 92–96
Abraham bar Hiyya, 111
Abraham ibn Ezra, 80, 111–12,
   142–43, 158–59
Accommodation (in the Law), 11–12,
   35, 69, 91, 104, 119
Adam, 109, 121, 135
Agriculture, commandments
   concerning, 4, 118
Albo, Joseph, 3
Al-Farabi, 90, 111
Al-Ghazali, 29–30
Al-Kindi, 111
Al-Mas'udi, 111
Antinomianism, 22, 36–39, 51–52,
   69–70, 78, 85, 120–21, 134
Aqedah, 11
R. Aqiba, 79
Arama, Isaac, 3
Aristotle (Aristotelianism), 8, 29–30,
   58, 69, 89, 90, 112, 128–30, 145
Ash'arites, 17, 37–38, 68, 71, 78, 113
Astrology, 6, 12, 110–12, 125, 131
   and fatalism, 127
   and *huqqim*, 58
   and theurgic magic, 111, 119, 121,
      128, 145
   as an ancient science, 146
   Maimonides' opposition to, 132
Averroism, 133
'*Azazel* (See Scapegoat), 110

Bahya ibn Paqudah, 111
Bereshit Rabbah, 22, 23, 24
Blood, prohibitions concerning,
   135–36

Bnei Keturah, 96
Bullock, burnt for consecration of
   High Priest, 123, 152
Buridan's Ass, 29

Causation, 129
Chapters of R. Eliezer, 151
Christians, 95, 97
Circumcision, 87–107, 114
   and friendship, 94–95
   and paschal sacrifice, 92
   and unity of God, 94–95, 100–2,
      104–5
   as preliminary to conversion, 92
   as means of communal
      differentiation, 92–93
   classification in *Mishneh Torah*
      and in *Guide*, 87–88, 105–7
   in Islam, 96
   reason why performed on eighth
      day, 96–97
Concealment, devices of, 10, 73, 114,
   120
Covenant, divine, 98–100
Crescas, Hasdai, 3
Crossbreeding (*kil'ayim*), prohibitions
   on, 146, 155

Day of Atonement (See *Yom Kippur*)
Decree of Scripture (See *Gezerat ha-
   katuv*)
Devarim shel ta'am, meaning of, 55

'*Eidim Zommimim* (false witnesses),
   57
'*Eglah 'arufah* (commandment to
   break the neck of a young heifer),
   138, 152